Japan in the World Economy of the 1980s

Japan in
the World Economy
of the 1980s

Saburo Okita

UNIVERSITY OF TOKYO PRESS

Contents

Preface

My previous book, *The Developing Economies and Japan* (University of Tokyo Press, 1980), dealt mainly with Japan's postwar recovery and issues in economic development. In the years since that book was published, Japan's economic growth and the yen's appreciation have combined to give Japan a per-capita GNP higher than even the United States in 1987. At the same time, chronic current account surpluses have generated a massive flow of capital out of Japan and made Japan a major player in international financial markets.

The changes in the world economy and the expansion of the Japanese economy that took place during this period have exacerbated economic friction between Japan and the industrialized countries of North America and Europe. By the same token, these developments have increased global expectations of Japan and fueled hopes that Japan could do more to stimulate world economic growth, especially in the developing countries.

This book is a compilation of the major academic papers and lectures I delivered between 1980 and 1987. Even though there have been substantial changes since some of them were written, I have resisted the impulse to rewrite and have instead had them reprinted here without the benefit of hindsight.

In a way, the turn of the decade marks a convenient turning point for me, since it was in November 1979 that Prime Minister Masayoshi Ohira appointed me his Minister for Foreign Affairs. As Foreign Minister, I accompanied the Prime Minister on official visits to China, Australia, New Zealand, the United States, Mexico, and Canada, among others, and held ministerial consultations with the Foreign Ministers of France, England, West Germany, and Italy. It was also as Foreign Minister that I represented Japan at the Venice Summit in June 1980, standing in for Prime Minister Ohira in the wake of his unfortunate death a mere ten days before the start of the Summit.

In July 1980 Prime Minister Zenko Suzuki asked me to become the Government Representative for External Economic Relations, in which capacity I was primarily responsible for negotiations on the trade friction with the United States and Europe. Although I resigned my government post in December 1981, I found myself a frequent participant at international conferences and seminars and, despite my private capacity, sometimes heading government missions. All of this, of course, offered me a continuing opportunity to discuss global economic issues with people from all over the world.

In 1980, the U.S. government came out with its report *Global 2000: Report to the President,* which impressed Prime Minister Suzuki and Minister of State for the Environment Hyosuke Kujiraoka and moved them to establish the Ad Hoe Group on Global Environmental Problems within the Environment Agency and to appoint me its chairman. The Group's 1982 interim report recommended the establishment of a United Nations blue-ribbon commission to study global environmental issues and called for increased emphasis on the environment in development aid programs.

Also in 1982, the United Nations Environmental Program held a Special Session in Nairobi (commemorating the UN Human Environment Conference held in Stockholm in 1972) at which the Japanese representative, Minister of State for the Environment Bunbei Hara, submitted a Japanese proposal calling for the establishment of a United Nations commission to study global environmental issues. This proposal was approved at the United Nations General Assembly the following year, and the World Commission on Environment and Development (WCED) was formed in the fall of 1984 with Gro Brundtland (later Prime Minister of Norway) as chairwoman and me as one of its members. Environmental issues have been a constant concern and are a major theme running through this book.

Another primary theme is that of Pacific economic cooperation. In 1968, a conference of Pacific economists and other concerned experts was held at the Japan Center for Economic Research, where I was serving as president. These conferences have since developed into the Pacific Trade and Development Conference (PAFTAD) with conferences held in various locations thoughout Asia and the Pacific—the 18th scheduled to be held in Kuala Lumpur in December 1989.

During Prime Minister Ohira's January 1980 visit to Australia, he and Prime Minister Malcolm Fraser agreed on the holding of a Pacific Community seminar in Canberra. This grouping soon developed into the Pacific Economic Cooperation Conference (PECC), and subsequent meetings have been held in Bangkok, Bali, Seoul, Vancouver, and Osaka. A tripartite organization composed of government officials, academics, and businesspeople, PECC has played an important role in promoting regional cooperation. I am presently the chairman of the Japanese PECC committee and chaired the May 1988 Osaka conference. This book thus contains a number of papers on Pacific cooperation.

Additionally, I have long been concerned with the North-South problem and the difficulties facing the developing countries, and the book includes my major works in this area as well.

This is, as I said, a record of papers written over the last decade. It is by no means a systematic treatment, yet I am hopeful that this book, like my last one, will find a receptive audience interested in the same issues that have interested me over the years.

July 1989   SABURO OKITA

Aspects of
Japan's Economic Maturity

Labor Productivity and Economic Development:
The Japanese Experience

Japan's economic experience from the end of World War II onward can give valuable insight into the relationship between labor productivity and economic development. Throughout the postwar period the Japanese economy has maintained a better economic performance level than any other country. This was made possible by a constantly high rate of increase in labor productivity—a clear indication of the important role of productivity as a supply-side factor in economic development.

There has recently been a surge of interest in productivity throughout the world. Both the developing countries and the stagflation-plagued industrial countries now view higher productivity as an effective means of revitalizing their economies. People who are interested in what elements affect productivity can probably learn much from Japan's experience.

The Japanese economy underwent rapid growth after World War II. In 1960, Japan's nominal GNP represented only 2.9 percent of the world total; by 1978 this figure had reached 9.5 percent. The OPEC countries may well be the only countries that have been able to match Japan's rapid growth in income levels. In 1973, their total nominal GNP was 2.8 percent of the world total but rose in the space of just three years to 4.3 percent in 1976 (Table 1).

True, both Japan and the OPEC countries have been successful in rapidly increasing their income levels. The methods used,

This essay was presented at the Conference on United States Productivity at Brown University, February 27–28, 1981. The author acknowledges the cooperation of Mr. Takao Komine in preparing the text.

3

Table 1   Japan and OPEC Shares of Global GNP

(billion U.S. $; %)

	1960	1970	1973	1976	1978
World total	1,500	3,222	4,755	6,820	8,786
Japan	43	200	411	574	836
(Percentage of world total)	(2.9)	(6.2)	(8.6)	(8.4)	(9.5)
OPEC	—	—	133	290	379
(Percentage of world total)			(2.8)	(4.3)	(4.3)

Note: GNP figures are based on estimates from the *World Bank Atlas*.

however, have been completely different. Japan has done this basically by improving its labor productivity. In contrast, the OPEC countries have done so by making their terms of trade more favorable.

Trends in Japanese Labor Productivity

The development of Japan's postwar labor productivity can be divided into two periods. The first was the period of rapid economic growth before 1973, when labor productivity increased rapidly. Labor productivity in terms of real GNP grew by an average 9.0 percent annually in 1964–73, an extraordinary figure compared with 1.9 percent for the United States, 3.2 percent for the United Kingdom, and 4.7 percent for West Germany.

The second period is the present period of 4–5 percent growth since 1976. After a sharp business slump in 1974–75 triggered by the first oil crisis, the Japanese economy has been growing at a stable rate of 4–5 percent, but with substantially lower growth in labor productivity. The annual average for 1976–79 was 3.9 percent (Table 2).

The reasons for the recent downturn in Japanese productivity growth are not yet fully understood. Probably a number of combined factors have been responsible—constraints on oil and other imported resources, rising energy prices, environmental problems, and constraints on export markets due to trade friction.

Table 2   Changes in Labor Productivity in Terms of GNP

(%)

	1964–73	1976–79
Japan	9.0	3.9
U.S.A.	1.9	0.7
F.R.G.	4.7	3.0
U.K.	3.2	1.4

Notes: 1. Based on OECD *National Accounts* and *Labor Force Statistics*.
2. Labor productivity = Real GDP/Number of employed persons

What should be stressed here, however, is that Japan's productivity growth rate is still relatively higher than those of the rest of the world: the 1976–79 figures for the United States, the United Kingdom, and West Germany were 0.7 percent, 1.4 percent, and 3.0 percent respectively.

Let me discuss the reasons why Japan's labor productivity has continued to grow at higher rates than other countries.

Reasons for Increased Productivity

Labor productivity increases are effected by various factors, both short-term and long-term. In the short term, fluctuations in the utilization rate due to the business cycle have some impact. However, let me focus on the long-term factors that have made the rate of productivity increase so high in Japan, starting with the economic reasons.

Increase in the capital–labor ratio

The first reason that one can point to is the increase in the capital–labor ratio. It is possible to define the rate of increase in labor productivity in terms of two factors: an increasing rate of productive capital stock per employee, and an increasing rate of production per unit of capital stock. Productive capital stock per employee in Japan's manufacturing industries rose from an annual average rate of 7.9 percent in 1955–73 to 8.3 percent in 1974–79 (Table 3).

This increase in the capital–labor ratio is of course attributable

Table 3   Increase in the Capital–Labor Ratio (Manufacturing Industry)

(%)

		Rate of Increase in Labor Productivity	Rate of Increase in Capital–Labor Ratio	Rate of Increase in Utilization Ratio	Output Coefficient
Japan	1955–73	8.5	7.9	1.5	−1.0
	1974–79	4.7	8.3	−1.3	−2.1
U.S.A.	1955–73	2.3	2.4	0.0	−0.1
	1974–79	1.3	0.9	0.5	−0.1

Notes: 1. Based on Economic Planning Agency, *Capital Stock Statistics*.
　　　2. Rate of increase in labor productivity = Rate of increases in capital–labor ratio + Rate of increase in utilization ratio + Output coefficient.

to active plant and equipment investment by industry. But we should not overlook the contribution made by the high rate of savings of the Japanese people: what is by international standards a particularly high rate of 20 percent out of personal disposable income has been maintained. It is only because of this high saving that the country has been able to direct a large proportion of its economic resources toward expanding future production capacity by investing in plant and equipment. Plant and equipment investment account for an extremely high 15–20 percent of GNP in Japan (Table 4). In other words, a national preference for saving for future (as opposed to present) consumption, and industry's willingness to invest in plant and equipment for the sake of efficiency, have combined to make possible an increase in productivity.

Table 4   Investment in Plant and Equipment as a Proportion of GNP

(%)

	Japan	U.S.A.	F.R.G.	U.K.
1960–65	18.5	9.4	14.2	8.2
1966–70	19.4	10.4	13.0	8.3
1971–78	16.0	10.1	12.1	8.0

Note: Based on Economic Planning Agency, *National Economic Statistic Yearbook*.

Table 5   Impact of Labor Shift: Productivity Trends by Sector
(average annual rate as %)

	1965–70	1970–75
All industry	10.7	6.0
Primary industry	6.9	4.1
Secondary industry	11.3	7.8
Tertiary industry	5.1	5.4
Percentage of increase due to labor shift	1.3	0.9

Note: Based on Economic Planning Agency, *National Economic Statistic Year-book*.

Shift in the labor force

The second reason is a shift in the labor force from low productivity sectors to high. This shift alone is enough to enhance the overall productivity of the economy, even without any increase in the productivity of particular industries. Looking at the labor productivity trends in individual industrial sectors (Table 5), we find that the effect of technological progress is greatest in the manufacturing industries, while it has been difficult to increase productivity in the primary and tertiary industries because of the slow pace of growth in the capital–labor ratio.

The proportion of Japan's labor force in primary industry started out, after World War II, at a fairly high level compared with other countries and subsequently declined sharply. This shift in the labor force had the effect of improving the productivity of the economy as a whole, and its effect was particularly apparent during the period of high economic growth. About one-seventh of the increase in overall productivity in 1965–75, for example, was brought about by such a shift.

Moreover, the fact that the proportion of the work force employed in the public sector did not expand greatly is thought to have played an important role in determining productivity trends. Because the market mechanism does not work well in the public sector, efficiency improvements are prone to lag compared with the private sector, thereby making productivity improvements difficult. An expansion of the public sector, therefore, impedes the growth of productivity in the economy as a whole. In Japan's case, the proportion of persons employed in the public sector rose

Table 6   Changes in Work Force Structure by Industry

(% of total)

	1965	1970	1975	1979
Japan				
Primary industry	23.5	17.4	12.7	11.2
Secondary industry	31.9	35.2	35.2	34.3
Tertiary industry	44.6	47.3	51.9	54.3
(Subtotal: Public sector)	8.2	7.7	8.7	8.9
Total	100.0	100.0	100.0	100.0
U.S.A.				
Primary industry	6.1	4.5	4.1	3.7
Secondary industry	30.7	33.2	29.5	30.1
Tertiary industry	63.2	62.3	66.4	66.2
(Subtotal: Public sector)	28.6	26.2	26.5	24.7
Total	100.0	100.0	100.0	100.0

Note: Figures for Japan are based on *Survey of the Labor Force*, those for the United States on *Statistical Abstract of the U.S.* and *Survey of Current Business*.

slightly from 8.2 percent of the total work force in 1965 to 8.9 percent in 1979—an extremely low percentage by international standards. Whereas the number of public servants per 1,000 population is about 80 in the United States and West Germany and over 100 in the United Kingdom, it is only 45 in Japan (Table 6). The fact that Japan has maintained a comparatively small government has probably helped raise the overall efficiency of the economy.

The role of technological progress

The third reason is greater production efficiency due to technological progress. Japan's technological level immediately after World War II was substantially behind that of the United States and Europe. This gap was rapidly closed by technology imports, and production efficiency improved in the process. Imported technology, linked with active plant and equipment investment, became widespread in all sectors of the economy.

Because of the rapid pace of growth in plant and equipment investment, Japan's production facilities are fairly young by international standards. Economic Planning Agency calculations show that the average age of production facilities is 10–11 years in the United States against 7–8 years in Japan. If the average age of capital equipment is low, it means that there is a correspondingly high proportion of production facilities that incorporate the latest technology and that efficiency is correspondingly greater.

One feature that has been prominent these last couple of years has been the spread of industrial robots that incorporate electronic technology. Industrial robots were born in the United States at the beginning of the 1960s and first appeared in Japan in 1967. Since then, performance has been improved and prices have declined as a result of microcomputers, and their fields of application have broadened rapidly. Initially robots were used in automaking welding processes, but they have since spread to the electrical appliances and machinery industries. Such robots are not limited to the large companies, but are becoming common even in the smaller enterprises. Today there are 75,000 industrial robots (including 7,500 multi-purpose robots) in Japan, more than half of the industrial robots in the world even at a conservative count.

There has been rapid growth in the robot-making industries. There are about 80 robot manufactures in Europe and the United States; in Japan, 130 enterprises are competing in the business of making robots.

The trend toward labor saving by the use of industrial robots is seen as growing in the future, and will contribute to an increase in labor productivity.

All other countries have had essentially the same opportunity to actively introduce technical innovations that Japan has had. Yet, why has Japan alone so actively incorporated such innovations? I feel that the characteristics of Japanese economic organizations have had a substantial impact in this regard.

Japanese management strategies

To begin with, the approach to management in Japanese enterprises is considerably different from that in U.S. businesses. The results of questionnaire surveys on business management in Japan and the United States conducted by Assistant Professor Kagono

Table 7   Comparison of U.S. and Japanese Management Goals

Goal	Japan	U.S.A.
Investment–profit ratio	1.23	2.43
Market share	1.49	0.73
New-product ratio	1.04	0.21
Increasing share prices	0.02	1.14
Rationalization of production and distribution systems	0.68	0.46
Owned capital ratio to liabilities	0.61	0.38
Improvement of product portfolio	0.65	0.50
Improvement of working conditions	0.08	0.04
Improvement of company's social image	0.18	0.05

Notes: 1. Based on Tadao Kagono, "Japanese Management, American Management," Keizai Seminar, Jan. 1981.
2. Respondents were asked to list three choices in order of preference, which were assigned values of three, two, and one point respectively. The results were then averaged.

of Kobe University and his colleagues are very interesting in this respect (see Table 7). Kagono observes the following differences between Japanese and U.S. management.

First, U.S. enterprises emphasize short-term management efficiency as measured by the investment–profit ratio and stock prices as their management goal, whereas Japanese enterprises emphasize goals relating to growth in the longer term, such as market share and new-products ratio.

The second difference observed by Kagono is that U.S. enterprises have clear working manuals, authority is concentrated in the upper management, and there is a strong degree of standardization of work content, while Japanese companies have vague work manuals, diffuse authority, and a low degree of standardization of work content. This is because Japanese enterprises make their decisions by gaining an overall consensus through repeated discussion starting from the bottom and working up. Moreover, they rely not on manuals for work procedures but on on-the-job training. U.S. management may be summarized in one word as "mechanical," Japan's as "organic."

Since Japan's management organization is based on a complex decision-making process and requires time in training, its short-term efficiency is poor. However, it does have the advantages of strengthening the individual worker's sense of participation and enabling him to gain a fuller understanding of the enterprise's position.

Third, a large proportion of U.S. businesses use the operating division system which emphasizes the profitability of each individual operation. This gives greater voice to the financial and accounting sector than the manufacturing sector. In Japan, by contrast, only a small proportion of companies have adopted the operating division system. The result has been that operations with high growth potential but low profitability can be covered by other high-profit operations. Moreover, the manufacturing sector has a strong voice in management decisions.

To sum up these points, U.S. businesses have a management framework that emphasizes short-term efficiency, especially current performance, while Japanese businesses have a more flexible management framework that aims at greater efficiency of the production system as a whole and over time. It is through such an approach to management that Japanese businesses have constantly sought out new technical innovations and have actively brought them into use.

Features of Japanese labor relations

Labor has also displayed little resistance to new technology; in fact it has actively welcomed it.

From the worker's viewpoint, technical innovation which leads to a rise in labor productivity appears to deprive workers of their workplace, which is why worker's resistance to the introduction of new facilities and technologies is so strong in Europe and the United States. When viewed over the whole national economy, however, improvements in labor productivity do not lead to an increase in unemployment. If productivity rises due to technical innovation, then business profits and wages increase; domestic purchasing power expands; international competitiveness is strengthened, thereby increasing exports; and all of these create new employment opportunities. Japan's economic experience is proof of this.

The reason that Japanese workers have actively accepted technical innovation is due to the unique relationship between the enterprise and the workers in Japan. For a start, labor unions are not occupation-specific but firm-specific. Secondly, a lifetime employment system in which employees work at the same firm until retirement is the general practice. Thirdly, a seniority-based wage system is standard throughout Japanese enterprises.

There has been a strong tendency to think of these features of Japanese labor-management relations as being based on cultural and spiritual traditions unique to Japan and qualitatively quite different from the labor-management systems in the West. However, it would be more natural to view the Japanese system as enjoying its longevity precisely because both labor and management have felt it to be to their advantage. In fact, there have recently been a number of attempts in Japan to explain the formation of the Japanese-type labor-management relationship as the product of economic rationality.

One of the keys to this relationship is the fact that Japanese firms invest heavily in the education of their workers in the form of on-the-job training. During the postwar period of high economic growth, Japanese firms had to make efforts to train their own workers in order to obtain skilled labor that was otherwise prone to be in short supply. Thus Japanese workers' skills became specialized to suit only one particular enterprise. Consequently, firms try to discourage workers from leaving in order not to lose any of their investment in worker education, and the workers, for their part, find it more advantageous to stay with the same company because they are unable to use their skills to the fullest elsewhere. Worker organizations therefore become built up around the enterprise unit. Moreover, since the training of young workers costs money and workers' skills improve with the number of years employed, it is an easy step from there to seniority-based wages.

The Japanese-type labor-management relationship that has evolved in this way makes it easier for workers to accept technical innovation flexibly. For a start, their sense of identity with the firm is strong and they are aware that the firm's development is to their own advantage, so they tend to cooperate at their own initiative to improve the efficiency of its production system and strengthen its competitiveness. Moreover, since their employment is guaranteed and they gain experience in a variety of workplaces as part of their on-the-job training, workers do not form a rigid attachment to a particular workplace, and it is therefore possible to relocate the work force flexibly when new technology is introduced.

Nor is it just a matter of there being little resistance. In Japanese enterprises, workers actively make proposals for the improvement of work processes, and these lead to improvements in labor productivity. To take a case in point, when one machine tool manufacturer set up a suggestion system, it received over 1,000 suggestions per month. One automaker receives an average of seventeen suggestions per worker each year; some 30 percent of these are actually adopted and contribute to increase productivity. Examples such as these are not at all uncommon in Japanese factories. Norman Macrae, writing in *The Economist*, describes this behavior on the part of Japanese workers as the "daily productivity hunt." Individually, the suggestions from the factory floor may be of little effect, but the fact that workers are dealing with the problem of productivity is without doubt the basis for the rise in productivity.

The role of economic policy

I would now like to turn to the role that has been played by economic policy in increasing productivity in Japan.

Much attention is recently being paid in the United States to economic policies that focus on the supply side rather than on demand management.

Looking back on the progress of Japan's economic policy since World War II, I suspect that, although the theoretical grounds may have been somewhat shaky, emphasis has always been placed on securing supply capacity: Japan has in fact been implementing supply-side policies. This has, I feel, contributed also to the increase in productivity.

There has not yet been any attempt, even in Japan, to analyze systematically the effect of Japan's supply-side policies. I would therefore like to examine here the role of industrial policy, which is one of the main policies in this regard.

Japan's industrial policy can be divided into a number of fields: industrial structure policy, energy policy, regional development policy, and technological development policy.

As its industrial structure policy, the Japanese government presents a studied vision of what sort of industries should lead the economy in keeping with the stage of economic development. In the 1950s, emphasis was placed on the recovery of the steel, coal, and other basic industries. In the period of high economic growth in the 1960s, an industrial structure was chosen that focused on the heavy and chemical industries which had high income elasticity and plenty of room to improve productivity. In the 1970s, as trade and investment became liberalized and the newly industrializing countries began to catch up in such fields as textiles, the choice fell on knowledge-intensive industries involving a high degree of processing.

The industrial structure policies based on such visions constitute neither central planning nor mere forecasts. They are what might be termed indicative planning policy in which taxation and financial inducements are used in keeping with the policy while leaving things basically to the market mechanism.

Energy policy has seen many vicissitudes. Immediately after World War II, the focus was on obtaining the energy to fuel economic reconstruction. In the 1960s, policy efforts were made to shift energy sources smoothly from coal to oil. This also entailed a process of adjustment in which the domestic coal-mining industry was scaled down smoothly. Since the 1973 oil crisis, emphasis has been placed on stockpiling oil, conserving energy, and developing nuclear power as constraints on energy growth.

Regional development policy has also played an important role in improving the supply base. The 1960s saw improvement of social capital and development of seaside industrial zones under the Pacific Coastal Belt Development and the Growth Center Development Program. In the 1970s, the government has been promoting the decentralization of industry to deal with worsening urban and pollution problems. Improvement of roads, communications, and other infrastructures has made such decentralization economically feasible.

As for technological development, ever since the 1950s, policies have been implemented to facilitate the introduction of overseas technology. But as Japan has come to catch up with the Western industrial countries, emphasis has come to be placed on developing our own technology.

An important factor in the implementation of these industrial policies has been that government and business have had little sense of confrontation with each other but rather one of cooperation. The government has at all times believed that promoting greater efficiency in the production system by giving full rein to private enterprise's vitality is essential to economic development. Business, for its part, has taken the government's vision as indicating the road the Japanese economy must take.

This relationship between government and industry is maintained by a close exchange of information between the two. The government is constantly collecting data on industry and seeks out the views of industry to take them into account in formulating important policies. Its visions of industrial structure, for example, were drawn up after repeated discussion with representatives from universities, industry, and labor.

I believe that Japan's industrial structure policy would not have been able to maintain its effectiveness had there not been a relationship of trust and cooperation between government and business.

The Role of Labor Productivity During the Oil Crisis

With this kind of background, Japanese labor productivity has continued to rise at what is in international terms a very high rate. The increase in labor productivity has sustained the development of the Japanese economy so far. However, successive oil price increases have meant that a different role is being sought for labor productivity.

Japan has almost no domestic energy resources. Moreover, since it has relied on cheap and abundant oil to sustain its high economic growth, the Japanese economy is now one of the most heavily dependent on imported oil in the world. Whereas the proportion of imported oil to total energy supplies was 35.2 percent on the average for the OECD countries, Japan's was as high as 73.4 percent in 1978. Thus the Japanese economy is

Table 8   Japan's Recent Economic Performance

(Percentage Increase over Previous Year)

	Real GNP Growth Rate			Rate of Increase of Consumer Prices		
	1979	1980	1981	1979	1980	1981
Japan	5.9	5	3 3/4	3.6	6 1/4	5 1/4
U.S.A.	3.2	−3/4	3/4	11.3	10 1/2	10
F.R.G.	4.5	1 3/4	−1/4	4.1	5 1/4	4
U.K.	1.6	−2 1/4	−2	13.4	15 1/2	12
OECD average	3.3	1	1	8.6	11 1/4	9 3/4

Notes: 1. Based on OECD *Economic Outlook No. 28*, December 1980.
   2. Figures for 1980 are expected performance, those for 1981 are projections.

particularly susceptible to increases in the import prices of oil.

In 1979–80, however, Japan's economic performance was good by international standards, despite a substantial increase in oil import prices (see Table 8). Although the average inflation rate in the OECD countries was 8.6 percent in 1979 and 11.25 percent in 1980, that of Japan was 3.6 percent and 8.0 percent respectively. The real economic growth rate in the OECD countries was an average of 3.3 percent in 1979 and 1.0 percent in 1980, but Japan's was 5.9 percent and 5.0 percent respectively.

One of the major reasons that Japan's heavily oil-dependent economy has been able to maintain a better economic performance than other countries has been the high rate of increase in labor productivity.

Higher oil prices pull up prices and put pressure on business profits. Increased labor productivity, on the other hand, is a factor that stabilizes prices and boosts profits. The labor productivity increase of Japanese manufacturing was 12.1 percent in 1979 and rose to 12.3 percent in the first half of 1980. At the same time, the per-worker wage increase rate stayed at 6–7 percent, so the unit labor cost went down 4–5 percent (Table 9). In other words, when there is an increase in production costs due to the rise in oil prices, wage costs go down and it becomes possible to hold down the overall cost increase. The pressure of prices is thus weakened, and it is possible to hold down to a considerable extent any deterioration in business profits and decline

Table 9   Productivity and Wage Costs

(%)

	Japan			U.S.A.		
	Rate of Productivity Growth	Wage Increase Rate	Rate of Wage Cost Increase	Rate of Productivity Growth	Wage Increase Rate	Rate of Wage Cost Increase
1978	8.0	6.4	−1.5	1.7	9.0	7.2
1979	12.1	6.2	−5.3	1.8	8.5	6.6
1980 (first half)	12.3	8.4	−3.5	1.8	7.7	5.8

Source: Main economic indicators, OECD.

of real income. This is what has sustained Japan's favorable economic performance: the increase in labor productivity has acted as a cushion to soften the blow of the oil crisis.

Conclusions

As we have seen, the increase in labor productivity has been an important basis for the strength of the Japanese economy and has sustained its development so far. However, there is the possibility that the rate of increase in labor productivity will gradually slow as Japan's economy and society mature. One of the reasons for this is that the average age of the work force will rapidly increase. The percentage of workers aged 45 years or more is expected to rise from 30 percent in 1965 and 35 percent in 1975 to about 40 percent of Japan's total working population by 1985. At that point Japan will have the oldest work force in the world. As the population grows older, it will gradually become more difficult to maintain the Japanese type of labor-management relationship as represented by seniority-based wages and lifetime employment.

The second reason is that as income levels increase, Japanese workers show a growing preference for increased leisure over higher income with longer work hours. At present the level of leisure time in Japan is low compared to other countries: only one-fourth of all workers enjoy a full two-day weekend. No doubt this poor level of leisure time will gradually be rectified. This means that the resources that have hitherto been directed to improving production efficiency will have to be allocated to boosting leisure time.

Third, the saving ratio is declining. Japan's saving ratio has been high so far because of the high rate of income increase, the low level of housing and financial asset stocks, and the continuing graying of the population. However, such economic and social conditions will probably gradually disappear, and the proportion of resources that can be directed in the form of investment to improve future production capacity will eventually dwindle.

All these factors combined lead us to predict that the rate of increase in Japanese labor productivity will gradually slow down. This would be a natural development as the Japanese economy finishes catching up with the Western industrial countries and matures.

Japan's experience with labor productivity has been that economic development ultimately depends on and is determined by the willingness of the people and businesses that compose the economy to make progress and the functioning of the economic systems that interconnect them. What has maintained the high increase in labor productivity and thus pushed up the level of economic activity has been neither a shogun-type loyalty nor any special feature of Japanese society. It is because Japan has an economic system in which the will to improve the economy itself can have free rein, to which end resources are being allocated rationally with government assistance.

Japan's Science
and Technology Reexamined

In a recent survey dealing with national identity, Japanese were most proud of what they perceived to be their nation's strength in science and technology. According to that survey, conducted by the Japan Research Institute, Japanese strength in science and technology was perceived as clearly something to be proud of in comparison with foreign countries by 50.2 percent of the 1,551 respondents, and relatively so by additional 33.7 percent. Also, 30.7 percent of respondents found Japanese economic strength to be most worth boasting about, followed by 30.4 percent who found it relatively worth boasting about. On the other hand, only 5.7 percent of total respondents believed that they could be most proud of Japan's political strength vis-à-vis foreign countries, and a large plurality (44.6 percent) disagreed with that assessment.[1]

More than a decade ago, Japan was dubbed "an economic super-state," primarily due to boosts in exports such as steel, color TVs, and, most notably, automobiles. The Japanese have increasingly seen economic strength as the most salient factor shaping their conception of national pride. Nippon Broadcasting Corporation's survey data illustrates this point. In 1964, 65 percent of those sampled responded by saying the West was economically superior to Japan, while only 17.0 percent disagreed. Seven years later, in 1971, however, the situation was reversed— that is, 40.0 percent believed Japan was economically superior

[1] Japan Research Institute, *Varying Indices of Industrial Society*, 1983.

This paper was prepared in June 1984 at the request of the Massachusetts Institute of Technology, Cambridge, Massachusetts. The author is grateful to Prof. Taizo Yakushiji of Saitama University for his assistance.

19

to the West, whereas only 15.0 percent took the opposite view.

Now let us turn to the American scene and ask how Americans perceive their country's greatness. The National Opinion Research Center provides more or less comparable data based on a different questionnaire. According to them, 46 percent of their 1,635 respondents saw America's technological know-how as contributing most to U.S. influence in the world, and 22 percent selected scientific creativity as most contributory. In stark contrast to Japanese opinions about their own government, the U.S. government's performance was rated by Americans as second to technological know-how. That is, 41 percent chose the form of their government as most contributory. American confidence in their science and technology has declined slightly and gradually. Harris Surveys show that the public's rating of industrial know-how as the major factor that will make America great went down from 87 percent (1973) to 86 percent (1975), and stood at 80 percent in 1977 and 80 percent in 1979. The rating of technological genius also went down from 78 percent (1977) to 73 percent (1979). This may reflect the stagnation of U.S. productivity which started in the late 1970s.[2]

Fluidity in Decision-Making

While public opinion data is interesting, it tells us little about the actual state of a nation's science and technology. And more importantly, it says very little about the relationship of a nation's science and technology to that nation's productivity. Unlike the public, scholars have to be more careful in asserting that a state's strength in science and technology is highly correlated with industrial productivity. Phenomenologically it may be so, or it may not be. Indeed, the late William Abernathy argued that the relationship of productivity to science and technology poses a dilemma.[3] The dilemma is that excessive stress on increasing

[2] Jon D. Miller, Kenneth Prewitt, and Robert Pearson, *The Attitudes of the U.S. Public Toward Science and Technology*, Chicago: National Opinion Research Center, University of Chicago, 1980; The Harris Survey, Releases dated 8/27/73, 11/27/75, 1/16/78, 3/6/80.

[3] William J. Abernathy, *The Productivity Dilemma*, Baltimore: Johns Hopkins University Press, 1978.

productivity (which is often called "labor productivity") tends to suppress otherwise "useful" intramural slacks that are often the key to creativity in scientific and technological endeavors. This view is supported by economist Burton Klein of Cal Tech, although he used a somewhat different conception of productive efficiency.[4]

I agree with these assessments and value of the retention of "fluidity" in decision-making as a means for retaining useful slack in the system. Moreover, in my view, social flexibility is vital to both industrial strength as well as scientific and technological strength. In a speech before an OECD Ministerial Conference on "The Longer-term Performance of OECD Economies: Challenges Facing Governments" in February of this year, I argued that the flexibility of Japanese society has been one of the prime causes for the level of Japanese economic success attained so far. One form of flexibility is found in competition, which gives people alternatives and which permits innovation through new combinations of resources. It is generally recognized that there has been strong competition in Japanese society and such competition has motivated entrepreneurs' positive attitude toward investment and the introduction of new technologies. This, coupled with the general social flexibility, has helped shape positive responses to changes in economic and industrial environments.

In my view, an effective society is one that is fluid enough so that market demands and entrepreneurial decision-making can be linked by a good feedback mechanism, and in which enough slack exists so that feedback can improve subsequent decisions. A good example along this line can be drawn from the case of pollution-controlled engine design during the early 1970s. As in the U.S., the stringent Japanese emissions standard initially aroused a rather hostile reaction from the auto industry due to the cost of add-ons and the enormous R&D investment required. But when industry finally came to recognize that society (i.e., the market) truly required it, they quickly shifted their attitude

---

[4] Burton H. Klein, "The Slowdown in Productivity Advances: A Dynamic Explanation," in Christopher T. Hill and James M. Utterback, eds., *Technological Innovation for a Dynamic Economy*, New York: Pergamon Press, 1979, Chapter 3, pp. 66–117.

and invested a great amount to implement what the government specified. Another example can be found in the way most Japanese companies quickly shifted their fuel dependence from oil to coal when the 1973 oil crisis erupted.

I am emphasizing Japan's cultural trait of social flexibility because transfer of one country's culture to another country is rather painstaking and, in most cases, impossible. Whatever the cultural context, government or other large organizations can reduce or expand the amount of practical flexibility in any society. I am arguing that coercive measures or regimented systems must be avoided. Furthermore I believe that policies based on the market mechanisms will always be conducive to meeting societal needs if the dynamic elements of the market economy are arranged in what I call a "virtuous circle" of non-inflationary sustainable growth, technical innovation, active investment, and creation of job opportunities. Thus, it becomes of vital importance that friction arising from the process of structural change and technological innovation be resolved in the long run by enhancing flexibility of all parties concerned. In this regard, let me illustrate one example below.

Rational Industrial Adjustment Policies: The Income Doubling Plan of 1960

Needless to say, policy flexibility is important in guiding the relationship between market and corporate entities. Whether or not foreign observers call Japanese economic and industrial planning targeting or non-targeting, modern Japan has relied on a flexible policy-making strategy for her economic upgrading. Among these policies, the most notable has been the famous Income Doubling Plan adopted in 1960.

The policy concept of the National Income Doubling Plan (for the period from 1961 to 1970) was originally drafted by the Kishi cabinet's Economic Deliberation Council in 1959, which was the advisory body attached to the government with the Economic Planning Agency (EPA) as its secretariat. It was further substantiated by the next Ikeda cabinet. The plan was officially announced on December 27, 1960. The aim of this plan was literally to double the national income in about ten years' time. Five areas designated for attention by this plan were: (1) strengthening of social overhead capital, (2) inducement to realize a highly industrialized structure for the economy, (3) promotion of exports and strengthening of economic cooperation with less developed countries, (4) development of human ability and advancement of science and technology, and (5) mitigation of the dual structure and securing of social stability.

On a post-hoc basis, some noticeable features of this earmarking plan are in order. First, this plan emphasized a long-range time perspective (i.e., ten years). Previously, economic planning normally had a five-year perspective. The longer period reflected the government's recognition that it was imperative to develop a social infrastructure, a task that required a greater time span. Secondly, the plan did not aim at fixing detailed targets for every sector of the economy but instead emphasized long-term policy measures. Thirdly, the manpower aspects received keen attention. Two committees, the Committee for Education and Training and the Committee for Development of Human Resources, were established before and after the announcement of the plan. In 1963, the latter committee recommended a manpower policy for economic development. In the context of this article, there are two points which deserve special attention. One is the flexibility and non-targeting of the government's economic planning, and the other is the role of manpower policy. I will briefly touch upon these two.

The government's plan had to be flexible because the Japanese economy was, and remains, internally competitive. Internal competition, in turn, posed the fluid environment in which government policy had to be implemented. Often foreign observers are puzzled to see a highly competitive society in Japan. They have a preconception of Japan as a country under strong governmental and economic leadership. Contrary to this prevailing image, Japan is characterized by keen competition among private enterprises, and even by competition among various governmental agencies. For instance, we have eleven auto-manufacturing companies, and seven or eight world-competitive consumer electronics firms. And the Ministry of International Trade and Industry (MITI) and the Ministry of Posts and Telecommunications, for example, continuously wrangle over a new concept of a future telecommunications-oriented society.

When one reviews Japan's postwar economic or industrial planning, he will find continuous readjustment of the original plans. This strongly implies that, unlike French indicative planning, the dynamic nature of the private sector and the uncertainty about future growth potential have put limitations on the use of economic plans for determining the level of investment in individual sectors of Japanese economy. If we put it differently, the government plans provide guideposts for decisions to be made by private enterprises, and they do not aim at fixing detailed targets for every sector of the economy. In Japan, there is growing recognition of the usefulness of planning in a free-enterprise economy, and the preparation of the economic plans itself has had an educational effect upon the various ministries, on business, on labor unions, and on the general public. In a word, Japanese economic planning is a great feedback lesson to steer the country's economy in adjusting to dramatic changes in the outer environment. I believe that the "virtuous circle" is a key to this state's learning process.

Manpower and Fluidity in R&D: Two Graphical Presentations

National university entrants during the 1960s

One of the key areas the Income Doubling Plan deemed vital was promotion of science and technology, which, of course, aimed at the forthcoming full economic liberalization in the 1970s. The plan proposed an increase in the state's R&D investment. It identified a shortage in scientific and engineering manpower and called for an increase of 170,000 such people during the period the plan encompassed. Furthermore, it advocated that many of the new high schools being built for the baby-boom generation in 1963–65 should be primarily engineering high schools to fill the foreseen shortage in the middle-level engineering work force on the order of 440,000.

During the period of income doubling, Japanese often heard

a slogan called the *"rikohka*-boom"—*rikohka* being a Japanese abbreviation of "the faculties of science and engineering," which literally means that high school graduates were attracted to apply to these faculties for college entrance examinations. Now let us see how this policy worked.

The *"rikohka*-boom" has been interpreted as responding to the state's need to increase the total number of college graduates in science and engineering, particularly in the latter field. The aim was not simply to increase in numbers but also to enhance in quality.

Since the Meiji Restoration in 1868, national universities have functioned as a key supplier of qualified manpower to the state's need. And since they are under the jurisdiction of the Ministry of Education, the number of new enrollees is annually controllable as a predetermined fixed number. This is a marked difference from the American educational system, where private and state educational institutions operate under their own policies. For example, President Reagan emphasized in his 1984 State-

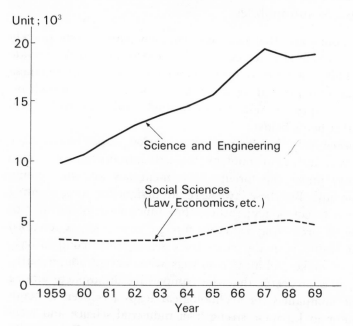

Figure 1   National university entrants by discipline
Source: *Basic School Statistics*, Ministry of Education.

of-the-Union address the reenhancement of the U.S. educational level. However, the U.S. educational system may not respond to his warning as quickly as the Japanese system did during the 1960s. The maneuverability of the Japanese system is partially evidenced in Figure 1.

The trend of the curve for science and engineering entrants (i) was much steeper, and the curve for social science students (ii) was suppressed, in the first half of the 1960s. Since there were natural increases in the number of applicants for national universities, the steeper trend in (i) implies that increments in those qualified applicants were absorbed mainly by science and engineering faculties. Given these observations, we may conclude that more qualified high school graduates entered national universities' science and engineering departments. Needless to say, Japan's succeeding dramatic increase in industrial productivity owes much to the success of manpower policy during this period.

Undulating pattern in industrial activities: The case of automobiles

I pointed out above that Japanese economic plans became quickly obsolete because of fierce competition and change in the private sector. This is a marked indicator of the liveliness of Japanese industrial activities during the 1960s. How can we see such industrial liveliness in relation to technological progress? I will discuss this point below.

Retrospectively, in the preceding period, Japan could have enhanced industrial technology through introduction of foreign technology under the foreign investment law and the foreign exchange laws. But these laws were not designed as implementing tools for a target policy; rather, they functioned to control (for the sake of preserving valuable foreign currencies) a so-called jammed traffic of many companies which were competitively rushing to make technical contracts with foreign counterparts. In fact, it is no secret that the competitive atmosphere among Japanese companies for technological leaps has been a major contributor to Japanese strength in industrial science and technology to date. Now let us see, in Figure 2, how Japanese industries could break with the practice of technological borrowing

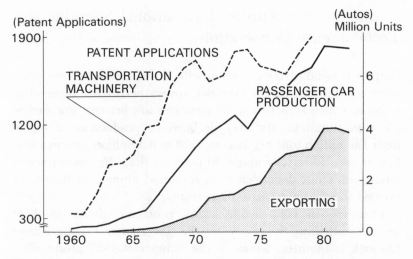

Figure 2   Patterns of automotive technology development, automobile production, and exports
Source: Keiichi Oshima, "Competition and auto trade: A technological perspective." Paper delivered at the University of Michigan's Auto Conference, 1983.

and enter into the period of development of indigenous technology.

This figure shows three things. First, the R&D activities, interpreted in terms of patent application thrusts in transportation machinery (composed mostly of automobile related industries) were most active around 1964 or 1965. The patent application curve forms a typical "logistic" pattern, and thus its first derivative has the highest peak around that year. This also implies that Japan's indigenous technology in the automobile sector "shook off" dependence on foreign precedents and sprang into full bloom in the mid-1960s. It is worth noting that this period also corresponds to the highest peak of the *"rikohka*-boom." Second, the production of passenger cars went up dramatically from about 1967, a couple of years after this lively period, which implies that the supply-side condition met that of the demand side, giving way to Japan's first auto-boom. Third, exports were bootstrapped in the early 1970s. Interestingly, these three curves took off systematically in undulating waves.

Selecting a New Future: International Scientific and Technological Cooperation

Despite the industrial success briefly described above, the prospects for Japan's future may not always be bright. Internally, many so-called sunset-industry problems are present. For example, the aluminum industry declined in production of ingots from 1.0 million tons per year in 1978 to 0.3 million tons in 1982, figures even lower (by about 50 percent) than the government's guideline. Thus, dependence on imported aluminum ingots increased from 43 percent to 82 percent.

Japan is, in fact, facing many problems. Some of them are illustrated in the study by the government's Long-Range Outlook Committee, which in the summer of 1982 produced a report entitled *Japan in the Year 2000*. Three salient problems are identified for the future of the Japanese economy. (a) The population is rapidly aging (the population aged 65 and above accounted for 5 percent of the total in 1960 and 10 percent in 1983, and will reach 16 percent in 2000 and 19 percent in 2010 —giving Japan, in the near future, the oldest age structure among OECD countries). (b) Japan, now one of the leading countries in the field of high technology, has a difficult task in developing new technological frontiers. (c) Japan has to live in a new and broader environment, responsive to the changing world economy, and interact in harmony with the other nations of the world.

Combining the above (b) and (c), Japan's future scientific and technological strength is certainly at risk. How it will fare depends on how successfully Japan can engage in international cooperation in science and technology. Let me further elaborate on this problem.

In 1983, the National Academy of Science (NAS) and National Research Council (NRC) jointly filed an important report on the future course of U.S. scientific and technological strength. The report, entitled *The Panel on Advanced Technology: Competition and the Industrialized Allies*, admitted that the U.S. could not expect to maintain its overwhelming market share in advanced technologies. This is a startling admission because advanced technology is perceived as a strong part of America's self-image. It denied, however, the desirability of protectionist measures to regain U.S. competitiveness. Instead, it stressed enhancement of the technical capacity of civilian sectors including not only productive technology per se but product planning and even marketing. The report concluded that the U.S. must initiate a two-part strategy to maintain its capacity for technological innovation and to foster an open healthy international trading system. In this respect, the panel recommended diplomatic prescriptions to negotiate with competing foreign countries in an international roundtable for instituting new trading rules with a focus on high technology. Coincidentally, a similar argument was made by John Zysman and Stephen S. Cohen in *Foreign Affairs*.[5] I do not know whether these views are indicative of U.S. official strategy in science and technology for the next generation, but let me present an argument in a Japanese context, given these American views.

Since the Ikeda-Kennedy meeting in 1960, the U.S. and Japan have been cooperating in science and technology at a governmental level. Today there are nine or ten clusters in which the U.S. and Japan cooperate: Among these areas are nuclear energy, medicine, energy, space, cancer, biochemistry, marine science, and environmental protection. If we include cooperative agreements by private firms, there are countless numbers of cooperative programs between the two countries. Furthermore, Japan has numerous ties with other OECD countries as well as developing countries in scientific and technological cooperative agreements. What are rationales for them?

In addition to the general reasoning that we are participating in the postwar liberal trade regime, there are other crucial reasons why Japan has to devote itself to international cooperation in science and technology. First, in the private sector, Japanese companies, although they are currently enjoying a good reputation, have to form cooperative ventures with foreign competitors in order not to be totally disappear from a future international competitive race. This is because some technologies are "over-

---

[5] John Zysman and Stephen S. Cohen, "Double or Nothing: Open Trade and Competitive Industry," *Foreign Affairs*, Summer 1983, pp. 1113–1139.

whelming" or "fatal" in a sense that if a company fails to adopt them, it becomes fatally vulnerable in international competition. A good example of this can be found in productive agreements among the world's giant corporations making video tape recorders and small passenger cars. This is a case where severe competition inevitably invites cooperation. Second, perhaps there are times when a donor country is better off releasing high technologies rather than enclosing them within their own borders. Releases are made to allied countries in the form of technical agreements with restrictions against transferring these technologies to third countries. This is a case of the so-called packaged or tied transfer of technology in developed countries. This strategy is sometimes applied both to government agreements for technologies with national-security implications and to private agreements for important know-how such as computer software and microprocessors. Whatever Japan's predilections in general may be, it has to comply when this type of technology is involved.

Thirdly, in order to achieve an economy of scale in production, Japan has to ask neighboring countries for joint ventures in parts and machine design and production. This is an internationally scaled counterpart of the zero-inventory system for continuous parts supplies which is currently being practiced among Japanese domestic industries. This strategy contains several advantages for both parties participating. In the first place, the technical level of these countries will be enhanced as they play the role of suppliers of qualified parts. It is a more or less identical role Japan played in the past during the days of American's Korean War procurement. Japan of course will gain considerably if supplied with good parts and machine equipment from nearby nations. Also, cooperating countries would gain economic benefits from OEM (original equipment manufacturers) products they manufacture bearing Japanese brand names. However, this is a view from the Japanese side. There is, of course, another view. It is the logic of technology transfer. Let me briefly describe its framework by referring to a report by the Task Force on Technology Transfer of the Pacific Economic Cooperation Conference, at which I represented Japan as a member of the standing committee.

The report sheds light on the following four major issues:

(a) proper choice of technology, (b) absorptive capacity, (c) contract and pricing, and (d) unpackaged transfer. For issue (a), the task force recommends that technology-receiving countries should develop their own technology-transfer policies, which should include the identification of domestic needs and the search for available technology. In essence, it is the issue of non-passiveness in technology transfer. Concerning absorptive capacity, the report emphasizes social investment for infrastractures such as technical and engineering universities and testing and research labs. To realize fair contracts and pricing, it has been pointed out that a feasibility study should be done by introducing alternative sources of technology and by identifying its cost segments. Finally, the issue of unpacked transfer of technology is best described by the statement that "new and sophisticated technology is mostly transferred by owner manufacturing companies coupled with direct foreign investment or with strict restriction of the use of transferred technology such as export restriction and tied purchases of specific equipment and materials." Thus, the report recommends strengthening the absorptive capacity of domestic industries for exploiting the potential advantages of unpacked and untied technology transfer free of direct investment and constraints on the use of transferred technology.

It seems to me quite possible to mingle Japan's logic of international cooperation and its logic of technology transfer. For example, the open-door policy of inviting able technical personnel from technology-receiving countries for study and training is one alternative from which both parties can benefit. In fact, before companies become internationalized, we Japanese need to be internationalized. In this regard, some measures must be taken to widen our absorptive capacity to welcome foreign researchers and engineers from both developed and developing countries. No country in history can become internationalized without an open-door policy to incorporate foreign nationals into various segments of society. Japan is truly on the verge of exposing itself to the outer world scientifically and technologically. Whether or not she will be able to cope with this new situation is a true acid test for Japan's future.

Theoretical Sources of Trade Frictions

Japan's trade practices have come in for considerable criticism from overseas during the past decade. It is the purpose here to analyze recent developments and attempt to assess the validity of that criticism. Japan has made rapid progress in further opening her markets and much of the criticism once levied against Japan is no longer relevant. An attempt is made to highlight these areas and to explain the various changes which have made much of the criticism obsolete. This article deals first with Japan's balance of payments as the macroeconomic target of overseas criticism and then looks at residual import quotas and tariff rates as indications of the openness of the Japanese market. It finally deals with some specific issues relating to (i) import-inspection procedures, (ii) distribution mechanisms and commercial practices, and (iii) trade in services.[1]

Balance-of-Payments Trends

Some people have charged that Japan is continuing to accumulate major surpluses in her current account and that these surpluses are having a deleterious impact on industry and employment in other parts of the world economy. In examining the

This article was first published in *The World Economy: A Quarterly Journal on International Economic Affairs*, Vol. 7, No. 3, September 1984. Reprinted with permission of Basil Blackwell Publisher Ltd. and of the Trade Policy Research Centre, the journal's copyright holder.

[1] The author appreciates the assistance of Noboru Nishifuji, of the Economic Planning Agency in Tokyo, in preparing this article.

validity of this argument, it is instructive, as a first step, to consider the current-account surplus as a percentage of gross national product (GNP) over the last twenty years (see Figure 1). The first point to be made is that Japan has not consistently been in surplus, the current account having fluctuated between surpluses and deficits.

Until the mid-1960s, the current account was a factor limiting GNP growth, for rapid growth quickly threw the current account into deficit. In the mid-1960s, however, the current account shifted to a surplus position, recording major surpluses in the periods 1971–72, 1977–78, and 1982–83. It is in these three periods that trade friction has been most heated. Because the current-account surplus exceeded 1 percent of GNP in each of these periods, it can be empirically demonstrated that this 1 percent of GNP is a threshold for trade friction. At the same time, it should be noted that the current-account deficit was approximately 1 percent of GNP after the oil "shocks" of 1973–74 and 1979–80.

Japan's dependence on energy imports in 1980 was 84 percent, the highest for any of the seven major industrialized countries and many times the United States's dependence of 15 percent or the United Kingdom's of 3 percent (see Table 1). Crude oil alone accounts for 37 percent of Japan's total imports. When coal, liquefied natural gas and other mineral fuels are included, the category "mineral fuels" accounted for 50 percent of Japan's

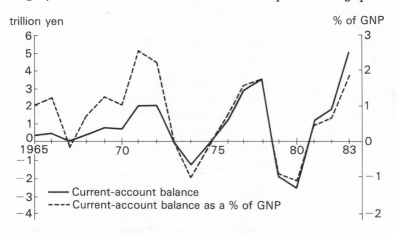

Figure 1   Japan's current-account balance compared with GNP

Table 1   Energy-import Dependence and the Share of Energy in Total Imports for the Major Industrialized Countries, 1980 (%)

	Energy-import dependence[a]	Share of total imports	
		Crude oil	Mineral fuels[b]
Canada	−6.2	10.2	12.4
France	72.6	19.5	26.5
United Kingdom	2.7	8.5	13.6
Italy	82.1	20.5	27.9
Japan	84.1	36.5	50.1
United States	14.5	25.8	32.9
West Germany	54.4	7.7	22.3

Source: *Statistics of Foreign Trade, Series B*, Organisation for Economic Cooperation and Development, Paris.

[a]Defined as the volume of energy imports divided by total energy consumption.
[b]Derived by subtracting electric power from Section 3 of the Standard International Trade Classification.

total imports in 1980. When oil prices soar, as they did during the two oil crises, Japan's crude-oil import bill also soars and the current account falls precipitously into the red. In the wake of the second oil crisis, for example, crude-oil imports rose by ¥7 trillion ($29 billion) between 1978 and 1980. As a result, the current account slipped from a surplus of 1.7 percent of GNP in 1978 to a deficit of 1.1 percent of GNP in 1980. This GNP shift of 2.8 percent is approximately equivalent to the increase in crude-oil imports (3 percent of GNP) over the same period. By contrast, the current account tends to go sharply into the black when real oil prices decline, as they have done recently.

Looking at current-account trends over the past ten years, in spite of the severity of the deficits in the wake of the two oil crises, Japan has regained balance in its current account by expanding exports of high-quality and high-value-added products manufactured with more energy-efficient technology. In short, Japan has regained a surplus position in its current account because its industry has been able to adapt.

The 1983 current-account surplus

In 1983, three years after the second oil crisis, Japan recorded a current-account surplus of approximately ¥5 trillion ($21 billion), or 1.8 percent of GNP. There are a number of special circumstances accounting for this large surplus.

The first factor is the decline in oil prices. At its general meeting in March 1983, the Organization of Petroleum Exporting Countries (OPEC) decided to reduce crude-oil prices by approximately $5 a barrel; the price to Japan fell to $30.77, a decline of 11 percent. This saving, a total amounting to approximately ¥1.5 trillion ($6 billion), went straight into the current account.

The second factor is the effect of the dollar's strength, and the yen's weakness, on foreign-exchange markets as a result of high rates of interest in the United States. This was especially true of 1983's current account. In 1982, the average rate of exchange was ¥249 to the dollar, a devaluation of approximately ¥30 from 1981's average rate. This difference served to boost export volume and to hold down import volume in 1983, and it combined with the "J-curve" shift to raise export unit prices in dollar terms as a result of the yen's appreciation through exchange-market adjustments in early 1983. Taken together, these currency-related factors added approximately ¥1.7 trillion ($7 billion) a year to the current account.

Had neither of these factors been present, the current-account surplus would have been held to approximately ¥2 trillion, which is only 0.7 percent of GNP and well below the "threshold for trade friction." In addition, the current-account surplus was higher because the American economy started its recovery (pulling in imports) before the Japanese economy did so.

With the bulk of the current-account surplus in 1983 due to such one-off factors, it may be assumed that Japan's current-account surplus in the medium term will be considerably lower and will stay within 1 percent of GNP as long as oil prices are stable, the rate of exchange finds a rational equilibrium (for example, purchasing-power parity), and the Japanese recovery takes off.

Long-term balance-of-payments fluctuations

Yet, while the major current-account surplus in 1983 was a one-off phenomenon, Japan's current account is expected to continue in the black for the long term. According to the hypothesis of "balance-of-payments stages," this long-term structural surplus in Japan's current account arises because she is at the immature creditor stage.

As the American economists Gerald M. Meier, Robert E. Baldwin[2] and Charles P. Kindleberger[3] and the British economic commentator Lord Geoffrey Crowther,[4] and others have argued at various times, a country's trade balance, investment income, and capital account fluctuate according to its stage of development and a country develops from a debtor position, in which capital inflow offsets the trade deficit, to a position in which the trade surplus enables the country to pay the interest on capital imports, to being a capital-exporting country, and finally to recording a surplus in its investment income.

Crowther further refined this to define an immature creditor nation as one which has a net capital outflow because of surpluses both in its goods-and-services balance excluding investment income and in its investment income and where, too, the current-account surplus and net capital outflow are both considered likely to continue strong in the long term. In other words, this stage may be explained as one in which the high rate of domestic savings generates a large savings surplus, which is made globally available through outflows of capital.

The United Kingdom was at the immature creditor stage from the early 1800s until around 1880 and the United States from around 1915 until the mid-1960s. Later-developing Japan achieved this stage only in the late 1970s and it is expected that she will continue for some time to supply considerable funds from

[2] Gerald M. Meier and Robert E. Baldwin, *Economic Development: Theory, History, Policy* (New York: John Wiley, 1957).

[3] Charles P. Kindleberger, *International Economics*, fourth edition (Homewood, Illinois: Richard D. Irwin, 1968).

[4] Lord Geoffrey Crowther, *Balances and Imbalances of Payments*, George H. Leatherbee Lectures (Boston: Graduate School of Business Administration, Harvard University, 1957).

her domestic savings surplus through her current-account surplus and capital outflow. Just as the United States and the United Kingdom did before her, Japan will continue to supply capital to the world and to contribute to global economic development (i) through industrial cooperation with other industrialized countries and the newly industrializing countries and (ii) through economic cooperation with the developing countries via official development assistance.

Again according to the hypothesis of balance-of-payments stages, the next stage after the immature creditor nation is that of the mature creditor nation, in which the goods-and-services balance excluding investment income is in deficit, but this deficit is more than offset by investment income accruing from past overseas investment and the country continues to have a new outflow of capital. This was the position attained by the United Kingdom after 1880 and by the United States after the mid-1960s. As a late-industrializing country, Japan may be expected to become a mature creditor nation in the early twenty-first century as a result of the decline in the savings ratio as a consequence of the rapid aging of her population and the shift to a service-oriented (and information-oriented) industrial structure.[5] When that happens, it is expected that a number of today's newly industrializing countries will be playing the same role in the world economy which Japan now plays.

Openness of the Japanese Market

Among the most useful measures for comparing the openness of different national markets are the number of items subject to "residual" import quotas and tariff rates. (Under the General Agreement on Tariffs and Trade [GATT], specifically Article XI, import quotas are meant to be eliminated and so those still in force are euphemistically described as "residual.") By either measure the Japanese market is very open.

[5] Long-term Outlook Committee of the Economic Council and Economic Planning Agency, *Japan in the Year 2000: Preparing Japan for an Age of Internationalization, the Aging Society and Maturity* (Tokyo: Japan Times, 1983).

Table 2   Residual Import Quotas, 1981

	Agricultural products	Mining and manufacturing	Total
Benelux	2 (10)	3 (4)	5 (14)
Canada	4 (3)	1 (1)	5 (4)
Denmark	5 (62)	0 (2)	5 (64)
France	19 (39)	27 (35)	46 (74)
United Kingdom	1 (19)	2 (6)	3 (25)
Italy	3 (12)	5 (8)	8 (20)
Japan	22 (55)	5 (35)	27 (90)
Norway	48 (54)	1 (1)	49 (55)
Sweden	5 (2)	1 (—)	6 (2)
United States	1 (1)	6 (4)	7 (5)
West Germany	3 (19)	1 (20)	4 (39)

Source: GATT Secretariat, Geneva.

Notes: Figures are as of December 31, 1981. The figures in parenthesis are as of December 31, 1970. Agricultural products have been classified in accordance with Customs Cooperation Council Notation 1–24 and mining and manufacturing products in accordance with CCCN 4.

Residual import quotas

Japanese residual import quotas now apply to only 27 products and product categories (see Table 2). This is less than one third of what it was ten years ago and it is considerably less, for example, than for France. Moreover, the number of residual import quotas is decreasing rapidly.

Japan has residual import quotas in only five mining and manufacturing categories and these are concentrated in coal, leather, and leather footwear. The Japanese market is at least as open as the other developed countries (and much more so than France, which has 27 residual import quotas in mining and manufacturing products alone). In agriculture, Japan has the second-highest number of residual import quotas among the developed countries, only Norway having more. As the "standard-bearer" for free trade, Japan is acutely aware of the need to move forcefully to eliminate these residual import quotas and to accelerate liberalization, but she is constrained by the political and social importance of the agricultural sector, as are the European Community, the United States, and other industrialized countries.

Tariffs

Japan has implemented a number of "packages" of market-opening measures and has taken the initiative in lowering her tariffs on a wide range of products. As a result, Japan's tariff burden is now on a par with that of the European Community and among the lowest in the world (see Table 3). According to statistics of the GATT Secretariat, the average tariff rates when the reductions agreed in the Tokyo Round of multilateral trade negotiations of 1973–79 are fully implemented will be approximately 3 percent for Japan, slightly over 4 percent for the United States, and a little under 5 percent for the European Community. Japanese tariff rates will be the lowest of any major signatory country to the Tokyo Round agreement.

In 1984, Japan is taking the further steps of (i) implementing Tokyo Round tariff cuts for mining and manufacturing products one year ahead of schedule, (ii) lowering tariffs on 47 items of export interest to her trading partners (including semi-conductors, reconstituted wood, perfumes, and bananas), and (iii) improving the Generalized System of Preferences by raising the GSP import ceiling by approximately 55 percent. Moreover, Japan is taking the lead in pushing for further tariff cuts through advancing the implementation of the Tokyo Round agreement and the initiation of a new "round" of multilateral trade negotiations.

In spite of this progress in eliminating residual import quotas and lowering tariffs, Japan is still accused of having numerous non-tariff interventions and remaining a closed market. Con-

Table 3   Tariff Burdens[a], 1977–81

	1977	1978	1979	1980	1981
Australia	9.1	10.1	9.5	9.5	9.0
Canada	5.1	5.2	4.6	4.5	4.5
European Community	3.3	3.7	3.3	2.8	2.6
Japan	3.8	4.1	3.1	2.5	2.5
United States	3.4	4.1	3.9	3.1	3.2

[a]Defined as the total revenues from tariffs and customs duties divided by the value of total imports.

sidered below are the areas on which this criticism mostly centers.

Import-inspection Procedures

A number of reforms have been made in Japan's import-inspection procedures in recent years and major progress has been achieved in opening up her market.

Standards and certification systems

In 1983 the Japanese Diet enacted amendments to sixteen laws. The amended laws, which went into effect on August 1, 1983, institutionalize fundamental improvements in Japan's standards and certification systems.[6] The main purposes of these revisions were (i) to allow self-certification by foreign companies and (ii) to make the inspection and certification procedures essentially the same for Japanese and non-Japanese companies. As such, the revisions institutionalized the principle of non-discrimination for a wide range of products, including foodstuffs, pharmaceuticals, chemicals, fertilizers, home electrical appliances, automobiles, and agricultural machinery.

Other improvements that have been effected, in addition to

---

[6] The sixteen laws which were revised and the products affected are as follows: the Pharmaceutical Affairs Law (pharmaceuticals, medical equipment, and cosmetics), the Nutrition Improvement Law (special nutrition foodstuffs), the Agricultural Chemical Regulation Law (agricultural chemicals), the Fertilizer Control Law (fertilizers), the Agricultural Mechanization Promotion Law (agricultural machinery and equipment), the Law Concerning Standardization and Proper Labeling of Agricultural and Forestry Products (agricultural, forestry, and fishery products such as foodstuffs and plywood), the Law Concerning Safety Assurance and Quality Improvement of Feed (feeds), the Consumer Product Safety Law (consumer products including helmets for motorcyclists and baseball players), the High-Pressure Gas Control Law (oxygen cylinders and other high-pressure containers), the Electrical Appliance and Material Control Law (household electrical appliances), the Law Concerning the Safety and Optimization of Transactions of Liquefied Petroleum Gas (LPG appliances), the Measurement Law (measuring devices), Gas Utility Industry Law (urban gas appliances), the Law Concerning the Examination and Regulation of Manufacture, etc., of Chemical Substances (seven specific chemical substances including polychlorinated biphenyls, polychlorinated naphthalenes, and hexachlorobenzenes), the Road Vehicles Act (motor vehicles), and the Labor Safety and Sanitation Law (machine tools and equipment, including press machines and gas masks).

these legal amendments, include: (i) enhanced "transparency" through seeking the views of foreign experts in the course of drafting standards and providing more information about what the standards are and how they are established; (ii) harmonization with internationally accepted standards where they exist and participation in endeavors to draw up international standards when necessary; (iii) greater acceptance of overseas test data; and (iv) simplification and streamlining of certification procedures. The fields of automobiles, pharmaceuticals, and household electrical appliances are typical.

1. *Automobiles*: Japan has taken the following steps with respect to type designation and standards for automobiles.

(a) It was made explicit that foreign car manufacturers are able to apply for, and receive, "type designation," thereby eliminating the need for the Ministry of Transport to inspect every vehicle individually.[7]

(b) The procedures and requirements for type designation were drastically simplified to enable foreign manufacturers to take advantage of this system.[8] One sample vehicle together with documentation usually suffices for type designation. Not only has this made type designation far more accessible; it has also shortened the time requirement by approximately one third.

Whereas manufacturers used to have to submit two vehicles that had been driven 30,000 kilometers (one for safety testing and the other for environmental pollution testing), this requirement can now be met with documentation.

The Japanese authorities are now able to accept data from tests performed by foreign testing organizations when the procedures are equivalent to those in Japan.

The paperwork has been radically simplified to require fewer details and to eliminate the need for strength-test data on specific parts.

---

[7] The Road Vehicles Act as revised in May 1983 to go into effect on August 1, 1983.

[8] Amendments to the Motor Vehicles Type Designation Regulation that went into effect on August 1, 1983.

(c) Japan is an active participant in the United Nations Economic Commission for Europe's Group of Experts on the Construction of Vehicles (Working Party 29) and is determined to see that the results of these meetings are reflected in Japanese standards and that her standards are harmonized with those in Western Europe and North America. Japan is also reviewing her standards for points of difference which would warrant revision and has already relaxed her safety standards to conform more closely to those in Western Europe and North America.[9] Harmonization revisions have been made for all items requested by countries in Western Europe and North America except for emission-control requirements.

(d) Efforts are also being made to hear the views of foreign manufacturers in the course of drafting automobile standards. Japanese experts made several trips to Western Europe and North America to explain the reasoning behind the revisions and their implications for these countries.

2. *Pharmaceuticals*: Foreign manufacturers of pharmaceuticals stand to benefit from the following five measures.

(a) Efforts are being made to meet regularly with representatives of the American Chamber of Commerce in Japan and to hear their views.

(b) Japan is taking an active part in efforts by the World Health Organization and other international organizations to formulate international standards for pharmaceuticals.

(c) Since October 1, 1983, Japan has been accepting foreign stability-test data as well as foreign data on specifications and test methods, and consideration is being given to which foreign clinical-test data are acceptable.

(d) The new regulations now permit the transfer of import approvals for pharmaceuticals from one importer to another when the foreign pharmaceutical manufacturer remains unchanged.[10]

---

[9] Amendments to the Safety Standards for Road Vehicles that went into effect on October 1, 1983.

[10] Amendments to the Ministerial Ordinance Implementing the Pharmaceutical

(e) Health drinks and herb sweets made of chamomile or valerians, which used to be treated as pharmaceuticals, are now treated as foodstuffs as of April 1, 1983, thus making their import easier.

3. *Electrical Appliances*: With respect to electrical appliances, there have been reforms in four main areas, these being set out below.

(a) Foreign representatives are included in the drafting procedure for the standards for household electrical appliances under the Electrical Appliance and Material Control Law.

(b) Work has been completed on harmonizing Japanese technical standards for electrical appliances with the standards of the International Electrotechnical Commission, as reported to the GATT in August 1983.

(c) Japan has arranged for cross-acceptance of test data with the United States and Canada.

(d) The new regulations now permit the transfer of type authorization from one importer to another when the foreign electrical appliance manufacturer remains unchanged.[11]

Office of the Trade Ombudsman

The Office of the Trade Ombudsman (OTO), formally the Headquarters for the Promotion of Settlements of Grievances Related to the Openness of the Japanese Market, was established as part of the January 1982 package of market-opening measures. Consisting of the administrative vice ministers from the fourteen government ministries and agencies concerned, the OTO is headed by the Deputy Chief Cabinet Secretary in the Office of the Prime Minister.

The OTO's mandate was broadened by the April 1984 package of market-opening measures for dealing with complaints regarding procedures for direct investment in Japan and related

Affairs Law as revised effective August 1, 1983.

[11] Amendments to the Electrical Appliance and Material Control Law as revised effective August 1, 1983.

matters. At the same time the office was renamed the Office of the Trade and Investment Ombudsman.

In the two years and four months from its establishment until May 1984 the OTO has received 149 complaints. Of these, 99 were from overseas—48 of them being from the United States and 29 from Western Europe. By area of jurisdiction, the main ministries involved were as follows: the Ministry of Health and Welfare (pharmaceuticals, food hygiene, etc.), which received 57 complaints; the Ministry of Finance (customs and tariff procedures, etc.), which received 36 complaints; the Ministry of International Trade and Industry (high-pressure gas containers, etc.), which received 30 complaints; and the Ministry of Agriculture, Forestry, and Fisheries (livestock and plant quarantine, etc.), which received fourteen complaints.

Of the 149 complaints received, processing has been completed on 143. Of these, 85 were resolved in an import-facilitating manner—41 resulting in improvements in import-inspection procedures and other provisions and 44 revealing misunderstandings which could then be resolved. In addition to judging complaints, the OTO is promoting an ambitious educational campaign for foreign firms and diplomatic missions in Japan as well as companies overseas through the Japan External Trade Organization (JETRO). The OTO is unique in bringing together high-level officials from a broad range of government ministries for the specific purpose of opening up a market. There is nothing quite like it anywhere else in the world and it is hoped that foreign manufacturers and governments will take advantage of the OTO's availability.

In January 1983 the OTO Advisory Council was established to oversee the operation of the OTO and to deliberate on complaints about access to the Japanese market. This eight-man board has Nobuhiko Ushiba as chairman, myself as deputy chairman, and such figures as Sony's Akio Morita and Honda's Soichiro Honda as members. Board members have traveled to the United States, the European Community, Australia, the Scandinavian countries, and countries in southern Europe in an effort to explain the OTO's revisions of Japan's standards and certification systems and other measures being taken to further open the Japanese market, as well as to hear firsthand any complaints which exporters in these countries might have. Although the Advisory Council does not have administrative authority, the stature of its members gives it considerable influence within the government of Japan.

Distribution Structure and Commercial Practices

Not so long ago, the *Financial Times*, published in London and Frankfurt, characterized Japanese distribution as a "Rubik's Cube" and said that the greatest problem facing foreign companies in Japan was their inability to solve the cube. There is a widespread belief overseas that foreign products are shut out of the Japanese market by an irrational distribution system.

One of the main foreign complaints about the Japanese distribution system is that it is multi-layered and highly complex, leading to higher distribution costs. This complaint essentially boils down to the complaints that (i) there is an inordinately large number of small retail outlets and (ii) there are many different distribution channels, even at the wholesaler level, the hefty commissions to be paid at each stage resulting in excessive distribution costs.

The existence of many retail outlets, however, does not inherently mean a complex distribution system and it is very much in the Japanese consumer's interest to have large numbers of retail outlets. On the second point, it is true that Japanese distribution is multi-layered and that the many layers do tend to drive up distribution costs. But it is not only foreign products or foreign companies which pay the high costs resulting from complexity in the distribution system. Japanese products are subject to the same costs. The only difference, if any, is that it may take foreign companies longer to understand the Japanese distribution structure and to devise ways of using it to their best advantage.

There is also criticism that, distribution systems aside, Japanese commercial practices are exclusionary. Although foreign companies may see the close personal relations between manufacturers and distributors as abnormal, these are not exclusionary. Rather they are the natural result of any long-term business relationship and a foreign company which has been in Japan a long time would most likely develop the same kind of close personal relations with its Japanese distribution (as, in fact, many have).)

Industry associations are also frequently cited as a factor tending to exclude foreign firms from the Japanese market, but these associations are primarily for friendship and networking of information; they are not where trading actually takes place. Even if they were, foreign firms are free to join Japanese industry associations and all members can use the associations for the same purposes of friendship and information networking for which Japanese companies use them.

Most of the complaints relating to commercial practices are based upon misunderstandings. Some reflect differences between Japanese practices and those in the United States and Western Europe. Yet the fact that Japanese practices are different is hardly grounds for criticism.

Most foreign companies have trouble with the Japanese market because they approach it in the wrong way. The first problem is generally the lack of a long-term export strategy. It is obviously impossible to hope for stable long-term expansion of exports unless the target market is studied thoroughly and products are developed which satisfy customer requirements. Taking the simple example of the placement of car steering wheels, Japanese drive on the left-hand side of the road and, therefore, the steering wheel in Japanese cars is on the right. Most cars imported to Japan, however, come with the steering wheel on the left. This demonstrates a lack of commitment and willingness to adapt to market conditions. As was pointed out in *Der Spiegel*,[12] published in Hamburg, any company which hopes to succeed in the highly competitive Japanese market has to work on exports in accordance with a long-term plan.

The second problem is that foreign firms tend to price high in order to generate large commissions. This is especially pronounced in automobiles, whisky, brandy, cosmetics, sports equipment, and clothing. While high prices and large profit margins

---

[12] *Der Spiegel*, Hamburg, January 3, 1983.

Table 4   Japanese Trading Offices Overseas and Foreign Trading Offices
in Japan

	Japanese trading offices overseas		Foreign trading offices in Japan[a]	
	Offices	Employees	Offices	Employees
United States	986	33,464	170	1,551
European Community	703	14,636	79	667
United Kingdom	151	4,294	28	189
West Germany	256	5,857	24	293
France	80	1,455	9	89
Italy	47	495	4	11
Southeast Asia	1,370	33,437	175	1,444
Other regions	1,364	28,427	95	1,478
Total	4,423	109,964	519	5,140

Source: *Boeki Gyotai Tokei-hyo* [Trading Sector Statistics], Ministry of International Trade and Industry, Tokyo.
Note: The figures are as of March 31, 1981, except for British trading facilities in Japan, which are as of March 31, 1980.
"Foreign trading facilities in Japan are those facilities of foreign corporations and Japanese corporations in which foreign investors hold a majority interest.

may be successful in the short term by creating an image of quality and exclusiveness, most of these companies have found that their growth potential is limited, that they are unable to compete in price, and that they get squeezed out of the market.

The third problem is the lack of sales effort. Foreign firms are quick to criticize the so-called exclusionary nature of the Japanese market, but they are far less anxious to discuss their own sales efforts. Looking at the numbers of overseas offices and overseas personnel as two measures of export sales effort, foreign firms have only one eighth as many offices in Japan as Japanese firms have overseas and only one twentieth as many people stationed in Japan as there are Japanese stationed overseas (see Table 4). American and West European firms are just not making the same effort in exports that Japanese firms are.

Nevertheless, there are numerous companies which have studied the Japanese market and have adopted successful marketing strategies in Japan, among them being IBM (computer equipment), BMW (automobiles), Schick (men's razors), Braun (electric shavers), and Max Factor (cosmetics).

Liberalizing Trade in Services

Liberalization of restrictions on international transactions in the services sector of the world economy has been hotly discussed in the Organization for Economic Cooperation and Development and the GATT in recent years. But it will be difficult to come up with specific guidelines for liberalization of services immediately because (i) every country's services sector is different due to the distinctive social and historical features which shaped it, (ii) there are major disparities in the level of development in the services sector between the developed and the developing countries, and (iii) it is not easy to predict what impact technological innovation in information processing and telecommunications will have on the services sector. Nevertheless, liberalization in the services sector is expected to become increasingly important in the 1980s and 1990s and it may well come to rival liberalization of trade in goods in importance.

While the services sector includes such disparate fields as telecommunications, information processing, engineering, consulting, education, finance, insurance, medical care, hotels and restaurants, mass media, and air and sea transport, I will focus on (i) telecommunications and information processing and (ii) financial services because of their significance for all economic activity.

Telecommunications and information processing

The dramatic advances in computer and telecommunication technology have recently sparked demands, both within Japan and from the United States, for deregulation of the use of telecommunication networks and information-processing services. With the partial amendment of Japan's Public Communications Law in October 1982, the use of telecommunication networks has largely been liberalized. Value-added networks are now permitted for small business organizations. In 1984, it is planned to overhaul the entire structure of telecommunications and data-processing utilization, a major undertaking which will entail moving the system from monopoly to competition and privatizing the Nippon Telegraph and Telephone Corporation (NTT). Although some degree of regulation will inevitably remain for such considerations as protection of privacy, software copyright, and national security, the trend is towards sweeping liberalization.

Financial services

The same wave of liberalization and internationalization is also evident in banking and securities where the main factors are (i) the electro-information revolution, as epitomized by electronic banking, (ii) the growth of financial assets and the trend wards greater sensitivity to differentials in rates of interest, and (iii) the expanded international flow of capital.

As in other fields, liberalization of the financial and capital markets is premised on ensuring non-discriminatory treatment for Japanese and non-Japanese firms alike (so-called "national treatment") and, too, on easing restrictions and reducing the government's role. Rapid progress has already been made since 1978 in ensuring non-discrimination, and the Revised Banking Law of 1982[13] provides that foreign banks shall receive exactly the same treatment as that accorded to Japanese banks. On the question of scaling down the role of government, efforts have been made since late 1980 to consolidate the framework for financial liberalization, including the shift from regulated, in principle, to unregulated, in principle, for external transactions.[14]

Yet, as illustrated by the major differences between the United States and the United Kingdom, on the one hand, and the Federal Republic of Germany, Switzerland, and the Netherlands, on the other, each country's financial system has been shaped by its distinctive social and historical circumstances. It would be folly to implement reforms so drastic that they destroyed the structure of Japanese society. But Japan is working steadily and unwaveringly for further liberalization and internationalization in this area.

In the autumn of 1983, the government of Japan announced its intentions to promote further liberalization of the financial

[13] The Banking Law as revised effective April 1982.
[14] The Foreign Exchange and Foreign Trade Control Law as revised effective December 1980.

and capital markets and a greater international role for the yen.[15] The medium-term directions are as follows:

(a) liberalization of short-term capital markets, including the creation of an active market for treasury bills, greater flexibility in amounts and maturities for certificates of deposit, and the creation of a market in yen-denominated bankers' acceptances;

(b) liberalization of the market for public and corporate bonds, including greater diversity in the kinds and maturities of national bonds, greater flexibility in the conditions of issue of corporate bonds, the issue of government bonds denominated in foreign currencies, and relaxation of the conditions of issue of Euro-yen bonds;

(c) liberalization of rates of interest, including efforts to promote market-determined rates of interest through liberalizing short-term capital markets, liberalizing bond markets, and gradually eliminating interest-rate ceilings; and

(d) a lowering of the barriers between financial institutions, including the gradual removal of the distinctions between ordinary banks, trust banks, securities companies, and other financial institutions.

The government of Japan and the United States administration reached agreement on measures for liberalization of Japan's financial market along these lines at the end of May.[16]

Summary

A brief review of the areas of contention in trade frictions with Japan discussed above may be in order.

[15] Comprehensive Economic Measures announced on October 21, 1983, and the Joint Press Announcement by Noboru Takeshita, Minister of Finance of the government of Japan, and Donald Regan, the Secretary of the Treasury in the United States administration, of November 10, 1983.

[16] Report by the working group of the Joint Japan–United States Ad Hoc Group on Yen-Dollar Exchange Rates and Financial and Capital Market Issues, May 30, 1984.

Because Japan is so heavily dependent on imported energy resources, its current account necessarily fluctuates greatly with changes in energy prices. When real prices of oil fall by 20 percent, the current-account balance readily shows a surplus of approximately 2 percent of GNP, but this swelling of the current-account surplus is a temporary phenomenon.

While Japan's current-account surplus is expected over the long run to show a surplus of within 1 percent of GNP, this outlook is consistent with her status as an immature creditor nation, beginning around 1970. As an immature creditor, Japan, like the United Kingdom and United States before her, is expected to be a capital-exporting country and to contribute to world economic development by making the capital surplus generated by the high rate of savings (equivalent to the current-account surplus) available to meet overseas needs for capital.

Her tariff rates already being among the lowest of any developed country, Japan is taking the initiative to lower the tariffs further through advanced implementation of the Tokyo Round agreement and through advocacy of a new round of multilateral trade negotiations.

The first criterion for market openness, aside from tariffs and residual import quotas, is that of fair (that is, non-discriminatory) treatment. Recent institutional changes in Japan, including the improvements made in her standards and certification systems, import-inspection procedures, and financial-market and capital-market trading requirements, substantially ensure national treatment in these areas.

The second criterion for market openness is that of liberalization and deregulation. Here, too, major progress has been made, as seen in the improvements in the standards and certification systems, the liberalization of telecommunications and information processing, the liberalization of capital transactions, and the establishment and activities of the Office of the Trade Ombudsman.

Rapid and wide-ranging reforms have been instituted to make the Japanese market more accessible. Most of the traditional foreign complaints about the Japanese market are now groundless. Japan is working to provide information on the actual openness of her market, but it would be encouraging if foreign firms recognized the major changes which have been wrought and moved to take advantage of this new situation.

In the twenty-first century the world economy will be characterized by extensive service and information sectors. Japan is taking the initiative in working with the United States and the countries of Western Europe towards establishing a framework for liberalization of international trade in services, telecommunications, and information in keeping with this long-term trend.

The Role of the Human Element in the Development Process:
Japan's Experience

I would like to begin by repeating an ancient and extremely important truth: economic development can only be achieved as the result of economic efforts by the people who actually live in a given country. In reiterating this, of course, I in no way mean to imply that the peoples of the developing countries are not making sufficient efforts for development. Nor do I intend to slight the importance of cooperating with these countries' self-help endeavors. Rather, I would emphasize that there is no magic formula for economic development. Every country has its own history, customs, religion, and cultural traditions, and this background must be taken into account in planning for economic development.

As an economist, I am sometimes asked if Japan's modernization was successful because Japan was blessed with favorable circumstances or because of some special strategy that the Japanese devised and implemented. Most of the people who put this question to me are clearly inclined to the latter view, and they hope to draw some lessons from the Japanese experience. While it is all very well to want to learn from experience, it should be remembered that the lessons of history may be misleading or even dangerous if taken out of context. Japan is neither an ideal model case nor an irrelevant example for today's developing countries. The truth lies somewhere in between.

Given this, one of the things I point out whenever I discuss Japan's economic development is that modernization is not

This essay was delivered as the Paul Hoffman Lecture Sponsored by the United Nations Development Programme (UNDP), in New York on May 8, 1986.

synonymous with westernization. Even today, Japan contains many elements setting it apart from the Euro-American countries, and Japan was the first non-western country to achieve a degree of success in its efforts at modernization. Many of Japan's traditional elements played an important role in our development process. Accordingly, I would like to briefly review Japan's economic development process with special attention to the human elements.

Post-Restoration Educational Policy

As is well known, Japan's modernization is generally said to have begun in 1868 when the feudal government was replaced by a government that was more open to the rest of the world and determined to promote modernization. This is true as far as it goes, but it should also be remembered that this new government inherited a number of elements that were very conducive to economic development. One of them was education, especially the emphasis on primary education. Even in the feudal era, there were a number of very good private educational institutions, and systematic education in the basics of reading, writing, and arithmetic was already widespread. Such education was by no means compulsory, but these basic skills were already recognized as essential. By the time the new educational system was introduced in 1872, 30 percent of the Japanese people were already able to read and write, indicating that education was by no means limited to the big cities.

The education policies adopted by the new Meiji government were thus designed to strengthen and supplement this tradition. Higher education at the university level was limited to the core elite needed for economic development and institutional modernization, and the bulk of the government's resources were devoted to improving elementary and vocational schools.

This decision to keep higher education relatively limited and to emphasize elementary education for the general population has set the tone for Japanese education ever since. On the negative side, this has resulted in charges that Japanese are lacking in creativity or intellectual curiosity; but on the positive side it has been a major factor in giving Japanese the practical abilities needed to adopt, adapt, and improve the advanced technologies necessary for economic development. In effect, Japan's educational system in the early decades of development was pyramidal in shape, with widespread primary and vocational education for everyone.

A little less than two years ago, in August 1984, an Ad Hoc Commission on Educational Reform was enacted and a council empaneled to review the educational system in today's context, to rectify the distortions induced by an outdated educational system, and to reform and reshape the educational system to better suit it to Japan's current situation. In discussing the economic friction that Japan has encountered as a trading nation, I like to say that Japan is today embarking upon a third national opening—the first having been the Meiji modernization and opening to the West sparked by Commodore Perry's arrival in Edo Bay and the second the great democratization that began after Japan's defeat in World War II. The same thing might well be said of Japanese educational policy, the first great change taking place in the Meiji Restoration's wake, the second after World War II; the third educational restructuring just now getting under way.

Looking Back on the Rapid-Growth Era

Japan's 1960 income-doubling program—a program that I was in charge of drafting as director-general of the Economic Planning Agency's Planning Bureau—is often cited as a key document in Japan's rapid postwar economic development. Yet, this plan was not conceived out of thin air. The postwar Occupation policies effectively eliminated the economy's quasi-feudal aspects and contributed greatly to putting Japan on the road to modernization. At the same time, these years were a time of great technological innovation worldwide, and the pace of innovation appeared especially fast and formidable to Japan as it strove to catch up with the industrialized countries of the West. Another factor that contributed to Japan's rapid postwar growth was the existence of a large pool of low-cost, high-quality labor that was well educated and capable of mastering sophisticated technology. All of these factors were taken into account in drawing up the national income-doubling program that was announced in 1960.

Under this program, we hoped to double Japanese national income within the decade. In fact, this goal was achieved in only seven years. With this, Japan entered upon a period of very rapid growth, the per-annum growth rate averaging better than 10 percent a year for fifteen years. As such, this program played an important role in consolidating the foundations for Japan's postwar economic development.

Drawn up within the framework of a free-market economy, this was a long-term plan significant for its seeking to avoid the tendency of much of modern policy planning and corporate management to make judgments solely on the basis of the immediate situation and tried instead to serve as part forecast and part encouragement so that people could focus on the long-term outlook. It was not so much a rigid plan as a set of policy-management directions. There is currently much debate about the feasibility of planning in a market economy, but I think it is recognized that invisible hands alone cannot be left to govern the market entirely unchecked. Even the United States, which is, if anything, even more devoted to free-market principles than Japan is, has implicitly recognized this with its participation in last September's G-5 intervention in currency markets and the passage of legislation mandating a balanced budget. Some degree of planning is needed in both national and international economies.

In 1982, Professor Lester Thurow coordinated a symposium on Japan's postwar economic performance at the Massachusetts Institute of Technology, the results of the symposium later published by MIT as *The Management Challenge: Japanese Views*. Commenting on the five priorities that we had set in the 1960 income-doubling program, Professor Thurow wrote:

Consider the five elements in the Japanse economic strategy at the beginning of the income-doubling decade: strengthen social overhead capital, push growth industries, promote exports, develop human ability and technology, and secure social stability by mitigating the dual structure of the economy. This list could easily serve as strategic objectives for the American economy by the year 2000.

Even back in the late 1950s, we recognized the promotion of science and technology and the development of our human resources as indispensable to economic development. There was a special emphasis on training people in the sciences, and in consultation and cooperation with the Ministry of Education we drew up a plan for educating engineers and other technical people. Japan today graduates more engineers than the United States does, but even in the early years we were aware of the human aspect as an important element for Japan's industrialization. In 1961, the year after the income-doubling plan was drawn up, a subcommittee was formed within the Economic Council to study ways of enhancing human abilities. After extensive deliberation on how to develop people in the scientific and technological fields—everybody from university graduates to skilled workers—a human-resources development plan was drawn up.

Until then, technology and education had been seen as essentially different concerns from economic issues, and there had been virtually no frontal consideration of these areas in economic planning. Rather, there was a tendency among teachers and other people interested in education to argue that education should not be thought of in economic terms. However, there must be some connection between society's needs, those abilities the economy requires of people, and the educational process that gives people these abilities. Otherwise, the schools will end up turning out large numbers of highly educated, overqualified, and unemployed people. At the time, I emphasized that education and economic planning are as two circles which, while not concentric, do overlap to a considerable degree. It was predicted that the pace of technological innovation would pick up and a major transformation of the industrial structure was predicted. As new technology is incorporated into the economy, it is necessary for engineers and other workers alike to be continually learning and mastering the new technology. We were convinced that, as population growth slowed and the labor pool stopped expanding so fast, the nation's overall economic strength would depend upon how capable each individual worker was.

Once one accepts that the economy works through the free activity of corporations and market mechanisms, it is clear that the private sector must be the driving force for the attainment of any goals or targets for industry in general. When people in the private sector realize how economic development is achieved, their creativity and efforts make it possible to solve numerous problems and to achieve the society's goals. The role of the government is to create a climate in which the private sector can act, to remove any barriers that may arise, and to indicate general directions. I have long maintained that, though the government may want to assist these corporate efforts, to offer stimulation, and to encourage industry to work toward set goals, its economic role can only be complementary and indirect. In education and scientific research, however, the government can take a central role.

Japan's Twenty-first-Century Issues

I would like next to mention a number of changes that will affect the environment for human-resources development in Japan in the twenty-first century. The first of these is the rapid graying of the labor population. In 1960, only 5 percent of the Japanese population was aged 65 or older. Last year that figure was 10 percent, and by the year 2000 it is expected to top 15 percent. Since most of the other industrialized countries now count 13–14 percent of their populations to be 65 or older, this means that Japan in the twenty-first century will have more of people 65 or older than these countries do. According to a study by the Economic Planning Agency, approximately one-quarter of the labor population will be aged 55 or over in the year 2000. Beginning in the year 2000, the total population cohort aged 15 to 64 will begin to shrink even as the cohort 65 and older continues to grow. Given these demographic trends, there will have to be some adjustment in the labor market if industry is to maintain its vitality. The West European countries that have chosen to respond with a welfare state providing early-retirement benefits are now beset with the dual problems of burgeoning welfare costs and a deteriorating will to work. If this fate is to be avoided, it seems clear that we need to restructure the labor market to respect old people's employability and will to work and to ensure that they have the job opportunities they need.

The second change facing Japan is the rising educational level and the increasingly ambitious influx of women into the labor market. Although the rapid increase in the numbers of people going on to junior colleges or full four-year universities has peaked somewhat since 1975 and is now stable at about 37 percent, the population cohort that has received higher education will continue to expand as a percentage of the total population. In the year 2000, it is expected that twice as many Japanese will have had higher education than do now. Given this tendency toward an ever-better-educated society, it is clear that we need to be thinking about the kind of education needed to train the people who will provide the welfare services an older population will need and how the educational system can best meet the needs of this older society. It should also be pointed out that the better-educated women tend to be more strongly represented in the labor force than their less-educated sisters. This trend is expected to grow even stronger in the years ahead as more and more women go to work part-time to supplement the family income or to utilize their specialist skills in the service sector.

The third change is that the longer life span obviously means that people have more time in their total lives, and this raises the question of what to do with that time. People now have nearly 100,000 more hours of useful life than they did just a quarter-century ago. At the same time, the average work year has grown 300 hours shorter, from 2,400 hours 25 years ago to 2,100 hours now. However, this is still more than the average 1,900 hours in the United States and the United Kingdom, the 1,700 hours in France, and the 1,600 hours in West Germany. On April 7 of this year, the Advisory Group on Economic Structural Adjustment for International Harmony, a private advisory group to the prime minister, released its report on what Japan should do to harmonize its economic structure with the world economic climate. As one of the members of the Group, I would like to quote from this report. "The total working hours per year," the report said, should be brought "in line with the industrialized countries of Europe and North America and early realization of complete five-day work weeks should be pursued in the private sector, while efforts should be made for speedy implementation of these policies in the public and financial sectors." Japanese are often accused of working too hard, but we are trying to restructure the economy so that people can make fuller use of their free time and improve the quality of their lives.

As a Partner in Development

While this has been and portends to be the Japanese experience, I would like also to touch upon some of the ways that Japan can help other peoples. When I visited Thailand last January, I had the pleasure of talking with Deputy Prime Minister Bhichai. During our discussion, I asked him what Thailand wanted from Japan. He told me there were three things. First are efforts to redress the trade imbalance. Second, he expressed the hope that private-sector direct investment from Japan would be directed toward increasing Thailand's foreign-exchange earnings. And third, while he said that funding from the Japanese Overseas Economic Cooperation Fund was appreciated for its contributions to infrastructure improvement, he wondered if some of that OECF capital could not be channeled to more directly help the Thai small-business sector and export industries. It was in response to this third request that Japan has since instituted two-step loans to Thailand whereby the OECF lends to the Industrial Finance Corporation of Thailand and the IFCT in turn lends to small businesses.

Upkeep is an important part of ensuring that a company or country is able to use its productive capacity to the fullest. Yet, in many places the shortage of qualified maintenance personnel has idled equipment installed at great cost. Here again Japan can help, this time by providing the necessary supplies and coupling this with educational programs for maintenance engineers. Technical cooperation is important to enhance people's capabilities and encourage the necessary organizational provisions. It goes without saying, of course, that all of this will go for naught if the recipient country is not aware of the importance of its small-business sector and the need to maintain and keep up existing plants and facilities.

Policy consistency is also important, and frequent policy flip-flops are detrimental to aid effectiveness. It is important that the developing countries recognize that private companies cannot survive unless they are able to earn a reasonable profit.

There was a time when virtually all economic development experts were agreed on the importance of import substitution. Yet, as these same experts have seen the success achieved by the Republic of Korea and the newly industrializing countries of Southeast Asia, they have gradually changed their song to sing the praises of export promotion. Today, however, these NICs face a bleak situation as a result of the protectionist tendencies in the industrialized countries. Which is better, import substitution or export promotion? There is no pat answer. Personally, I would tend to favor export promotion incorporating some elements of import substitution. It seems clear that a mix is needed, the exact proportions finally depending upon the individual country's size, resource endowment, technological level, and other factors. There are some countries which promote import substitution and self-sufficiency at any cost. Yet, if these countries decide, for example, that they need a high-cost steelworks, the costs of this decision will eventually permeate the entire economy, starting with steel-using industries, and it is important to consider these economic ramifications in setting policy. By the same token, if a country decides to concentrate on export promotion, the need to compete in the international marketplace will preclude much other investment. The developing countries have a great need to get maximum mileage out of their limited financial resources, and they should do all they can to formulate development plans firmly grounded in practical competitiveness.

There are a number of ways that Japan can and is helping in such development. The $50 billion Japanese current account surplus that is so much in the news these days is being recycled overseas in the form of long-term capital outflow. In 1985, the actual long-term capital outflow was $82.1 billion and the inflow $17.3 billion, leaving a net outflow of $64.8 billion. This net capital outflow is clearly in excess of the current account surplus of $50 billion. Much of this money has been invested in dollar-denominated securities, and the dollar's recent fall has thus had a double, even triple, impact on the Japanese economy. Looking to the developing countries, it should be possible to direct some of this money to these countries, especially to the countries beset with crisis-proportion debts, and to refinance their high-interest short-term debt with low-interest long-term loans so as to lighten their interest burdens and hence promote their economic development. Likewise, it should also be possible to allocate some of this surplus for long-term relief for the hunger-wracked countries of Africa. A new medium-term target was announced last September to double Japanese official development assistance in seven years, and this is another way that Japan can make its very considerable economic might, technological prowess, and experience available to the developing countries to help make this a better world.

Enhanced provisions for accepting foreign students in Japan are also important. In this vein, the Council on Foreign Student Policy for the Twenty-first Century was established in May 1983 at Prime Minister Nakasone's suggestion to look into this issue. After wide-ranging discussions, the other members and I submitted our report to the prime minister in August 1983. So far, Japan has concentrated on learning from the other industrialized countries, but it is now time we worked to make our experience and expertise more readily available to other peoples. According to UNESCO statistics published in 1982, there were 310,000 foreign students at American colleges, universities, and graduate schools in 1980, 120,000 in France (1982), 57,000 in West Germany (1979), 53,000 in the United Kingdom (1980), and only 8,100 in Japan (1982). The Council thus proposed that an effort be made to expand foreign student acceptance in Japan to British and German levels—about 50,000 students—by 1990 and to the French level of somewhat over 100,000 by the year 2000. Major efforts will be needed if these targets are to be met, but it is incumbent upon Japanese colleges and universities to make this effort for internationalization. As the report of the Advisory Group on Economic Structural Adjustment for International Harmony that I mentioned earlier has succinctly pointed out, "The time has . . . come for Japan to make a historical transformation in its traditional policies on economic management and the nation's lifestyle. There can be no further development for Japan without this transformation" to a more international society.

I have tried in the time alloted me to briefly review the history of Japanese development from the late nineteenth century onward with special attention to those human elements that have made this possible, and then to look at what Japan can do as a partner in development to help other countries. I would like to close by stressing once more the importance of education, and to do this I would like to quote an ancient Chinese saying that I am sure you are all familiar with: If you give a man a fish, he can eat it once; if you teach him how to fish, he can eat fish for the rest of his life.

PART II

Diplomatic and
International Relations

Japan, China, and the United States:
Economic Relations and Prospects

I

Interest in the future of the Pacific region has been increased in the past year by dramatic events, notably the conclusion of a peace treaty between China and Japan and the normalization of relations between the United States and China. And, over a longer period, the realization has grown that the Western Pacific region—which includes Japan, Korea, Taiwan, Hong Kong, the ASEAN countries (the Philippines, Thailand, Malaysia, Singapore, and Indonesia) and China—is one of the most dynamic areas in the world in terms of economic growth and development.

Although Japan's rate of economic growth since the 1973–74 oil crisis has been reduced from around ten percent to about five to six percent, the country still maintains a higher growth rate than any of the other industrial nations. South Korea, Taiwan, and Hong Kong have been growing at about ten percent per annum, even since the oil crisis, and their trade volumes are expanding rapidly. The ASEAN countries are also performing well, growing at a rate of six to seven percent a year, which is higher than the rest of the world's developing countries. China's annual rate of economic growth has been estimated at 5.3 percent for the 1970–75 period, and China's new ten-year economic development plan which was announced in February 1978 (covering the period 1976–85) projects a growth rate of about eight percent a year (although, as we shall see, this figure may be re-

This chapter was first published in *Foreign Affairs*, Summer 1979, pp. 1090–1110.

duced somewhat in subsequent reexaminations of the plan).

In contrast to the performance of these Western Pacific countries, economic growth in other parts of the world, with the exception of Latin America, has been much lower. With the cumulative effect of these different rates of growth, the Western Pacific will have a much larger share of the world economy by the end of this century. Already in 1977 American trade with Pacific countries exceeded that with Europe for the first time in her history.

Inevitably, Japan is playing a central role in what has been called this "great transformation."[1] This is particularly true of economic relationships: Japan's postwar economic ties to the United States have been fundamental to Japan's own progress as well as to the wider regional and world economies; Japan's trade and aid have in the past 15 years come to reach throughout East Asia; and, most recently, Japan has assumed a major external part in the new economic programs and policies of China. Yet today there is concern over the difficulties that have arisen in U.S.–Japanese economic relations, and a sense that both countries need to assess carefully the significance of China's new course and the role that each should play in relation to China. It is the purpose of this article to examine these issues as objectively as possible, from the standpoint of a Japanese who has tried for years to think and work in terms of what is best not only for Japan but for the Asian region and the world.

II

In 1978, Japan's gross national product reached almost half that of the United States; the level of overall trade between the two countries continued to rise, to a total of $39.7 billion, making Japan, next to Canada, the largest single trading partner of the United States.

However, recent relations between Japan and the United

[1] Stanley Karnow, "East Asia in 1978: The Great Transformation," *Foreign Affairs*, America and the World issue, 1978, pp. 589–612.

States have been increasingly acrimonious, marked by repeated confrontations over various economic issues. In the United States, characterizations of Japan's trade policy as "unfair" and as damaging to both the United States and the world economy can be frequently heard. A recent editorial in *The New York Times*, for example, commented critically on Japan's economic policy and concluded by saying, "American consumers have a stake in open trade with Japan, which the White House should defend. But if Japan does not look inward for future growth, our great Asian ally may become a victim of its success."[2]

At the risk of oversimplification, the causes for American irritation with Japan seem to fall principally into three categories. The first concerns the trade balance: Japan's global current-account surplus of $16.6 billion in 1978 contrasts with an American current-account deficit of nearly equal magnitude. Japan's surplus in trade account amounted to $24.6 billion, $11.6 billion of which arises from the bilateral U.S.–Japanese trade account itself. Japan is seen as having promoted exports regardless of their impact on others. Similarly, Americans argue that while their markets are open to foreign suppliers with minimal restraints, Japan in practice makes the way difficult for imports generally, and in some instances keeps the door closed completely.

Japan's so-called free ride on defense matters is a second source of irritation in the United States. The argument is that while the United States annually spends more than $120 billion on defense, Japan only spends about ten billion dollars. As a percentage of GNP, Japan's expenditure is much lower than that of either the United States or European countries. Another complaint along these same lines concerns the amount of foreign aid extended by Japan to poorer countries. Also, on a variety of international issues Japan seldom takes the initiative or leadership, and this is interpreted by Americans as "narrow selfishness."

Each of these first two causes of irritation is of long standing. The third is more recent. It relates to American anxiety about

2 *The New York Times*, February 19, 1979, p. A14.

future competition from Japan in high-technology industries. A typical expression of this concern can be found in the following sentences taken from the Jones Report, a Task Force Report prepared in January 1979 by the Subcommittee on Trade of the Committee on Ways and Means, U.S. House of Representatives: "If Americans perceive that our strongest industries— computers, aircraft, advanced electronics, etc.—are being overtaken unfairly, the domestic political reaction is likely to be strong." "We believe that the Japanese threat in these high-technology areas may soon become the most explosive economic issue between our two nations."

Related to this concern, Americans tend to see in their past and present relationship with Japan a ready model for future difficulties with other countries in East Asia, arising from the growing volume of American imports of industrial manufactures from "new Japans." We find in the same report the following: "Further, we foresee 'Japan trade crises' recurring with other developing countries—the so-called 'new Japans' of the Far East such as Taiwan, Korea, Hong Kong and Singapore—and later other developing nations throughout the world. . . . These recurrent and developing trade crises are destructive to international goodwill and injure other aspects of American foreign policy."

Coming back to U.S.–Japanese economic relations in themselves, there have been, and are, complaints on the Japanese side as well. Not only in the celebrated cases of the Nixon 'shocks" of 1971, but more recently, the United States has tended to engage in what seem to Japanese to be abrupt actions or pressure, sometimes touching politically sensitive areas, which create a sense of frustration and sometimes even anger in Japan. It is true that many of the shocks so far administered were to prod Japan into adopting policies which are necessary for the maintenance of harmonious relations with other countries and for delivering benefits to the Japanese consumer. In this context good advice from a close friend is often appreciated. However, if the advice becomes too frequent it may create a sense of frustration. The problem is compounded by the fact that Japanese people usually do not react immediately when they have objections or feel slighted. Instead they concede something on the particular issue—but with the result that stress builds up inside them. If such accumulated stress reaches a certain level, it may explode in an irrational form.

More basically, from a Japanese point of view American economic policy has for many years left much to be desired. The major Japanese complaints have concerned the continuing high rate of inflation in the United States and the relatively weak policy measures taken to stop or reduce it, and (closely related) the failure of the United States to economize on the use and import of oil—to the point where America's bill for imported oil in 1979 is now estimated at $50 billion. Behind these specific concerns, moreover, lies a deeper concern, that inflation rates and balance-of-payments deficits in the United States reflect low productivity growth and structural difficulties and habits. These seem reflected most strikingly in what informed Japanese see as a dangerously low rate of personal savings in the United States—now estimated at about five percent of personal disposable income, as compared with 13 percent in France, 15 percent in Germany, and 22 percent in Japan herself. I hope it will not be misunderstood if I say that some Japanese look at the American economy in a little of the same spirit that the ant reproached the grasshopper in the fable of Aesop.

The third category of irritants on the Japanese side concerns American demands for achievement of major changes, in a very short time, in the basic characteristics and thrust of Japanese economic policy and social habits. In suggesting that Japan "look inward for future growth," Americans seem to be asking that the Japanese people change abruptly the very habits that have produced the high levels of personal savings to which I just alluded, becoming in effect more oriented to immediate consumption, with a higher emphasis on imports and reduced emphasis on investment for export. I shall discuss in more detail in a moment the relationship between savings and investment, on the one hand, and the balance between exports and imports on the other. The broader point is that to bring down Japan's high rate of savings in a short period of time would be just as difficult as raising the rate of savings in the United States. Both are intricately related to broader economic and social structures.

Structural changes usually take a decade or more, not one or two years.

The fourth category of Japanese complaints concerns the occasional lack of understanding by the United States of the historical and social background of many of the Japanese government's policies and practices. One such factor which influences government policy is the sense of uncertainty about the future and a feeling of vulnerability concerning the economy. Frequent earthquakes and other national calamities combined with high dependence on foreign supplies for such essential commodities as food, energy, and raw materials may be the cause of this sense of uncertainty. In any case, this factor often produces a more prudent policy in the spending of foreign exchange than that found in countries endowed with abundant natural resources.

To take an immediate example, the political upheaval in Iran and resulting sharp oil price increases and supply uncertainty have led the International Energy Agency to recommend recently that its members reduce their oil consumption by five percent in 1979. Japan fully supports and accepts this policy. At the same time, since a very large part of Japan's oil consumption is for industrial production, there is bound to be some impact on Japan's growth rate in 1979, and this point does not appear to have been understood by those Americans urging that Japan speed up its growth rate sharply in order to reduce its balance-of-payments surplus.

III

Let us return in more detail to the causes of American irritation with Japan, starting with the issue of Japan's large balance-of-payments surplus. Undoubtedly, the size of that surplus—both in global terms and bilaterally with the United States—does reflect in part the policies of successive Japanese governments, designed to meet the sense of vulnerability and need to build up foreign exchange that I have just mentioned.[3] But the present surplus also stems from certain structural factors, including the

[3] For a closely parallel discussion of this point, see James C. Abegglen and Thomas

steady rise in technical advances and productivity (both in absolute terms and relative to other countries) and especially the very large surplus in domestic savings that has existed for some years.

Japan's high rate of savings—not only the personal rate just mentioned, but rates of saving by institutions—was until recently matched by very high rates of investment (almost entirely domestic), so that there did not exist that excess of savings over investment that, in standard economic analysis, goes hand in hand with an excess in exports over imports.[4] However, in the period since the 1973–74 oil crisis, Japan's growth rate and rate of investment have tended to drop, while the rate of savings has remained high. One could put it that Japan's transition from a production-oriented low-consumption economy to a consumption-oriented affluent society—which might have got under way in the early 1970s and tended to follow roughly the similar evolution of the U.S. and other economies at earlier periods—was held up by the uncertainties of the post-1974 economic climate. The result is that a large surplus of savings over investment now exists and will not readily be dispelled.

In large part for this structural reason, a five-year projection of the Japanese economy published by the Japan Economic Research Center (JERC) in February 1979 has concluded that for at least the next few years the surplus in Japan's global current account is likely to continue at an average annual rate of about ten billion dollars—less than the $16.6 billion surplus of 1978 but somewhat higher than the surplus now forecast for 1979— $7.2 billion, according to the JERC estimate.[5]

One policy measure designed to reduce this surplus of savings is to absorb excess domestic savings by issuing government bonds to finance budget deficits. However, in fiscal year 1979 this deficit amounted to 40 percent of the government's budget (about

---

M. Hout, "Facing Up to the Trade Gap with Japan," *Foreign Affairs*, Fall 1978, pp. 150–52.

[4] Among economists, the standard equation for this relationship is S (savings) minus I (investment) equals X (exports) minus M (imports). The lay reader may recognize some of the contributing factors: that low savings tend to increase consumption and thus imports, and the same for high investment.

[5] JERC, *Quarterly Forecast of Japan's Economy*, May 1979.

$75 billion in absolute amount), up from 37.6 percent in fiscal 1978 and 32.9 percent in fiscal 1977. It is simply not realistic to expect significantly higher percentages of the budget to be financed by the deficit mechanism.

A second trend that would be logical at this phase of Japan's economic development would be a marked increase in capital exports, tending in effect to soak up domestic savings as well as to bring the overall external accounts into better balance. It is now fairly clear that the Japanese economy has indeed been transformed from a capital-importing to a capital-exporting economy. Signs of that shift are already evident in the statistics of the long-term capital account. In the first quarter (January–March) of 1978, Japan's long-term capital account showed a surplus of $0.34 billion while the statistics for the second, third, and fourth quarters of 1978 registered deficits of $3.6, $4.1, and $5.0 billion respectively. The JERC's five-year projection of the Japanese economy forecasts a deficit in the long-term capital account of about ten billion dollars annually, reflecting the net outflow of long-term capital from Japan. This capital outflow will take the following forms: (1) increased development aid to the poorer countries; (2) lending by Japanese banks to foreign customers; (3) issuance of bonds in the Japanese capital markets by foreign governments and enterprises; and (4) direct foreign investment by Japanese companies. Ten billion dollars of capital exports will roughly correspond to one percent of Japan's GNP, a relatively low figure when compared with the past experiences of the United Kingdom or the United States. At one point during the interwar period, for example, Great Britain exported capital amounting to almost six percent of its GNP. And, during the Marshall Plan period after World War II, U.S. net capital outflows accounted for about four percent of the U.S. GNP.

In short, the Japanese economy is in basic transition both in domestic terms and in terms of its external relations. But—and this gets back to my earlier point about demanding change more rapidly than is conceivable—it is unrealistic to expect a rapid reduction in the current accounts surplus in the near future, although there will be fluctuations based on short-term business cycle movements.

It should be kept in mind that apart from these domestic structural factors the high rate of inflation in the United States and its low productivity growth might also contribute to Japan's current account surplus, in particular in the bilateral trade account between the United States and Japan. At the present time, Japanese exports to the United States are leveling off (in the case of cars, actually declining in terms of units sold), while Japan's imports from the United States are sharply increasing.[6] This kind of short-term improvement in the bilateral trade balance, however, cannot deal with the underlying problem. As James Abegglen has noted: "To the extent the United States tends to consume, rather than save and invest, it will consistently lose competitive advantage in the higher value-added sectors where trade among the advanced economies is concentrating."[7] While Japan's economy is evolving in the direction of the American one, it remains predominantly a production-oriented economy.

The same point bears directly on the American perception that Japan's economy is unfairly closed to the exports of other countries through both visible and invisible trade barriers which prevent cheaper products from flowing into the domestic market. The result can be seen in the high prices Japanese consumers are forced to pay for imports even though the country has large reserves of foreign exchange.

Unquestionably, this American complaint has some basis. As a latecomer to the industrial world, Japan has had government policies designed to encourage and protect both industry and agriculture. Although there has been substantial progress in reducing trade barriers in recent years, old habits persist, and behind many government positions lies the reality that the ruling Liberal Democratic Party now has only a precariously slim margin over the opposition parties; it does not have the perfect control of the economy suggested by the catch-phrase "Japan, Incorporated" and must weigh very carefully the consequences of liberalizing imports, notably in such currently sensitive areas as agriculture or the procurement of state corporations.

---

[6] January 1979 exports to the United States were up 1.0 percent and imports up 45.2 percent compared with a year ago, and for February 1979 up 10.5 percent and 39.8 percent, respectively.

[7] Abegglen and Hout, *loc. cit.*, footnote 3, p. 166.

But apart from such specific areas of political sensitivity—which have their counterparts in the United States and in Europe—the underlying balance of popular pressures in Japan is different from that in the United States, where consumer interest in low prices plays a much greater role than in Japan. Today there are signs of change in Japan—such as the recent protests raised by labor unions against the high cost of agricultural products. But until the basic transition to a consumer-oriented society has moved far enough to produce strong domestic pressure for removing trade barriers, governments in Japan will find it politically difficult to move as far as Americans and Europeans demand.

The second major category of American irritants toward Japan—concerning Japan's "free ride" on defense matters—is of course partly economic but also heavily strategic in its implications. The complaint that Japanese expenditures are too low and that Japan's security is too dependent on the American taxpayer sometimes leads to an argument that Japan's economic performance has been as strong as it has been in large part because of the absence of a significant defense burden. It is true that Japan's defense budget has consistently been less than one percent of GNP (currently it is about ten billion dollars), whereas that of the United States stands currently at $120 billion, or six percent of GNP, and has in the past been a still higher percentage.[8] Undoubtedly, Japan has been able to devote to economic investment some substantial part of the resources not employed for defense, but at the same time, Japan has not had the benefit of some of the civilian economic "spin-offs" that the United States has had, for example, in aircraft and electronics development.

But the real question is one of strategic wisdom. Most senior American officials familiar with East Asia over the years have seemed to share the conclusion that any substantial increase in defense expenditures by Japan—which by the way already has the eighth largest defense budget in the world in absolute terms—

---

[8] Actually, Japan's defense budget does not include some expenditures that are classified as defense expenditures in the uniform NATO estimates procedure. Under that procedure, a recent calculation is that Japan's defense expenditures would now be 50 percent higher than the figures and percentages given here.

would be upsetting to the stability and military balance in East Asia, and thus actually contrary to American interests. And in Japan itself, although discussion of defense issues has become more open in recent years, and support for present Self-Defense Forces more widespread, there remains very substantial opposition to any large increase in military spending and to the more assertive and nationalistic policies that would almost necessarily be implied by such increases. At the same time, it is true that recent changes in the international environment have defused domestic political sensitivity toward the military alliance with the United States—especially China's recent change in policy toward welcoming the Japan–U.S. Security Pact. With Japan's GNP now almost equal to that of the United States on a per capita basis, one reasonable measure to reduce tensions and share the cost of defense more fairly might be for Japan to assume a larger share of the burden of U.S. military expenditures incurred in the area of Japan and related to Japan's defense.

Next let us turn to the problems surrounding Japan's development assistance to poorer countries. In terms of official development assistance (ODA), Japan's contribution has been rather modest as a percentage of GNP. In 1977 it was 0.21 percent. While this figure is not much different from the assistance given by the United States (0.22 percent of GNP) and West Germany (0.27 percent), it is far below the international target figure of 0.7 percent of GNP and even below the 0.30 percent average achieved by the member countries of the Development Assistance Committee (DAC) of the OECD. In absolute terms, Japan's ODA contribution in 1977 was $1.42 billion. This places Japan third, behind the United States ($4.16 billion) and France ($2.27 billion).

Recent events, however, point toward an increase in the Japanese figure. At the Bonn summit meeting in July 1978, then Prime Minister Takeo Fukuda promised to double Japan's ODA in three years. After some bureaucratic haggling within the government, it was decided that Japan's ODA of 1977, measured in U.S. dollar terms, would be doubled by 1980. Now it appears that even that ambitious target will be surpassed. Because ODA figures are calculated on the basis of disbursement and not the commitment base, the appreciation of the yen exchange rate, the sharp increase in the aid commitment, and an accelerated disbursement in recent years are likely to combine to produce a doubling of Japan's ODA by 1979, one year ahead of schedule. If the Japanese government continues expanding aid to attain, say, another doubling in three to five years, then Japan's absolute ODA figure may exceed that of the United States and make Japan the top contributor of ODA among DAC members.

In view of the enormous capital requirements of the developing countries for increased food production, energy resource development, expanded transportation and communications networks, improved urban facilities, etc., it might be desirable to have Japan continue its high rate of saving in order to fill these needs. Both Japan and West Germany are well placed to take the lead in this regard. Indeed, such an initiative on the part of Japan would contribute not only to the material betterment of the developing countries but also to the improvement of Japan's international image and, in an indirect way, to an easing of tensions between the United States and Japan. Moreover, Japanese aid should over a period of time be less and less tied to Japanese procurement sources (a problem, again, common to all donor countries); thus it would constitute a genuine form of capital export tending to siphon off domestic savings and reduce the imbalance that now contributes structurally to Japan's current-account surplus. In short, a leading role in international aid fits Japan's current and future situation in somewhat the same way that a similar role fitted the situation of the American economy in the early postwar period.

The third category of irritations I have identified relates to present and future competition in high-technology industries, and the issue of whether such industries are being unfairly subsidized in Japan. On the basic issue of Japanese policy, I must be totally frank. The Japanese government has announced on a number of occasions its policy of encouraging the development of knowledge-intensive industries and the high-technology sector. This is an absolutely necessary policy in view of Japan's paucity of natural resources—88 percent of our energy needs, more than 60 percent of grain consumption, and virtually 100 percent of such vital minerals as iron ore, bauxite, and copper are imported. Given this almost total dependence and the instability of foreign supplies, the development of high-technology, knowledge-intensive industries is, for Japan, a matter of life or death. The development of this sector is also necessitated by the rapid industrial progress, and consequent competition in more traditional labor-intensive industries, that has been evident in other Asian countries such as South Korea and Hong Kong—and possibly China in the future.

The issue of government subsidies is perhaps more complicated. For example, the previously mentioned Jones Report charges that Japanese government support for research and development in some areas, notably those involved with very large-scale integrated circuits (VLSI), has amounted to an "unfair" subsidy. But the problem, from the Japanese standpoint, is that the costs and risks of this kind of research are now too great to be assumed by private concerns; in this respect, and perhaps in others as well, they are analogous to the research and development expenditures for defense-related projects that have traditionally been funded initially by the American government—later leading in many cases to widespread civilian sales. What is "unfair" in this kind of situation is surely very hard to define; to Japanese conscious of the vulnerability and resource-dependency of their economy, expenditures designed to permit that economy to adapt and remain competitive, while accommodating the growth and progress of other Asian nations, take on a very substantial national security character.[9]

This brings us directly to the problem of the rapidly industrializing nations and their increasing exports of manufactured goods. In Europe these countries are known as NICs (newly industrializing countries), whereas in the United States they are sometimes referred to as the "new Japans," as we saw earlier in the Jones Report. In any event, the emergence of these countries is often interpreted as an inimical and disturbing element in the world economy, particularly for the industrialized nations. This interpretation is based on the low wage structures found in these economies, and it reminds many Japanese of the time when,

---

[9] A recent estimate puts Japan's research and development effort in 1976, official and private, at about 1.7 percent of GNP, slightly lower than the 2.2 percent figure estimated for the United States in 1977.

during the 1930s, Japan's rapidly expanding exports of cheap cotton textiles and other manufactures were characterized as "sweatshop exports."

Because the per capita GNP of these countries is still quite low, it is natural that their average wage rate is also low. Capitalizing on their comparative advantage over high-wage countries, poorer countries start exporting a variety of labor-intensive manufactures. But it is rather biased and misleading to characterize such exports as "unfair." In time the exporting countries' income and wages will rise, and the comparative advantage will shift—as part of a natural process I call the "dynamic change in the international division of labor."[10]

As early as the 1930s a Japanese professor of economics, Kaname Akamatsu, invented a theory concerning the stages of development. Literally translated from the Japanese, it is called "The Flying Geese Development Theory." In brief outline the theory explains that a country (1) starts as an exporter of primary products and an importer of simple manufactured goods. It then (2) becomes an exporter of these simple manufactured goods as it (3) begins importing more sophisticated industrial products. Finally, it (4) begins exporting these advanced products. This development process takes place at different times among different countries, thus creating a changing international division of labor.

This process is an inevitable part of the development of the world economy. No measure can stop it artificially and the advanced industrial nations would be well advised to adapt themselves to it as best they can. The newly industrializing countries also have responsibilities. They must proceed at a gradual pace in order to allow time for the advanced nations to adjust. But in the end it cannot be denied that the basic pattern of a changing international division of labor will continue into the future.

One final point of anxiety regarding the newly developing nations concerns the so-called boomerang effect, the process by

---

[10] I develop this idea in "Dynamic Division of Labor and the International Order," in Antony J. Dolan and Jan Van Ettinger, eds., *Partners in Tomorrow: Strategies for a New International Order*, New York: E. P. Dutton, 1978.

which an industrialized country exports capital, technology, and advanced equipment to a newly developing country and eventually makes a competitor of the latter. It is true that over time certain sectors of industry in the advanced countries will lose competitiveness to the products of the newly developing nations. But, at the same time, increased competitiveness will bring with it increases in foreign exchange earnings and purchasing power in the poorer nations, and this will contribute to expanded trade and an increase in the entire global product and income.

It is equally clear that the evolution of this process will create problems for the advanced nations where growing rigidity in the social, economic, and industrial structures will prevent smooth and rapid adjustment. This rigidity is aggravated by the onset of a period of low growth. The task before the industrial nations, including the United States, Europe, and Japan, is to work out policies to provide for reasonable levels of employment even in a period of relatively slow economic growth.

These last paragraphs may seem to have strayed from our original concern with bilateral economic tensions between the United States and Japan. But it is important to bear in mind that our bilateral economic problems occur in a wider international context, and in fact relate to the ways each of our two countries—along with the other advanced industrialized countries—are adapting to the basic and far-reaching changes in the worldwide division of labor that have been under way for the past decade or more, and that seem likely to speed up in the future.

As for the Japanese economy itself, I return to the point that its evolution over the next few years likewise contains basic problems of structure as well as history and habit. Changes in the economic structure of Japan should, over time, tend to reduce some of the frictions that now exist in bilateral dealings with the United States. But I am bound to note also that, if the two nations should find themselves out of step in their efforts to cope with changes in the international economic structure, new and more serious frictions may arise in this respect. Japan feels itself bound to move forward in the high-technology area as a necessity if it is to remain economically healthy.

IV

Now let us turn to the question of China. Early this year I had the opportunity to visit Peking to discuss economic planning and related problems with Chinese officials. Previously, in February 1978, the Chinese government had adopted a ten-year Development Plan for the National Economy which targets a four-point modernization of agriculture, industry, technology, and defense. The plan, which was announced in a statement by Chairman Hua Guofeng, aims at achieving a four to five percent annual growth rate in agriculture and a growth of over ten percent in industry during the ten-year period from 1976 to 1985. The estimated total investment required for this plan is one trillion yuan (approximately $600 billion). The plan includes a target for steel production of 60 million tons in 1985 and calls for the construction of 120 large industrial projects.

At the same time that this ambitious plan was announced, the Chinese also introduced sweeping changes in their policy toward the outside world. However, because many of these changes and shifts in policy were so fundamental, and because they came so suddenly, there are a number of outside observers who doubt the permanence and reliability of this new course. Some even doubt the stability of the present regime. However, based on some of the key documents published by the Chinese government and what the author observed in Peking, it is my judgment that the present course will continue. Even if there are periodic shifts and variations from time to time, the basic task of rapid modernization will be pursued.

One of the major problems facing the Chinese in their quest for modernization has been the quality of leadership. The leadership qualities required during revolution are different from those needed for construction. For construction and modernization, and for the preparation and implementation of the plans and projects, technocrats such as planners, statisticians, and efficient administrators are absolutely essential. Unfortunately these represent precisely the skills which have been neglected during the past decade or so. Under the previous revolutionary leadership these technocrats were considered anti-revolutionary or lacking in revolutionary spirit, and many people possessing such skills were purged to the villages. Intellectuals and scholars, who are needed in the new modernization effort, were downgraded and many suffered through a very difficult time. Chinese leaders now openly admit that 15 years were wasted as a result of policies which denigrated administrative and technocratic skill. Now, however, these people are coming back to the center and they are busy establishing the governmental structure which will be needed to carry out the modernization.

The organizational problems for the realization of this plan are also immense. The Chinese are aware of this. In an article which appeared in the November issues of *Peking Review*, for example, Hu Chiao-mu, President of the Chinese Academy of Social Sciences, evaluated some of the basic problems likely to be encountered in carrying out the plan and the theoretical base for the modernization policy.[11]

Some of the problems the Chinese are likely to face in implementing the modernization plan include a severe shortage of trained and experienced manpower at all levels of government and enterprise, and a need to improve greatly worker efficiency and to increase the quality of work at all levels of production. And, in quantitative terms, China has a serious shortage of domestic savings for investment, as well as a serious shortage of the foreign exchange necessary for the purchase of modern equipment and know-how from abroad. The Japan Economic Research Center has recently conducted a comprehensive study of the Chinese economy which includes an analysis of the Chinese savings and investment balance. The tentative conclusion of this study is that China will experience a capital shortage of around $200 billion over the remaining eight years of the plan if it is to be implemented fully. This corresponds to about one-third of the total investment called for in the plan.[12]

In attempting to deal with this shortage, the policy alternatives available to Chinese leaders are likely to be: (1) to increase efficiency in the use of capital; (2) to raise the level of domestic savings; (3) to borrow from abroad; (4) to lower the plan's tar-

[11] Hu Chiao-mu, "Observe Economic Law, Speed Up the Four Modernizations," *Peking Review*, November 10, 17, and 24, 1978.
[12] Japan Economic Research Center, *Study on Japan–China Economic Relations*, January 1979.

gets, particularly in heavy industries; (5) a combination of the above four alternatives.

It should be noted that despite these problems, in certain respects China is well prepared to begin the modernization effort. In particular, the far-reaching social reforms carried out after the revolution have provided an egalitarian base for the work ahead. In a sense China has succeeded in distributing poverty equally— not wealth. Everyone is equally poor. But the basic necessities of life such as food, shelter, primary education, and medical care are available to the majority of the population. If China succeeds in carrying out its modernization without jeopardizing this egalitarian society, it will be a unique accomplishment in human history.

At the moment, the Chinese government seems to be in the process of reexamining the modernization plan to make it more realistic and feasible. In the beginning the planners may have underestimated the costs involved, particularly the foreign exchange costs. At the same time, the Chinese authorities may have over-encouraged the ministries and enterprises involved to produce their respective modernization plans. The result was a rush of activity with many of these ministries and enterprises approaching foreign suppliers to discuss procurement and other projects. Now that the government has begun a reappraisal, many outside observers doubt the intent and seriousness of the entire Chinese modernization effort. Based on the various announcements by the Chinese government and interviews given by the leaders, it is clear that the Chinese are aware of this problem and are making an effort to allay such misgivings.

In the post-revolution period, China has succeeded in establishing an organized agriculture and in developing small- and medium-scale industries. But experience in the building of modern, large-scale industries seems to be insufficient. As a result, the Chinese are now setting aside the first two years of the plan as a preparatory period during which time they hope to absorb foreign know-how, technology, and management techniques as quickly as possible.

Until recently, the Chinese government seemed to believe that the export of China's abundant natural resources would provide all the foreign exchange needed for the importation of modern equipment. For example, at one point the Chinese offered to vastly increase the export of oil, coal, and other natural resources to Japan in order to pay for the import of machinery. However, it is likely that if they succeed in modernizing their economy, domestic consumption of oil will inevitably increase. In addition, further pressure on the foreign exchange reserves will occur as a result of China's likely need to continue importing sizable amounts of food grains, steel, etc., for some years to come. In view of the above it will be necessary for China to explore the possibility of stepping up its export of manufactures.

The volume of Chinese foreign trade continues to be relatively small, although it is estimated that a 40 percent increase in the value of trade was registered last year. Chinese exports and imports in 1977 were $6.8 billion and $6.3 billion respectively. These figures are small when compared with the exports of South Korea ($10.05 billion) and Taiwan ($9.35 billion). Although Japan accounts for 20.9 percent of China's exports and 33.9 percent of her imports, China's share in Japan's foreign trade in 1977 was only 2.4 percent for exports and 2.2 percent for imports.

Some Asian countries express concern over the fact that China may soon become a serious competitor with their labor-intensive manufactured goods industries. Basically, however, China will remain an inward-looking country economically and, partly because of its political system, exports of manufactured goods may not increase very rapidly even though the government recognizes the need for them to do so. Moreover, larger exports from China when they do occur will result in larger imports as well, and this will contribute to the general expansion of trade in Asia and the world at large. In addition, more frequent contact with the outside world through foreign trade will make China and the Chinese less mysterious and will facilitate a better understanding with foreign nations.

In short, China's industrialization and modernization will move forward. Even if the current ten-year plan is overly ambitious (as admitted recently by Chinese officials),[13] the generally realistic and pragmatic approach to policy issues shown by the new leadership will ensure that China will eventually push its

---

[13] *The People's Daily* of February 24, 1979, carries an editorial to this effect titled "Emancipate Ideas and Attain General Balance."

modernization plans forward. By the end of this century, Chinese production of steel and other industrial products will rank it with the United States, the Soviet Union, Japan, and West Germany, even though per capita productivity and income will remain far below that of the other industrial countries because of the immense size of its population.

V

On the basis of this analysis, it seems clear that the unfolding of China's economic programs over the next twenty years should be one of the great constructive developments in East Asian and, indeed, in world history. What are its implications for the rest of East Asia, and what role can be played by Japan, the United States, and other industrial countries?

I have just noted that China seems unlikely to be a competitive threat to the industrializing countries of East Asia. Concern is also expressed in some Asian countries that if Japan directs an increasingly large share of its capital, including concessional loans, to China, then there will be substantially less available to other Asian nations. However, in view of China's limited absorptive capacity for foreign loans and the very cautious attitude China is likely to adopt in borrowing from abroad, Japan's ability to supply capital to the rest of the world will not be seriously affected.

At the same time, the modernization of China, with its population of 900 million, is an enormous task that will require the participation of all industrial countries. Through the enlarged economic ties formalized most recently in the agreements of early 1978, Japan expects to play a significant role, and the Chinese government has already turned to Japanese, including the present author, for advice on its current ten-year program running to 1985.[14] Proximity as well as deep historical connections have naturally stimulated Japan's interest in effective cooperation with China.

[14] For an interview with the author on this subject, see *The New York Times*, January 9, 1979, p. D3.

Yet, as others have noted, "China's socialist system of government and economy does not lend itself readily to the incentive-driven industrial expansion that Japan obtained."[15] China will undoubtedly wish to retain its own system, and will wish at the same time to diversify its sources of modern equipment. American and European interests—and in some cases governments acting directly—are already deeply engaged in developing greater economic ties with China. There should be ample room for all to play useful parts.

VI

As pointed out at the beginning of this article, the Western Pacific region, including China, will be the most dynamic part of the world during the last part of this century. The United States, facing both the Atlantic and the Pacific, will have to measure the relative importance of these two sides of the country. Japan, for many years to come, will play a crucial economic and political role in the region.

It would be unfortunate for both the United States and Japan if our two countries were to drift apart because of continuing conflicts over economic issues. If the previously mentioned economic irritations between the two countries continue, they may damage the underlying political, social, and security relationship as well. Imagine the case of a Japan, grown frustrated under repeated American shocks and pressures, becoming hostile toward that country. Such a development could endanger the very security of the United States itself. It would also mean the complete bankruptcy and ruin of the Japanese economy. This would have wide-ranging political repercussions not only in Japan but in other Asian countries as well. In a letter to *The New York Times*, Mr. J. Owen Zurhellen, Jr., former Deputy Assistant Secretary of State for East Asian and Pacific Affairs (1975–76) and U.S. Ambassador to Surinam, recently wrote concerning the current U.S.–Japan trade dispute:

15 *Ibid.*, comments by the writer of the article.

American negotiators must be firm and must work for reasonable trade terms with Japan. If we exceed those bounds and deal with Japan as an ill-intentioned malefactor while courting China with credits and most-favored-nation treatment, then we run the grave risk of convincing our principal ally and support in East Asia that we place a higher value on a vivacious and captivating new friend than we do on an old stalwart who, however stolid and sometimes hard to work with, has stood firmly with us on the world stage and with whom we have a set of relationships, including security as well as political and commercial, of fundamental national importance.[16]

The present author does not agree with all that is said here because he feels that it is crucial for the stability of the Pacific region for the United States to maintain friendly relations with *both* China and Japan. Neverthless, it is clear that a falling-out between the United States and Japan would have grave repercussions.

In recent years a new concept called "comprehensive security" has gained wide currency among Japanese. This concept is based on the notion that Japan's security is vulnerable in energy and food supply as well as in military terms. Hence the need for "comprehensive security measures" which include not only the improvement of military capability but also research efforts for the advancement of science and technology, stockpiling of food and energy supplies, and assistance to developing countries. These measures are seen as contributing to the overall security of the nation.

Japan has a highly organized and tightly compacted economy. (Japan's per acre GNP, for example, is about ten times that of the United States.) Thus, a few hydrogen bombs could completely devastate the entire country. Under these circumstances the best strategy for Japan is to avoid any possible military attack by following a prudent diplomatic course.

However, even without a direct military attack on Japanese territory the severing of Japan's energy and food supply lines

---

[16] *The New York Times*, February 28, 1979, p. A22.

could easily paralyze the nation. Thus, one aspect of the comprehensive security measures, in addition to the stockpiling of supplies, calls for the advancement of science and technology. This will give Japan some bargaining power and enable her to guarantee the imports of food, energy, and other raw materials necessary for her survival.

The security of Japan is also fundamentally dependent upon Japan's relationship with the United States. In thinking about this relationship it is necessary to stress its broad social, political, and military as well as economic foundations. Stress on these broad foundations will keep us from being overly distracted by the day-to-day business and economic problems that catch our attention. Senator Sam Nunn wrote in a recent report to the Congress as follows: "Economic problems between Japan and the United States are also of great concern in both nations. [But] they should not be permitted to disrupt United States–Japanese security relations. Both the United States and Japan must ensure that resolution of trade problems does no permanent damage to security relations."[17]

If the United States and Japan concentrate too heavily on current bilateral economic issues and overlook the comprehensive long-term relationship, there is a danger of our two nations moving onto a collision course. Americans must keep in mind that, for Japan, pressure from abroad is welcome if it is for the sake of broader regional and global interests, but not if it is for the narrow and sectoral interests of one country. Japan, on the other hand, must understand that her domestic policies have far-reaching repercussions on her international relations.

The visit of Japanese Prime Minister Ohira to Washington in early May seems to have served to dispel some of the misgivings on both sides and helped the two peoples to recognize their long-term and broad interests in the relationship. The Joint Communiqué on the occasion of that visit set an appropriate keynote: "Productive Partnership for the 1980s."

As for relations with China, the following remarks made by

---

[17] "United States–Japan Security Relationship—The Key to East Asian Security and Stability," Report of the Pacific Study Group to the Committee on Armed Services, United States Senate, March 22, 1979, Washington, D.C.

Prime Minister Ohira at the National Press Club, Washington, D.C., on May 3, 1979, are relevant: "The development of friendly relations between Japan and China, as between the United States and China, has broadened the foundation for our Asian policies. Japan will act in close concert with the United States and Western Europe to extend appropriate cooperation to China's economic development efforts."

Foreign Policy Speech for the Ninety-First Session of the National Diet

At the resumption of this Ninety-First Session of the National Diet, I should like to express my views on our country's basic foreign policy.

We stand today on the threshold of the 1980s.

Although the 1970s witnessed important moves made for the stabilization of international relations, they also saw the outbreak of new conflict and new tension.

Japan and the United States both normalized our relations with China. In Indochina, the long war was stilled, only to be replaced by new discord and new conflict. In U.S.–USSR relations, there were moves toward the relaxation of tensions as seen in the Strategic Arms Limitation Talks (SALT) agreements, but these relations have recently entered a new phase over the issue of Afghanistan. In the Middle East, too, a peace treaty was concluded between Egypt and Israel, but the road to a comprehensive peace remains rough, and the Iranian situation does not allow complacency.

Likewise, the international economy has experienced major structural changes with the 1971 "dollar shock," the 1973 oil crisis, and other developments. Many nations have been faced with prolonged recession, inflation, and other difficulties, and there is special concern with the energy problem as an important issue which should be overcome.

Looking ahead to the 1980s from this perspective on the 1970s,

This speech was delivered as the Diet began a new session on January 25, 1980; the author had just been appointed Minister of Foreign Affairs by Prime Minister Masayoshi Ohira.

it may be expected that international efforts will continue for global peace and the stability and development of the world economy, yet a number of difficulties may be anticipated in both the political and economic spheres, and the 1980s will be a very trying decade for global peace and economic development.

Within this context, Japanese foreign policy's mission must truly be termed both important and difficult.

The first need of any foreign policy is to protect the lives and livelihoods of the Japanese people.

On protecting the lives of the people, it goes without saying that our basic policy is one of firmly maintaining our security arrangements founded in a moderate yet high-quality self-defense capability and the Japan–U.S. Security Treaty. At the same time, it is also important that we acquaint the world with Japan's dedication to peace in international relations and strive to maintain and develop friendly relations with all countries. Viewing Japan's security from the broader perspective and in the overall context, it must be noted that foreign policy has an extremely important role to play.

As Japan is dependent upon overseas sources for the vast bulk of its energy resources and for the majority of its main mineral resources and foodstuffs, maintaining and expanding free and diversified trade and economic relations is the basic means to protect the foundations of the people's livelihoods. Accordingly, it is of crucial importance that we promote a comprehensive foreign policy that is not restricted to the economic realm but, rather, considers political, cultural, and all other aspects.

Further, it is essential that Japan do more to contribute positively to the maintenance of world peace and to international economic prosperity.

Japan's international importance has recently grown to reflect the sharp increases in our economic strength, and this trend may be expected to accelerate in the 1980s. The world expects Japan to take a more positive political and economic role in the international community. Although Japan has played a considerable role in the 1970s, we must further fulfill a role and responsibilities commensurate with our international position in the 1980s.

On the maintenance of world peace, it is imperative that Japan, based upon our basic policy of dedication to peace, participate in the creation of an international climate conducive to the preservation of world peace and contribute even more than ever to eliminating elements of instability in the various problem-ridden regions of the world.

At present, the global economy is in the midst of increasing inflation, and the outlook is increasingly grim because of the large number of problems which must be solved, including the slowing of growth rate, the harsh employment situation, the dulling of productivity increases, and the widening imbalances in international balances of payments, and because of recent oil developments. Recognizing our responsibilities as a major support for the global economy, Japan especially must seek to deal with these international economic difficulties in concert with the other countries concerned and, in particular, seek to contribute positively to the economic construction of the developing countries.

Thus our basic foreign policy stance in the 1980s must be one premised upon the perspective of Japan within the world community. Recognizing that Japan needs international peace and stability, we must pay greater concern to events in the world and must be prepared to take our responsible part. To contribute more positively to the maintenance of world peace and economic development from this perspective is thus to further enhance Japan's credibility in the international community and, I would submit, to protect the lives and livelihoods of the Japanese people.

I am determined to conduct future foreign policy on the basis of this realization, and I should like next to speak about our specific policy areas.

Japan–U.S. Relations

The continued maintenance and strengthening of friendly and cooperative Japan–U.S. relations founded upon the Japan–U.S. security arrangements remains the cornerstone of Japanese foreign policy.

As Japan takes on ever-increasing responsibilities as a member of the international community, it is most important in strengthening Japanese diplomatic efforts for world peace and stability that we further develop our cooperative relations with the United States as a trusted partner in the global perspective.

On the Japan–U.S. economic relationship, in addition to faithfully implementing the various agreements included in last May's Japan–U.S. joint communiqué and steadily steering the various issues in Japan–U.S. economic relations to conclusion, both countries must formulate a medium-term outlook for the Japan–U.S. economic relationship, and much is expected here of the work of the Japan–U.S. Economic Relations Group.

Although there has been some friction between the two countries over the past decade, it has fortunately been possible, through awareness of the coincidence of our basic interests, to keep this friction from developing into a more serious situation. For the future, it is imperative that the two countries continue to work unceasingly for the maintenance of friendly relations between them.

Relations with the Asian Countries

Overview

Asia is a region in which Japan should play a leading role for regional peace and development.

As well as further strengthening Japanese foreign policy efforts aimed at the peace and stability of the entire Asian region, we are resolved to further promote Japanese cooperation for these countries' expansion of their agricultural and industrial production, expansion of employment, trade development, human resources development, and more.

The Korean peninsula

On the Korean Peninsula, Japan will continue to work for deepening exchanges of opinions among all countries concerned in order to contribute to the stability and relaxation of tensions in that area, and with this in mind we will cooperate for the creation of an international climate for the resumption of substantive dialogue between North and South.

The Republic of Korea is currently striving for orderly reform to unite its people, and Japan both hopes that these efforts will bear fruit and seeks to additionally develop our mutual relations of friendship and cooperation. In our dealings with North Korea, we intend to continue the gradual building of exchanges in the trade, economic, cultural, and other fields.

China

I have recently accompanied Prime Minister Ohira on an official visit to China. During our stay in China, the leaders of our two nations held candid exchanges of opinions on the situation in Asia and on the Japan–China relationship in the 1980s. In these meetings, we indicated Japan's preparedness to cooperate positively with the building of the Chinese economy and, in so doing, we conveyed Japanese policy and obtained Chinese understanding that we will not cooperate in military areas, that we will not sacrifice Japan's relations with the other countries of Asia, especially our traditional relations with the ASEAN countries, and that the Japan–China relationship is not an exclusive relationship but a relationship of cooperation in concert with the other advanced industrial countries. There was also agreement seen in our opinions on intensifying cultural exchanges between our two countries.

Based upon the successes achieved in this visit to China, I intend to continue to work for the further development of this Japan–China relationship of peace and friendship.

ASEAN

Support for and cooperation with the efforts of the ASEAN countries as they make steady progress for the stability and development of Southeast Asia is an important pillar of Japan's Asian foreign policy. I intend to add to our continuing efforts to enhance relations of friendship and cooperation with these countries based upon the existing good Japan–ASEAN relations.

The Refugee Problem and Indochina

The Indochinese refugee problem has become an important humanitarian and political question.

Japan has undertaken to bear half of the expenses incurred by the office of the United Nations High Commissioner for Refugees in its Indochinese Refugee Relief Program for 1979, to mount major public- and private-sector relief activities including medical assistance for Cambodian refugees, and to promote resettlement in Japan and other efforts to solve this problem, and we intend to extend increased cooperation in all of these areas in the future.

However, no fundamental solution to the Indochinese refugee problem can be achieved without peace and stability in this region, and it is thus necessary that lasting peace be restored to Cambodia. Japan intends to play a part for peace by calling upon all countries concerned in cooperation with the ASEAN countries.

Southwest Asia

On the Southwest Asian region, we are determined to promote more mutual understanding with these countries and to cooperate in every way possible with their economic development.

Middle East

The situation in the Middle East is showing further signs of tension over such countries as Iran and Afghanistan, and future developments there should be watched carefully for the major political and economic impact they will have upon the world. In view of this situation, Japan's policy toward the Middle East should be conducted as one of the important pillars of Japanese foreign policy in the 1980s.

Relations between Japan and the countries of the Middle East have become increasingly close in various fields against the background of growing recognition of the importance of this relationship. The interdependence of Japan and these countries has accordingly deepened rapidly. Under these circumstances, we feel it necessary on Japan's part to establish a truly welcome Japanese presence in the Middle East by maintaining and promoting friendly and cooperative relations with the area.

Accordingly, it is necessary for Japan to contribute to nation-building and human-resources development in the countries of the Middle East as well as to deepen our mutual understanding with these countries in the historical, religious, and cultural spheres.

Moreover, Japan intends to extend all possible cooperation for the realization of Middle East peace with a view that the Peace Treaty between Egypt and Israel should lead to a just, lasting, and comprehensive peace, and it is also our policy to continue to strengthen the dialogue which we have been conducting with the PLO.

The Afghan problem

The Soviet military intervention in Afghanistan is an act contrary to international law and international justice and one to be deeply deplored, and we cannot but express our deep concern about the Soviet action and for the peace and stability of the international community. It is our earnest hope that the people of Afghanistan resolve their internal problems on their own, in accordance with the principles of non-interference in domestic affairs and respect for self-determination. Japan for its part demands prompt withdrawel of the Soviet forces from Afghanistan, and strongly calls upon the Soviet Union to seriously reconsider its attitude. Japan strongly supports the resolution adopted by an overwhelming majority at the recent emergency special session of the United Nations General Assembly. As a country devoted to the cause of peace and freedom for the international community, Japan considers it necessary to give expression in concrete fashion to this position, in concert with the United States, the countries of Western Europe, and other friendly nations. From such a perspective, we are reviewing Japan–USSR relations.

At the same time, the Soviet military intervention in Afghanistan has a direct impact upon the neighboring countries in the region and we consider that international efforts should be made to maintain the peace and stability of these countries. In this sense, should there be a request from the government of Pakistan, Japan intends, together with the other countries concerned, to give positive consideration to the expansion of cooperation in the economic field for the well-being and stability of that country's economy. Nearly half a million refugees from Afghanistan have recently poured into Pakistan, including large numbers of women, children, and aged people. In response to the call of the United Nations High Commissioner for Refugees (UNHCR), Japan has recently decided to contribute relief supplies worth ¥1 billion.

At the same time, Japan understands the grave view taken by the Third World countries, especially the Islamic countries, on the situation, and I would like to express our support for these countries.

The Iran problem

I am deeply concerned that the seizure of the United States Embassy in Teheran and the holding hostage of American diplomats has been so prolonged with no solution in sight.

This incident constitutes a serious threat to the inviolability of diplomatic missions, a fundamental rule of the international community. In this sense, it is an issue which cannot be ignored, not only by the U.S., our ally, but also by the international community as a whole, including Japan. The holding of hostages is unacceptable also from the humanitarian viewpoint.

Japan will actively support the international efforts, including those of the United Nations. Also, as the situation requires, Japan will act appropriately, in cooperation with the United States as well as European and other countries, regarding ways to achieve an early release of the hostages.

I strongly hope that the hostages will be released without loss of time, that the situation will be resolved in a peaceful manner, and that the bonds of friendship between Japan and Iran will be consolidated.

Relations with the Countries of Western Europe

On our relations with the EC member countries and the other

countries of Western Europe, cooperation between Japan and the West European countries is desirable to contribute to world peace and prosperity in the 1980s, and we intend to build broader relations of cooperation with these countries.

Relations with the Countries of Oceania

I accompanied Prime Minister Ohira on his visits to Australia and New Zealand from January 15 to January 20, and I feel we were able on these visits to affirm our relations of friendship and cooperation to date and to deepen mutual understanding with these countries. Both of these countries are good partners for cooperation in the Pacific region, and Japan intends to further develop our relations of friendship and cooperation with these two countries and with the other island countries of the South Pacific for continued peace and prosperity in the Pacific region.

Likewise, we also held significant discussions on the promotion of diversified relations of cooperation among the countries of the Pacific region, and it was agreed to further study the Pacific basin cooperation concept from this perspective based upon broad consensus within the region.

Japan–USSR Relations

Relations with the Soviet Union have entered a difficult phase due to the Soviet military intervention in Afghanistan and other events. Moreover, the problem of the Northern Territories still remains the largest pending issue in our bilateral relations with the Soviet Union, and particularly the Government cannot but view with grave concern the recent Soviet military buildup on these territories. It is the Government's firm intention to persist in demanding prompt withdrawal of such military measures and making untiring efforts in keeping with our consistent basic policy toward the solution of the Northern Territorial issue and the conclusion of a peace treaty.

Relations with the Countries of Eastern Europe

We intend to promote our efforts for mutual understanding and friendly relations with the countries of Eastern Europe, with whom relations have developed remarkably of late.

Relations with the Countries of Latin America

Likewise, in our relations with the countries of Latin America, now that the organizational and actual capability for developing a positive foreign policy toward Latin America has been completed with the establishment of the Latin America and Caribbean Affairs Bureau in the Ministry of Foreign Affairs with your approval in the last Extraordinary Session of the Diet, the Government intends to renew its determination to make efforts to further broaden the foundations of mutual cooperation and to strengthen the bonds of friendly and cooperative relations with these countries of such rich potential.

Relations with the Countries of Africa

As indicated by the moves to a solution of the Rhodesian problem, the countries of Africa are as one in their strong desire and aspiration for peace and prosperity. I am confident that positive cooperation with this desire and aspiration is the basis for further strengthening our relations of friendship and cooperation with the countries of Africa.

The International Economy

With today's increasing interdependence among the different countries' economies, it is only when all countries concerned coordinate their efforts to strengthen international cooperation that it will be possible to deal with the difficulties entailed in the global economy.

On oil and other energy issues, the most important and urgent tasks facing the advanced consuming countries at present are to hold down oil demand, to take measures to stabilize oil markets, and to lower our dependence on oil by developing and expanding the use of coal, natural gas, nuclear power, and other alternative energy resources. As a major consumer country, Japan must also respond responsibly in close cooperation with the other leading industrialized consumer countries in the IEA and other forums.

On the other hand, it is also extremely important that Japan secure the necessary supplies of oil, and it is thus necessary that we build broad relations of friendship and cooperation with the oil-producing countries.

At the same time, it is important for overcoming stagflation that we promote investment for improved productivity and for research and development as agreed at the Tokyo Summit and other occasions and that each country implement economic restructuring policies in coordination with other countries to strengthen its economic structure.

Moreover, Japan intends to work in cooperation with other countries to deter protectionism and to further promote the open-trade system. It is especially important for Japan that we effect those Tokyo Round agreements scheduled for first-stage implementation this year as soon as possible, and the Government intends to make every effort for the earliest possible acceptance of these agreements.

The North-South Problem

The adverse effects of soaring oil prices upon the development of non–oil-producing developing countries have recently become a problem, and the international community is being strongly pressed to deal positively with the overall North-South problem, including this issue. Japan intends to continue to participate positively in the North-South dialogue in order to seek to build constructive North-South relations in the 1980s.

At the same time, the Government is determined to meet its goal of doubling ODA [official development assistance] within three years in this final year as well as to seek continued qualitative and quantitative improvements in Japanese ODA.

In improving ODA, we intend especially to contribute to human-resources development, agricultural development, energy development including alternative energies, infrastructure construction, and other basic areas.

Likewise on that commodity question which is of great concern to the developing countries, it is our policy to make every effort for the prompt conclusion of those Common Fund negotiations which are now under way.

United Nations

On our multilateral foreign policy at the United Nations, and with special reference to the recent situations in Iran, Afghanistan, and elsewhere, Japan hopes to contribute positively with creativity and imagination so as to enable the United Nations to make fuller use of its peacekeeping functions.

Likewise, it is the policy of the Government to continue to contribute positively to promote disarmament, centering on nuclear disarmament, which is of primary concern.

Cultural Exchange

In today's global society of heightening exchange and interdependence among countries, the importance of expanding mutual understanding and trust through wide-ranging and frequent cultural contacts is increasingly realized. Especially for Japan, heavily dependent on the maintenance of smooth relations with other countries, the promotion of positive cultural exchanges is an important link in our foreign policy. Accordingly, the Government is determined to make untiring efforts to further expand our international exchanges in the cultural field.

Conclusion

These have been my views on the important foreign policy issues facing Japan. In view of the severity of the international situation and the position in which Japan finds itself, it is no exaggeration to say that the 1980s will truly be a time of trial for Japanese foreign policy. Looking ahead to this era, the further strengthening of our structure for foreign policy implementation is an urgent matter. Likewise, in the promotion of foreign policy, it is crucial to obtain even broader public understanding and support than before, for it is only then that Japanese foreign policy can squarely meet the trials of the 1980s.

I would like here to request the further understanding and support of all of the people in this endeavor.

How Can Japan and the United States Reduce Economic Frictions?

Conflict in Japan–U.S. trade relations has been intensifying since last year. Japan and the United States are important free-world partners. It would be most unfortunate should friction in their bilateral trade relations damage the basically cooperative relationship between the two countries. Today I would like to review the background of the Japan–U.S. economic friction of recent years and suggest some remedial steps. Cool reasoning has never been more necessary than at present, when debate has grown so heated.

In delving into the background of Japan–U.S. economic friction, it is necessary to differentiate between long-term, structural problems and short-term, cyclical ones. We must also avoid factual misunderstandings and inaccurate perceptions, and should not allow specific phenomena to make us lose sight of the overall picture.

Trade Imbalance

According to U.S. statistics (FAS base), in its trade with Japan the United States recorded a deficit of $9.9 billion in 1980 and $15.8 billion in 1981 (Table 1). This appears to be largely responsible for stirring up American public opinion resulting in the recent criticism of Japan.

Often overlooked in this argument is the fact that international

This speech was given before the National Press Club in Washington, D.C., on May 19, 1982.

Table 1   Comparison of Japan and U.S. Balance of Payments

(billion dollars)

	1977	1978	1979	1980	1981
1. Japan					
Current Balance	+10.9	+16.5	− 8.7	−10.7	+ 4.7
Trade (goods)					
balance	+17.3	+24.6	+ 1.8	+ 2.1	+20.0
Services	− 6.0	− 7.4	− 9.5	−11.3	−13.7
2. U.S.					
Current Balance	−14.1	−14.1	+ 1.4	+ 3.7	+ 6.5
Trade (goods)					
balance	−29.1	−31.1	−27.6	−24.2	−27.6
Services	+16.8	+19.4	+28.7	+36.1	+41.2
3. U.S.–Japan Trade (Goods) Balance					
U.S. deficit (−)	− 8.0	−11.6	− 8.7	− 9.9	−15.8

trade requires multilateral dealings, and so should not be judged on a purely bilateral basis. Concentrating attention on a particular bilateral relationship tends to invite misunderstanding of the real situation. In 1980, for instance, the United States had a deficit of $9.9 billion in its visible trade with Japan but ran up a surplus of $17 billion with the EC. In the same year Japan had a trade deficit of $30 billion with the Middle East and a deficit of $6 billion with Canada and Australia combined.

Another important point is that while the visible trade balance is highly emphasized, balance in service trade, another important factor, is being ignored. In 1981 the United States sustained a deficit of $27.6 billion in its visible trade with the entire world but had a surplus of $41.2 billion in service trade and, with other items added and deducted, recorded a net surplus in its current account of $6.5 billion. By contrast, in the same year Japan had a $20 billion surplus in visible trade but a $13.7 billion deficit in service trade, closing its current account with a surplus of only $4.7 billion. In the same way, the United States had a current account surplus of $3.7 billion in 1980, while Japan ran up a deficit of $10.7 billion. Thus, in terms of the current account, which signifies the overall balance of a country's external dealings, the United States was in better shape than Japan. In these circumstances, many Japanese find it difficult to understand why Japan alone must be on the receiving end of criticism.

Exchange Rates and Trade Balance

Judging from the relationship between visible and invisible trade and the structure of the world's multilateral trade, America's running up of a trade deficit of $10 billion or so with Japan is nothing out of the ordinary. The most important reason this deficit climbed to $15.8 billion last year was the fluctuation of foreign exchange rates in favor of the dollar and against the yen. At the beginning of 1981 the dollar was worth only ¥200. The yen began to weaken later, and in the summer of last year it took ¥247 to buy a dollar. Later the yen showed some signs of strengthening, but even now the dollar is worth around ¥240.

Not a few American economists say that last year's drastic jump in America's trade deficit with Japan would not have occurred if the value of the dollar had been kept at around ¥200. On the basis of the international competitiveness of products, the yen should have been quoted at higher levels because inflation is lower and the rate of productivity rise is higher in Japan than in the United States. But the high level of U.S. interest rates increased the gap between Japanese and American interest rates, with the result that dollars began flowing out of Japan into the United States, leading to the weakening of the yen against the dollar. The cheaper yen helped Japanese exports while discouraging imports. The Japan–U.S. trade imbalance grew as a result. Thus foreign exchange rates led to a dichotomy between the competitiveness of products and the movement of capital.

Meanwhile, some are of the view that the yen is weak because Japan has not sufficiently liberalized capital transactions, thus refusing to make the yen an international currency. This charge may be justified from a long-term viewpoint. In the short term, however, it is undeniable that the measures taken by the Japanese government in the spring of last year to liberalize capital transactions combined with the rising interest rates in the U.S. encouraged the outflow of yen, which led to the weakening of the Japanese currency. We fully understand that America's high interest rates are the result of America's tight money policy to combat inflation. But we cannot understand why the rate has to remain at a substantial 16 percent today, when inflation has been forced down to a relatively mild 6 percent. America's high interest rates are one of the major factors in America's, and for that matter the world's, recession.

We should not overlook the fact that high U.S. interest rates are making it difficult for European countries to take reflationary steps, intensifying Japan–U.S. trade friction, and making the interest burden almost unbearable for developing countries, which are already up to their ears in debt. In the United States, interest and foreign exchange rates are left to the market mechanism. The result has been wide and frequent fluctuations. These fluctuations in turn have helped push up interest rates, discouraging productive investment. Frankly speaking, we wish the United States would exercise a little more discretion about how its economic policy administration affects the world economy. The majority of the Japanese think high interest rates are the main cause of unemployment and low growth in the United States.

The Closed Nature of the Japanese Market

Particularly in recent years, there has been growing criticism of the closed nature of the Japanese market. More and more arguments are being heard that the closed nature of the Japanese market is a major cause of the trade surplus Japan has built up with its trading partners. Despite historical and cultural factors that stand in the way of its opening its market to foreign goods, Japan has continued its efforts to open its market to foreign imports. The progress made in this direction is apparent when the situation today is compared with that ten or twenty years ago. Recently, Japan decided to move up by two years the across-the-board tariff reductions agreed to in the Tokyo Round of Multilaterial Trade Negotiations, remove or lower sixty-seven nontariff barriers, set up the Office of Trade Ombudsman to deal with foreign suppliers' complaints, and take other measures to open its market. These steps are being implemented one by one.

Japan is a parliamentary democracy. In my view, Japan deserves praise for taking these steps despite the host of complaints politicians are receiving from constituents whose interests are adversely affected by the moves. The Japanese government intends to continue negotiations with the United States concerning the relaxation of residual import restrictions and the expansion of import quotas, and to enforce what is agreed on. In the United States it is often said that Japan should take dramatic steps to open its market. Social tradition and custom, however, dictate that Japan make decisions by consensus. For this reason it is difficult to make any dramatic decision. But I consider that Japan's continued efforts to open its market and its policy of persisting in such efforts in the future deserve favorable evaluation by foreign countries. For example, imports of beef from the United States more than doubled and those of citrus fruits increased by 50 percent during the last four years.

There is also criticism of the fact that the ratio of manufactured products in Japan's total imports is around 24 percent, which is low compared with the United States and European countries. The ratio temporarily dipped in the wake of drastic oil-price increases. But with the economy's absorption of the effects of the higher oil prices, the ratio has returned to the trend of increasing yearly. The very structure of its economy requires Japan to import massive amounts of food, energy resources, and raw materials. Even if Japan doubled the ratio of manufactured products in its total imports, it would not be able to reduce its imports of food and raw materials. The increased imports of manufactured products and undiminished imports of food and raw materials would require Japan to step up its exports by some $30 billion to pay for the increased imports. Such an export drive by Japan would only exacerbate trade friction.

These circumstances notwithstanding, I consider that opening its market is in Japan's own interest, and accordingly, Japan should cooperate in strengthening the free trade system based on GATT. If the present rules of free trade are lost, requiring countries to negotiate ad hoc on individual cases of trading and transactions, every country stands to lose. It is necessary to increase the resilience of GATT management, and in compliance with changes in competitive advantage among countries, both importing and exporting countries will be required to share the pains of adjustment. Countries needing time to adjust should be allowed a reasonable period in which to do so. We in Japan have been watching with concern the development in the U.S. Congress on so-called reciprocity bills. The testimony by U.S. Trade Representative William Brock on March twenty-fourth explaining the position of the Administration by pointing out the necessity of abiding by existing multilateral agreements was most encouraging.

Growth Based on Domestic Demand

We are fully aware of the criticism that Japan's recent economic growth, which has been heavily dependent on exports, is undesirable from the viewpoint of promoting the harmonious development of the world economy. It is true that both in 1980 and 1981 Japan's growth in GNP was heavily based on external demand increase. Reducing interest rates to encourage private sector investment, however, involves the risk of intensifying trade friction because it will widen the interest gap between Japan and the United States and weaken the yen on the world's foreign exchange markets. Looking at the domestic aspects, stimulating the economy by pumping in treasury money is difficult and ill-timed now, for the following reasons. Government finance has been in deficit for some years now, and the government's public debt outstanding has reached 40 percent of GNP. In the current fiscal year, 20 percent of the budget expenditures constitute deficit spending, and the government has publicly pledged to rid itself of this bulging deficit as soon as possible. Due to the worldwide recession and Japan's voluntary export restraints—in auto exports to the United States and auto, TV, and machine tool exports to Europe—recently Japan's export performance has shown a definite slump. Japan's exports for the fourth quarter of last year posted a decline from the preceding quarter. (The March 1982 export figure was 8.2 percent below that of a year ago). Although domestic demand showed some recovery in that quarter, GNP growth was −0.9 percent on a quarterly basis and −3.5 percent on an annual basis. As a result, tax revenue decreased, which tended to swell the budget deficit. In view of sluggish exports and the government's determination to expand domestic demand, these factors will result in domestic demand-oriented growth this year.

Linking the Trade and Defense Issues

One of the causes of friction in Japan–U.S. relations is the feeling in the United States that Japan should assume a larger share of its own defense, commensurate with its increased economic power. We are aware that some Americans argue that Japan, by spending only about 1 percent of its GNP for defense, compared with America's 6 percent, is investing the funds saved on defense in private industries so that Japanese exports will be more competitive on the world market. But the main reason for the relatively high level of private investment in Japan is not so much the difference in defense spending between Japan and the United States as the Japanese people's high propensity to save— 20 percent compared with 5 percent for the American people.

After World War II, Japan declared in its new constitution that it would not use force as a means of settling international disputes. The country subsequently adopted the basic policy of improving its self-defense strength only within the framework of an exclusively defensive and non-nuclear capability. For Japan to participate in a collective security arrangement would require constitutional amendment, which calls for passage by a two-thirds majority in the national legislature, followed by a national referendum. I do not see such a likelihood in the near future. We understand that U.S. government authorities have agreed to this basic Japanese policy of improving its defense capability. From their past experience, the majority of Japanese people strongly wish that nuclear weapons will never again be used. We hope that the United States and the Soviet Union will successfully negotiate a large-scale reduction of nuclear weapons that will lead to worldwide disarmament.

Although Japan will never have the capability of attacking other countries, it will continue its efforts, by applying high technology, to guarantee the capability to defend itself effectively, with the help of the Japan–U.S. security treaty, if attacked by a foreign country. The United States may not be satisfied with the speed with which Japan undertakes to improve its defense, but this is an issue that must be judged in the light of the world situation, and one that requires a national consensus. A sudden and sharp increase in defense expenditures may destabilize domestic politics and invite suspicions of neighboring Asian countries.

In tandem with its effort to its strengthen self-defense capability, Japan should direct its vast economic power to world development, especially through assistance to developing countries in such fields as the production of food and energy and in developing infrastructures such as transportation and communication. Japan has more than fulfilled Prime Minister Takeo Fukuda's pledge to double Official Development Assistance (ODA) in the three years ending in 1980. Prime Minister Zenko Suzuki has publicly declared a plan that would increase the ODA total for the five years ending with 1985 to more than double the total for the preceding five years. I personally think it is desirable that Japan accelerate this plan and become, in the not too distant future, the world's largest aid donor. Moreover, Japanese companies, instead of just exporting their products, should enter into business tie-ups with foreign companies as often as possible to create job opportunities abroad by building factories in host countries and to share profits with foreign business partners. In fact, there are more than 200 factories with Japanese participation in the United States and they are directly creating employment for 65,000 people. Further expansion in this area is expected.

Conclusion

Japan and the United States are bound together not only by common economic interests but also by common political values, such as free elections, freedom of speech, and respect for human rights. Japanese prime ministers have repeatedly stated that Japan–U.S. relations are the backbone of Japanese diplomacy. U.S. presidents have stated that relations with Japan form the basis of America's Asian policy, and have stressed Japan's importance as a democratic partner. It would be most unfortunate if the relations between these two countries were to suffer due to economic friction and mutual misunderstandings. Both nations must strive to maintain and develop their friendly relations by deepening mutual understanding from a long-range and comprehensive viewpoint. I hope that the Japan–U.S. relationship will develop into a truly productive partnership.

Cooperation and Development in the Pacific Region

Looking out over the international situation today, the horizon is a mix of dark clouds and some bright prospects. Among the darkest clouds is the global economy, especially the recession in the advanced industrial countries. The United States alone now has 12 million unemployed, and the European Community another 10 million. This recession in the industrialized countries has heightened economic friction and strengthened protectionist trade tendencies in these countries. At the same time, the global recession has resulted in lower prices for many commodities exported by the developing countries and has thus been a major blow to those countries which rely heavily upon exports of primary commodities. Even the OPEC nations have been thrust from a position of foreign capital surplus to one of shortfall by the reduced demand and lower prices for their oil. The countries of Eastern Europe and many developing countries have been forced to curtail their imports sharply in the face of burgeoning debts and high interest rates. As a result of this global recession, the world trade volume of both 1981 and 1982 was less in real terms than the year before. Some countries are having difficulty repaying their external debts, and this is raising questions about the viability of international finance mechanisms. These are all very pressing, very disconcerting problems.

In the longer term, it should also be noted that little progress has been made in narrowing the gap between the affluent North and the impoverished South, and that poverty and starvation

This chapter is the text of remarks at the graduation ceremony of the University of the South Pacific, in Suva, Fiji, on December 16, 1982.

113

are widespread in the least developed countries. According to one FAO study, there are 450 million people worldwide who are deprived of the minimum nutritional levels necessary for sustenance. In ghastly contrast, $600 billion is spent every year on armaments and the military, and the threat of nuclear war continues to haunt mankind's future.

There is seemingly no end to the gloom clouding our horizons, but despair should not be allowed to obscure the positive elements of hope. First, there is the fact that the world has generally managed to live in peace for the last thirty-seven years. Although there have been a number of local conflicts, there has been no large-scale war since the end of World War II. The threat of nuclear war remains, but there is increasing awareness worldwide of the urgent need to somehow stave off this disaster. The global recession, serious as it is, has not sparked a major social and economic breakdown. At the same time, there are hopes that the declining inflation rates and consequently lower interest rates in the industrial nations will lend themselves to a measure of economic recovery starting sometime next year. If this happens, it is not unreasonable to expect recovery in commodity prices and expansion of world trade levels. While most of the developing countries remain poor, a number of them have graduated to the ranks of the newly industrializing, and these NICs are achieving very rapid economic growth to narrow the gap with the advanced industrial countries. Also, even as rapidly expanding populations impose new economic burdens on the developing countries, many of these same countries have made rapid progress in expanding food production. India, for example, has doubled its production of foodstuffs over the last quarter-century. Rice production is up in the Southeast Asian countries, and some countries have been able to move from being rice importers to become rice exporters. The developing countries are also making rapid strides in nutrition, hygiene, and the diffusion of education, and steady progress is being made in prolonging life expectancies, lowering infant mortality rates, and reducing illiteracy. The development of modern transport and communications has drastically reduced time-distances around the globe, and technological innovation has engendered a convenience which was unimaginable only a few decades ago. Micro-electronics technology, for example, can link the scattered islands of the South Pacific and make instant communication with the rest of the world a reality.

In looking toward the future, it seems to me that we should work to diminish the gloomy aspects and enhance the bright prospects. Promoting cooperation among the nations of the Pacific is significant in this positive sense in promoting the development of this region. Just as the famous American journalist Walter Lippmann could say at the end of World War I that the Atlantic had become "an inland sea," so may it be said that modern communication and transportation technologies are rapidly making an inland sea of the Pacific.

The potential for cooperation in the Pacific region is already widely recognized. The Pacific Development Conference of economists from the region, for example, has met twelve times so far since its establishment in 1968 to analyze and advance this topic, with the next meeting scheduled for Manila next month to discuss energy issues. Businessmen have also shown great interest, as in the Pacific Basin Economic Council (PBEC), which was founded in 1967 and has met frequently throughout the region. Last year, the PBEC met in Hong Kong, this year in Nagoya, Japan, and next year it will meet in Santiago, Chile.

One of the major stimuli to international interest in the issue of Pacific cooperation came when the late Prime Minister Masayoshi Ohira of Japan made Pacific cooperation a major policy theme for his government. To begin with, Prime Minister Ohira established a private study group to examine the issue of Pacific cooperation, a group which I was asked to chair. This study group of about a score of scholars and experts issued its report in May 1980, pointing out that, while economic relations may be expected to grow steadily closer in accordance with actual economic workings, it is necessary to make conscious efforts to supplement these economic relations with cultural and other cooperation for enhanced mutual understanding. Not only is the Pacific region geographically vast, it is a very heterogeneous region encompassing great historical, religious, cultural, climatic, economic, and other diversity. Moreover, efforts to promote mutual understanding among the various parts of the Pacific region have been wanting so far. Frankly, the Japanese people are largely ignorant of conditions in the South Pacific, and I suspect the reverse is also true. The same may also be said of relations between the South Pacific nations and the Southeast Asian nations. If economic interaction proceeds at too fast a pace in the absence of mutual understanding, there is the real danger that this could lead to misunderstanding and friction. In this sense, it is very important that we work actively for exchanges of students and teachers among universities in the Pacific region, exchanges of people in various fields, and other programs to introduce each other's cultures and societies more widely.

The late Prime Minister Ohira stressed in his policy program the following guiding principles for Pacific Basin cooperation:

(1) that Pacific Basin cooperation be promoted as a long-term policy aiming at the twenty-first century,
(2) that the emphases of this cooperation be in the economic and cultural fields and that the political and military be excluded,
(3) that Pacific Basin cooperation be open to all countries of the region, and
(4) that the promotion of Pacific Basin cooperation be premised upon consensus and agreement among the Pacific countries.

In September 1980, the Pacific Community Seminar was held at Australian National University under the auspices of ANU Chancellor Sir John Crawford. Academics, businessmen, and government officials from the five developed Pacific countries (Australia, Canada, Japan, New Zealand, and the United States), the ASEAN five (Indonesia, Malaysia, the Philippines, Singapore, and Thailand), and the Republic of Korea and the South Pacific participated in this Seminar. The government officials took part as experts in their own right and not as representatives of their governments, and the Seminar itself was nongovernmental in character. This Seminar was noteworthy in further advancing the concept of Pacific Basin cooperation; yet, at the same time, there was concern expressed by some ASEAN countries that such cooperation may serve great-power domination of the region or may be injurious to the process of ASEAN consolidation. The ASEAN countries, however, have given further study to this issue of Pacific Basin cooperation, and progress was seen on a number of fronts at the second Seminar held this June in Bangkok at the invitation of Thailand's Deputy Premier Thanat Khoman. For example, an interconference standing committee was appointed with eight members from the various Pacific countries, and task forces on trade and investment were set up. There was also agreement that the Seminar's third meeting should be in Indonesia and its fourth meeting in South Korea. While the concept of Pacific Basin cooperation is thus being promoted on a nongovernmental basis for the time being, the possibility is open that it may develop into an intergovernmental organization sometime in the future if the countries involved agree. Among the many themes to be discussed are trade and investment (already the subject of task-force studies), energy, foodstuffs, transport and communications, tourism, and marine development.

Mr. Zenko Suzuki, then Prime Minister of Japan, made a speech on June 16 this year at the East-West Center, Honolulu, Hawaii, titled "The Coming of the Pacific Age." He stressed the following five principles of the Pacific cooperation: first, "Ocean of Peace"; second, "Ocean of Freedom"; third, "Ocean of Diversity"; fourth, "Ocean of Mutual Benefits"; and fifth, "Open Ocean." He also spoke in the same speech about Pacific island nations, as follows:

The island nations in the Pacific have already achieved, or are now in the process of achieving, their independence. Despite their tiny populations, their limited land mass, and their distance from foreign markets, these countries have chosen the democratic form of government and are strengthening dialogue and cooperation through such organizations as the South Pacific Forum. I find their wholehearted devotion to nation-building of great interest.

Because the South Pacific region consists of many small islands scattered over a broad expanse of ocean, many of their problems are not shared by the Pacific rim countries. By the same token, even in the South Pacific, there are some countries which have large islands and others which are primarily congregations of coral reefs. Accordingly, it is imperative that cooperation for regional development be attuned to the needs and circumstances of each nation. At the same time, the difficulty of achieving economic viability mandates assistance and cooperation from the developed Pacific rim countries, especially Australia, Canada, Japan, New Zealand, and the United States. There is a special need, since the South Pacific has long been isolated from the rest of the world, to promote the development of human resources in administration, business, technology, medicine and hygiene, and other modern specializations. Moreover, cooperation from the developed countries should include not only the development of human resources but also improved transport and communication among the islands of the South Pacific, technical cooperation in fisheries and agriculture, environmental protection, and energy development suited to their island circumstances (such as Ocean Thermal Energy Conversion, or OTEC).

Japan is also a Pacific island nation, and there has been increasing interest in Pacific cooperation in recent years. Chastened by the horrors of World War II, Japan has adopted a constitution renunciating war, has vowed not to become a military power, and has adhered steadfastly to the principles of an exclusively defensive and non-nuclear capability. At the same time, Japan has achieved remarkable economic growth, and the Japanese share of world GNP has grown from 3 percent in the early 1960s to 10 percent today. Given these developments, it is incumbent upon Japan to use its economic resources and technological capability for the good of the global economy, and especially for the economic development of the poorer countries, and for the maintenance and furthering of world peace. Such efforts are clearly also in Japan's own interests. I am therefore most hopeful that the cooperative relations between Japan and the South Pacific nations will continue to expand to all our benefit in the years ahead.

Yet, no amount of outside help can—or should—do the job for you. The primary impetus for developing your countries and integrating them into the broad Pacific community must come from yourselves. That is why I am especially happy to have had this chance to talk to you and to outline the state of Pacific cooperation. Now it is up to you as the leaders of the future to build upon these foundations to create a better life for your people. The responsibilities which you graduates will bear are very heavy, but I am confident that you will be equal to them.

Allow me in closing, then, to simply extend my warmest congratulations and very best wishes for your future.

U. S.-Japan Economic Relations

It is both an honor and a pleasure to be able to speak to the Rotary Club of Chicago. Actually this invitation to me was extended in a very roundabout, and very Japanese, way. Mr. Keijiro Oto, an old friend of mine from high school, was chairman of the reception committee when your Chicago Rotary Club visited Japan last year. When the Chicago Rotary group came to Tokyo, Mr. Oto gave them a copy of a speech I had given to the National Press Club in Washington last May. After he read the speech, President Getzoff asked if this man Saburo Okita could be prevailed upon to speak to the Chicago Rotarians.

As you can see, I was very ready and willing to be prevailed upon because I know how important Chicago is in international trade and how influential your "heartland" views are in America. Even if we were having this luncheon in Tokyo, for example, much of the good food would have been bought through Chicago's grain, meat, and other commodity markets. Thus it was that I was glad to leave Tokyo a couple of days early and stop off in Chicago today on my way to Washington to attend a meeting of the Group of 30.

In Washington, the Group of 30 will be discussing international financial issues, but I suspect you are more interested in U.S.-Japan trade friction, so let me talk about trade. After reviewing the points at issue, I will try to explain why I think that, for all of the emotions it arouses, trade friction is a relatively minor issue being blown all out of proportion.

This chapter is the text of an address to the Chicago Rotary Club, delivered on September 27, 1983.

To begin with, let me review the history of our bilateral trade friction.

In the 1950s and 1960s, the trade imbalance was not a problem. These were, if you will recall, years of American dominance in the global economy, and the United States argued that any country which was running a deficit—and that included Japan—just was not trying hard enough.

In 1969, however, textiles became a problem. After long years of negotiations, it had finally been agreed that Okinawa would revert to Japanese administration, and Prime Minister Sato went to Washington in November 1969 to meet with President Nixon and finalize the agreement. During this Sato–Nixon Summit, President Nixon pressed for some restraints on Japanese exports of textiles and textile products to the United States. Although the Japanese industry argued strongly against restrictions, agreement was finally reached in late 1971 amid heavy media coverage and aroused public opinion on both sides.

Yet more trade problems quickly sprang up.

Steel was one. In the steel case, the U.S. industry's complaints to the International Trade Commission as well as to the courts resulted in the decision that, even though there had been no Japanese dumping, a floor price should be established for steel exports to the United States and anything below that price should be considered de facto dumping. This floor price—or "trigger price," since it would trigger retaliation—was set to the cost of production at Japan's ultramodern mills plus a reasonable profit, and the furor died down for a while.

Another issue that you may remember was color television sets. Again, a sudden spurt in Japanese exports to the United States sparked charges of dumping, and ultimately a ceiling was imposed on U.S. imports of color television sets from Japan. However, this time the Japanese industry was quicker on its feet, and much of this Japanese production was moved to U.S. factories. Today, in fact, Japanese companies produce over three million color television sets a year in the United States, and exports are well below the 1.75 million limit.

A more recent issue has been that of automobiles. While I will not detail all of the reasons why Japanese automobiles' popularity took off in the United States, I recall a visit by UAW

Chairman Douglas Fraser in February 1980, back in the days when I was foreign minister, when he asked me to use my influence to get Japanese automakers to produce more cars in the United States. As you can see, I did not have a whole lot of influence, and the UAW and Ford ultimately took their case to the ITC. However, the ITC's finding that there had been no serious damage to U.S. industry and that import quotas were therefore not justified under the Antitrust Act ended things temporarily. Yet, in its stead, the U.S. administration argued that the U.S. industry needed time, money, and reasonable market prospects to finance the extensive retooling necessary for downsizing—and that Japan had a responsibility to provide three years of "breathing space." Congress was also very vocal on this issue, and the Japanese industry reluctantly announced in May 1981 that it would institute three years of unilateral and "voluntary" export restraint. Under these restraints, Japanese exports were limited to 1.68 million vehicles the first year, with the understanding that this figure would be indexed to the market to enable Japanese automakers to maintain their share when the market expanded. Well, we are still at 1.68 million in the third year, and no decision has been made yet on the measures to be taken after next May.

Other problems that you may remember have included machine tools, semiconductors, and motorcycles.

Yet this friction is not solely because of Japanese export strength. Much of it is also because of the poor competitiveness of American industrial products.

Even though America's share of total world trade has slipped over the past decade, many Americans tend to blame America's weak export performance on what they see as a "closed" Japanese market. We in Japan find this very disconcerting, and we are working hard to remove any substantiation for such charges. For example, five years ago, when the U.S. complained of Japanese restrictions on beef and citrus imports, United States Trade Representative Robert Strauss and Japanese Minister for External Economic Relations Nobuhiko Ushiba signed a five-year agreement establishing increasing quotas for these products. This agreement, which expires next March, is currently being renegotiated by the two governments.

Inspection procedures and industrial and consumer standards have also been cited as non-tariff barriers, and the Japanese government has moved aggressively to simplify import inspections and to harmonize Japanese standards with those prevailing in other industrialized countries. This May, the Diet—our Congress—passed a package of seventeen amendments to internationalize Japanese standards and inspection procedures. Other efforts to dismantle non-tariff barriers are under way.

Nor have we neglected the tariff barriers. Japan was active in promoting agreement in the Tokyo Round of Multinational Trade Negotiations, and we subsequently moved up two years' worth of tariff reductions. The tariff on automobiles and auto parts was cut to zero, and that on integrated circuits was lowered to the U.S. level—well below the European tariff level. All told, some 323 tariffs have been reduced or eliminated ahead of schedule. This we have done without asking for reciprocal concessions from our trading partners.

Nevertheless, the trade friction persists. I think there are a number of reasons for this persistent friction, and I would like to suggest half a dozen of them for your consideration.

First is the fact that the U.S. bilateral trade with Japan seems to be going deeper and deeper in the red. In 1980, the U.S. trade deficit was $10 billion; in 1981, $16 billion; in 1982, $17 billion; and the forecast for 1983 is $20 billion. However, these U.S. figures are only part of the story, and are misleading on at least two counts. For one thing, the international balance of payments also includes such "invisible" trade as services and capital transfers. When these factors are taken into consideration, the U.S. balance was in surplus. Service income, including interest and dividends from American foreign investments, plus the inflow of foreign capital are enough to wipe out your global trade deficit. For another thing, it must be remembered that trade is multilateral. The United States is running a deficit in its trade with Japan but enjoying a surplus in its trade with Europe. Japan, on the other hand, is in the black in its trade with both the United States and Europe but sharply in the red with the Middle East. If balance-of-payments comparisons are to mean anything at all, they must be based upon the total global balance for all categories.

Just to confuse things, different countries also have different trade patterns. For example, when the U.S. economy recovers, this recovery is reflected in surging sales for imports, which pushes your current account further into the red temporarily. In Japan, however, imports are still down—even with lower oil prices—and our exports have started to pick up. Thus it is forecast that Japan's current-account surplus will top $20 billion this year. However, this current-account surplus is largely offset by increased long-term capital outflow as Japanese companies rush to invest overseas, and Japanese foreign exchange holdings are actually down slightly during the past five years. Nevertheless, most people who look beyond the trade balance look only as far as the current account, and the spectacle of the U.S. going deeper in the red just as Japanese surpluses soar further exacerbates the trade friction.

The second cause of the trade friction's persistence is this idea that some Americans have that Japan has somehow contrived to evade its just international responsibilities and is getting an unfair "free ride." This "free-ride" theory comes up most often in relation to defense, and it is often pointed out that the United States spends more than 6 percent of its GNP on defense but that Japan spends less than 1 percent—0.98 percent in the 1983 budget. (Actually, this is more like 1.5 percent if you calculate it according to the NATO formula, but it is the 1 percent figure that gets all the publicity.)

While this is easy to understand emotionally, it is less plausible when you look at the facts. Fact one is the Japanese Constitution's unequivocal statement that "land, sea, and air forces, as well as other war potential, will never be maintained." Although this has been broadly interpreted to mean that Japan will not possess the means of aggression and will not abet aggression elsewhere, it still restricts Japan to a non-nuclear, exclusively defensive stance. Any sizable expansion of Japanese military spending would first have to build a popular consensus in favor of changing this—changes which would be resisted both by the Japenese public and by Japan's many Asian neighbors whose bitter memories of Japanese military expansionism are still all too vivid. Personally, I do not see how this can be done quickly.

Nor do I think it is what the United States really wants. It is noteworthy that even U.S. government calls for a greater Japanese role in defense do not go so far as to advocate Constitution revision and the acquisition of nuclear arms. Rather, the U.S. is calling for greater "sustainability" and stronger air and naval defenses within the current conceptual framework. There are currently moves afoot to have Japan assume responsibility for defending the sea lanes to a distance of about 1,000 nautical miles. Although Japan has been and will be making continued efforts to strengthen its self-defense capability and steadily increasing its defense expenditures, I do not expect any major increases.

The third factor which contributes to trade friction is the competition in high-technology fields. As you know, Japan is dependent upon imports for its foodstuffs, fuel, and other natural resources. This means we must export manufactured goods to earn the "hard" currency to pay for these vital imports—and these manufactures must be technologically innovative if they are to survive in the global marketplace. This life-or-death requirement has inevitably thrown Japan into competition with the United States in such fields as electronics.

Caught by surprise, many Americans have sought to explain Japan's technological competitiveness with the theory of "unfair industrial targeting policy." Basically, this theory holds that Japanese government and business have conspired to target select industries for domination and that the government protects and nourishes the Japanese entries in these industries to give them an unfair market advantage. Whatever validity this theory might have had in the past when Japan was still struggling to get back on its feet and Japanese industry was adapting off-the-shelf technology—and I grant that there was some protection during this catch-up period—it is much less important today. As I have already noted, Japanese tariff and non-tariff barriers are being dismantled step by step. Even more important, the pace of change in electronics and other state-of-the-art technologies is so rapid that no amount of protectionism could put a company or country on the cutting edge. There is broad cooperation to share the costs and risks of some research, but there is no more of it in Japan than there is in the United States. By way of comparison, the United States government is estimated to finance approximately 43 percent of all research done in the United States. Much of this is classified as military research, which does not mean it does not have commercial applications, but even if you discount the military portion, the U.S. government still puts up approximately 33 percent of America's research money. By contrast, the figure for Japan is about 28 percent.

Nevertheless, this is not an argument which dies easily, and I expect the competition in high technology to be a continuing source of friction between Japan and the United States.

The fourth factor which has exacerbated Japan–U.S. friction is unemployment. With the U.S. economy stagnant for three years and an unemployment rate of around 10 percent, this is a potent force. These people, who number over 10 million, want to know why they cannot find work, and the easiest answer is to blame it on Japanese imports in steel, automobiles, and other things. Never mind that Japanese auto imports have been artificially held to 1.68 million for the last two and a half years. Never mind that Japanese competition has stimulated the U.S. industry to innovate and resulted in better products at lower prices for all Americans. Never mind that imports are a result of other economic factors and not a cause of recession. It is far easier to blame imports than to blame such things as high labor costs, inefficient production, and an unwillingness to invest in capital improvements.

However, I am still hopeful that this will be less contentious when the U.S. economy recovers and employment picks up again.

The fifth factor aggravating trade friction is that many Americans think the U.S. is an open market and Japan a closed market. The only major area where Japanese imports are substantially restricted today is agriculture—and even here Japan is still the largest foreign customer for American agricultural products. Japanese agricultural imports from the United States last year were some $6 billion. That does not look like a very closed market to me.

When American industry runs into trouble, quotas are applied, tariffs tripled, and "voluntary" agreements sought to narrow the door to imports. Let me tell you what happened when the Japanese aluminum industry ran into trouble. To begin with, Japanese aluminum refining does not use cheap energy such as natural gas and hydroelectric power. It is almost totally dependent upon oil-generated electricity. As oil prices soared over the last decade, Japanese aluminum prices became less and less competitive. Production last year was only 350,000 tons—30 percent of what it was five years ago. During the same five years, the total market has grown 15 percent, and imports are up 2.8-fold from 466,000 tons in 1977 to 1,289,000 tons in 1982. There is obviously some government industrial hospice care to keep the retreat orderly and to avoid undue social disruption, but there is no effort to reverse the tide. Moreover, this same story could just as easily have been told about plastics, cotton textiles, coal, or any number of other Japanese "sunset" industries.

Currency exchange rates are the sixth cause of today's intense trade friction. Some people in the United States have charged that the Japanese government is manipulating the markets to help exports by keeping the yen undervalued. Yet, to have any impact, such manipulation would have to be both massive and sustained. It is significant that nobody has found any evidence of such manipulation. The United States Treasury Department studied this and said no. The Economic Report of the President in February 1983 also reported no evidence of Japanese manipulation.

However, we are all agreed that the Japanese yen is undervalued. Why is the yen undervalued? Basically, the yen is undervalued because the dollar is overvalued, and the dollar is overvalued because of its attraction, first for the high interest rates prevailing in the United States and second as a safe haven in times of international turmoil. Yet, the dollar's attractiveness as a safe haven is largely psychological, and it is interest rates which draw the professional money-men.

In turn, these high interest rates, although effective in wringing out inflation, have been sustained by the prospect of massive federal deficits. As the recovery builds, more and more companies will be going to the capital markets—where they will run into a United States government seeking to borrow to finance its huge deficit. This can only push interest rates still higher. Already there is talk of "crowding out" in the market, and we hear repeatedly that U.S. interest rates will not come down appreciably—or exchange rates to change much—so long as the federal government continues to run a large deficit.

Not only do these high domestic interest rates inhibit U.S. capital spending, they also make it more difficult for Japan and the European countries to stimulate their own economies by reducing interest rates since that would only widen the interest differential and further distort exchange rates and trade patterns. In addition, they make debt refinancing increasingly difficult for such developing countries as Brazil and Mexico. Indeed, it is difficult to see how we can hope for sustained recovery unless interest rates come down.

None of these problems which I have cited as contributing to Japan–U.S. trade friction—the U.S. trade deficit, the "free ride" theory, high-technology competition, unemployment, false-perceptions of a closed market, and exchange disparity—lends itself to an easy solution. As a result, I expect that some friction is inevitable.

However, I very strongly believe that this friction between friends must not be allowed to disrupt the friendship. The relationship between Japan and the United States is far too important—both to the principals and to the Free World as a whole—to allow it to self-destruct on such irritants.

Japan and the United States share a belief in the basic political values of democracy—free elections, freedom of speech, respect for human rights, and the other fundamentals of democracy. Some of these may have been learned from the United States and other Western nations over the last century, but they have all taken strong root in the Japanese consciousness. This alliance for freedom and democracy is buttressed by the vast proliferation of cultural exchanges between Japan and the United States. From baseball to judo, hamburgers to tofu, we have so much in common culturally that it is inconceivable that we cannot work out our differences. Added impetus for agreement comes from our shared security and strategic concerns. Japan is a bastion of political stability and economic prosperity in Asia, and this contributes importantly to the stability and prosperity of all of Asia.

Little wonder that successive U.S. presidents have called Japan the cornerstone of America's Asian policy—just as relations with the United States have long been acknowledged as the cornerstone of Japanese foreign policy. Two mighty industrial democracies on opposite sides of the Pacific, both benefit immensely from this alliance.

Some trade friction may be inevitable, but we must not let it distract us from the more important shared values underlying the relationship. I know that is the message which Prime Minister Nakasone took to Washington this January and again to Williamsburg in May, and I trust it will be the same message which President Reagan takes to Japan in November. These friendly relations at the highest level are important, yet friendly relations at lower levels are just as important, for it is only by actively promoting friendship and mutual understanding at all levels that we can immunize the relationship against emotional tirades and ensure peace, freedom, and prosperity for all. That, after all, is what the Japan–U.S. relationship is all about.

Asian-Pacific Affairs

My first meeting with John Crawford was in September 1967, when I attended an Australian National University–sponsored conference on Australia, Japan, and India.

Several months later, in January 1968, we were again thrown together when Crawford attended the first meeting of the Pacific Trade and Development (PAFTAD) Conference held at the Japan Economic Research Center in Tokyo, and I subsequently had the pleasure of working with him on a number of PAFTAD conferences. As we met more and more frequently over the years, especially since the initiation of Australia-Japan Research Committee in 1972 with Crawford chairing the Australian side and me the Japanese side, we got to know each other better, and my respect for his vision, intelligence, integrity, and pragmatism increased.

Short by Australian standards and with an unusually large head, he had an excellent sense of humor which he kept bridled when discussing important issues. Once he made up his mind, he was determined but not dogmatic, and he was always attentive to others' ideas and opinions.

In May 1970, Crawford and I were speakers at a Sydney seminar commemorating the bicentennial of Captain Cook's discovery of Australia. In listening to his remarks, I heard him say that Japan's future was "enigmatic," and when I asked him later what he had meant by that, he said that the term was in reference to the unpredictability of Japan's future course. However, I

This paper in memory of Sir John Crawford was prepared at the request of the Australian National University, Canberra, in January 1985.

noticed that he became more optimistic about Australian-Japanese relations in later years as developments allayed his concern about Japan's unpredictability.

I also recall a letter he sent me in 1977 introducing Robert Hawke, then on a visit to Japan, in which he predicted that Hawke was destined for the Australian prime ministership some day. This prediction was proved right six years later. Crawford was respected by Australian politicians, scholars, businessmen, and journalists, as well as by the many foreigners who had contact with him. He was also active as a trustee of the International Food Policy Research Institute (IFPRI), and I was honored by his recommending me as his replacement when he retired from the IFPRI.

The man's sense of principle is illustrated by his insistence that Australian National University, as publisher, destroy all copies of *Japan's Challenging Years: Reflections on My Lifetime* when an error was found in the foreword. This book, a translation and adaptation of my Japanese-language *Tohon Seiso—Watakushi no Rirekisho*, had been done by two Australian National University students who were studying Japanese. Quite inadvertently, the printer had dropped the italicized portion of the sentence "By the end of the 1940s, he had established himself as one of the leading figures in economic planning and policy analysis in Japan and an architect of Japan's *rehabilitation into the international community after a* devastating war" from Peter Drysdale's kind foreword to the English edition. Obviously, the omission completely altered the sense of the original, and Crawford was insistent that all erroneous copies be destroyed lest the misinformation gain currency.

On the concept of Pacific cooperation, I have heard from Drysdale that Crawford predicted this eventuality even before World War II. In Japan, Hitotsubashi University Professor Kiyoshi Kojima advocated the idea of a Pacific Free Trade Area in the early 1960s, but Crawford was clearly way ahead of him and broader in foreseeing this cooperation in non-trade areas as well.

Although the idea had gestated in many minds for many years, the Pacific cooperation concept was first brought to major world attention in May 1967, some eighteen years ago, by Takeo Miki in a speech entitled "Japanese Cooperation in Asia-Pacific Foreign Policy." Then Japanese minister for foreign affairs under Prime Minister Eisaku Sato, Miki highlighted four main needs in this speech[1]:

First is the need for enlightenment. Pacific cooperation is essential to Asian stability and prosperity, and there can be no stability and prosperity for the Pacific countries unless there is also security and prosperity in Asia. Cooperation is in everyone's self-interest. This is a forceful statement of the all-in-the-same-boat theory, and an attempt to make people realize that we share a common fate.

Second is the need for Asian regional cooperation. Recognizing that the Asian countries are aware of the need for regional cooperation and independent self-help efforts in accordance with economic laws, Miki argued that Japan should provide capital, technological, and planning cooperation in line with this momentum.

Third is cooperation among the industrialized Pacific countries. While it is crucial that Pacific cooperation among these countries not be seen as a "rich-man's club" or an exclusive economic bloc, it is important to strengthen the structures for cooperation and the emerging cooperative relations among private-sector interests in Australia, Canada, Japan, New Zealand, and the United States.

And fourth, and perhaps most important, is cooperation within the Asia-Pacific region to resolve the North-South problem. The developing countries of Southeast Asia tend to be forgotten countries, and there is a constant need for the industrialized countries to increase their assistance to Asia. Repeated efforts are needed especially to draw enhanced assistance from the Pacific countries.

Asked by Foreign Minister Miki to help flesh these ideas out more fully, Kiyoshi Kojima and I planned to hold a conference of economists on Pacific cooperation, and Kojima visited scholars in the various countries of the Pacific region and exchanged opinions with them. One of the people whom he visited in 1967 in this cause was Crawford, and it should be noted that from the

---

[1] As reported by *Nihon Keizai Shimbun*, May 25, 1967.

very beginning Crawford was a strong supporter of the concept and the cooperative spirit which it embodies.

In January 1968, the Japan Economic Research Center, of which I was then president, held the first Pacific Trade and Development (PAFTAD) Conference bringing together economists from the six countries of Australia, Canada, Japan, New Zealand, the United Kingdom, and the United States. Among the leading participants were Crawford, Drysdale, Ted English, Harry Johnson, Kojima, Hugh Patrick, Arthur Paul, and myself, and these same people also served as the main participants in subsequent PAFTAD conferences. (It should be noted, however, that Johnson, Paul, and now Crawford have since passed away.)

The focus of the first conference was on the examination of existing and future possible trading arrangements, and specifically the feasibility of a Pacific free trade area, among the economically advanced market-oriented nations of the Pacific—Australia, Canada, Japan, New Zealand, and the United States. The impetus emanated from a general concern at the time that the European Economic Community might develop into an exclusive trading bloc for Europe and Africa, with detrimental consequences for developed and developing nations.

The conference produced very good papers and an extremely useful dialogue among the economists who participated. Several points emerged, most importantly that the need for analysis of Pacific economic policy problems and communication among researchers around the region was far greater than had been initially perceived. Most participants had viewed Pacific economic relationships in bilateral rather than regionally multilateral terms, and most knew more about the United States than about the other countries. A Pacific free trade area appeared very much a second-best solution, but it was thought extremely worthwhile to consider other possible economic policies and institutional arrangements for greater regional cooperation. Participants at the first conference felt it was important to address explicitly the needs and interests of the developing countries of Asia and the Pacific in the analysis and discussion of regional cooperation. The significance of the issues raised and the challenge they presented led to an immediate commitment to work towards holding a second conference and to pursue these research themes over the next year.

The second Pacific Trade and Development Conference was held in the northern summer of 1969 at the East-West Center in Hawaii. At this conference representatives from Australia proposed a further conference, and the third PAFTAD Conference was held in Sydney in August 1970, on issues of private direct investment in the Pacific region. A pattern had emerged that has resulted in the continuing series and their organizational arrangements.

The fourth Pacific Trade and Development Conference, on obstacles to trade in the Pacific area, was held in Ottawa in October 1971; the fifth, on structural adjustments in Asian-Pacific trade, was held in Tokyo in January 1973; the sixth, on technology transfer in Pacific economic development, was held in Mexico City in July 1974; the seventh, on relations among the larger and smaller nations of the Pacific, was held in Auckland in August 1975; the eighth, on trade and employment, was held in Thailand in July 1976; the ninth, on the production, processing, financing, and trade of natural resources in the Pacific, was hosted by the United States Federal Reserve Bank in San Francisco in August 1977; the tenth was held at the Australian National University in Canberra in March 1979, on the emergence of ASEAN and its role in a changing Pacific and world economy; the eleventh examined the spectacular economic performance of the newly industrializing economies of Northeast Asia and their economic relations with other Pacific countries, and was held at the Korea Development Institute in Seoul in September 1980; the twelfth, held in Vancouver in September 1981, examined the subject of the development of and trade in renewable resources; and the thirteenth Pacific Trade and Development Conference, on energy adjustment problems in the region, was organized jointly by the Philippine Institute of Development Studies and Asian Development Bank in Manila in January 1983.[2]

The fourteenth conference, on Pacific growth and financial interdependence, was organized by the National University of Singapore and Economic Society of Singapore in June 1984; and the fifteenth conference, on industrial policy, will be held in Tokyo in August 1985.

In 1976, Crawford and I co-authored a joint report entitled *Australia, Japan, and the Western Pacific Economic Relations*. Published both in Australia and in Japan, this report brought together research undertaken by numerous economists in both countries. While Crawford and I were responsible for steering the project through to completion, Kojima and Drysdale were responsible for the research programs in their respective countries. This report is now considered one of the standard reference materials for study of the Japanese-Australian economic relationship and its implications for the Western Pacific Region. Chapter 8 of the report specifically deals with "Relations with Western Pacific Countries: Trade, Aid, and Investment."

The following paragraph from the report illustrates the shared interest of Japan and Australia in the development of the Western Pacific countries.

Both Japan and Australia have large responsibilities towards the developing world, and especially towards the Western Pacific developing countries with whom their trade, investment, aid and political relations are closest. They must take account of the increasingly strong and legitimate claims being made for more opportunities in trade, for controlled foreign investment activity, and for softer and more flexible aid terms. Recent developments in both countries' approaches to development assistance, although they start from a very different base, are encouraging in this respect.[3]

---

[2] *The Pacific Trade and Development Conference: A Brief History*, Peter Drysdale, Australia-Japan Research Center, Pacific Economic Papers, No. 112, Australian National University, June 1984, pp. 1–2.

[3] *Australia, Japan, and the Western Pacific Economic Relations*, Crawford and Okita, Australian Government Publishing Service, Canberra, 1976, p. 127.

In the fall of 1978, Japan's Prime Minister Masayoshi Ohira made the Pacific Basin Cooperation Concept one of his main policy platforms. Following up on this, he appointed a study group on this issue in the spring of 1979 with me as its chairman. When Ohira later appointed me minister for foreign affairs that November, Professors Seizaburo Sato and Tsuneo Iida took over the duties of acting chairmen until the study group's formal report could be issued in May 1980.[4]

Prime Minister Ohira made an official visit to Australia and New Zealand in January 1980 for talks with the leaders of these two countries. I accompanied him as foreign minister. When Prime Ministers Ohira and Frazer met in Canberra, they discussed the issue of Pacific cooperation as one item on their agenda and agreed that, assuming Crawford would agree as chancellor, it would be useful for the Australian National University to host a seminar to explore and promote the idea of Pacific cooperation. Since Crawford and I were old friends by then, I went out to the campus and consulted with him on this idea. Happily, he said that he would be glad to have the seminar at Australian National University provided the Japanese and Australian governments agreed to the following two conditions: that he be given complete discretion over whom to invite, the agenda, the running of the symposium, and other details, and that the Japanese and Australian governments support the seminar. When the two prime ministers accepted these conditions, he energetically undertook full responsibility for organizing and holding the seminar.

Although Ohira died that June, the seminar was held as planned at the Australian National University in Canberra from September 15 through September 18. This seminar, first called the Pacific Community Seminar but later known as the Pacific Economic Cooperation Conference (PECC), laid the basic framework for promoting Pacific cooperation.

Prior to the seminar, Crawford voiced his thoughts on the Pacific Basin cooperative concept in a speech which he gave to the Pacific Basin Economic Council (PBEC) meeting in Sydney on May 6, 1980. While not blind to the possibilities for the future,

---

[4] Report of the Pacific Basin Cooperation Concept; Pacific Basin Cooperation Study Group, May 1980.

he called for a pragmatically gradualist approach in light of the realities of international relations. Because the ideas which he expressed in this speech formed the basis for the basic approach taken toward the subsequent formation of PECC, it is illuminating to quote a few of Crawford's ideas from his Sydney speech:

> Discussion and consultation about economic problems and opportunities arising from inter-dependence must involve developing and developed countries in an organic unity. This inter-dependence automatically includes North-South relations as an integral component in any co-operative effort on the part of the Pacific Basin countries.
>
> The apparent forces of distance and diversity of language and cultures are the negatives. I have suggested they are weaker negatives than used to be thought. . . . Fundamentally inter-dependence in the Pacific Basin arises from complementarity of resources and trade among the countries of the Basin.

This quotation is indicative of Crawford's basic thinking on the significance of Pacific cooperation. Once this was established, Crawford went on to suggest a number of alternatives for the institutional framework for that cooperation:

> We can put the range from do nothing [bilateralism is sufficient] through variants of the loosely knit organization of the [British] Commonwealth of Nations and of the OECD [most rigorously put forward as OPTAD]: and to the idea of complete integration of the Pacific Region in the form of the European Economic Community.
>
> I believe we can eliminate the two extremes.

Stressing the trade and economic development issues, he pointedly excluded strategic and security questions within the framework of this Pacific cooperation. While recognizing the individual countries' concern with these questions, he maintained that

> nevertheless, there is not the close intermesh of strategic interests and concerns as would warrant confusing them in

the one organization with the economic issues, which call more clearly and easily for a single Pacific Organization to promote co-operation. One thing can be said: it is probable that improved co-operative effort in the economic field which promotes economic growth in the Pacific is likely on the one hand to lessen political friction and political misunderstanding and, on the other, to strengthen the economic base required for effective strategic and defence policies for member countries.

On the question of who should take the initiative for promoting Pacific cooperation, Crawford acknowledged the United States and Japan as the economic superpowers of the region but suggested the following approach should it prove difficult for either of them to take the initiative.

But [if it proves unfeasible for the economic superpowers to take the initiative] because of unnecessary sensitivity on the part of the U.S.A. or Japan, who will? I believe someone will—perhaps in the form of quietly arranged semi-summit of ASEAN members and the five developed countries under the heading of considering the state of present economic relations. Such a meeting would certainly serve.

This was a very prescient prediction of how, four years later, Indonesian Foreign Minister Mochtar would propose that Pacific cooperation be put on the agenda of the July 1984 ASEAN-plus-five foreign ministers' meeting and how the foreign ministers of all the countries concerned would concur.

The preparations for the September 1980 Canberra Seminar were done in line with Crawford's thinking as just explained, and the Seminar was attended by a total of twelve delegations: the five Pacific industrialized countries (Australia, Canada, Japan, New Zealand, and the United States), the then five ASEAN countries (Indonesia, Malaysia, the Philippines, Singapore, and Thailand), the Republic of Korea, and the South Pacific island countries. In order to make the exchanges of views as efficient as possible, each delegation was limited to three delegates, one each from government, academia, and business, and it was understood that all of these delegates attended not as representatives of their governments or institutions but in their individual expert capacities and were therefore able to speak their minds freely. Delegates were also in attendance from PAFTAD representing academia and PBEC representing business. This same government-business-academia tripartite structure has been retained for PECC.

The agenda for the Seminar as drawn up by Crawford included the following four main points:

(1) What are the forces promoting the Pacific community idea?
(2) What are the issues for substantive cooperation?
(3) Which countries are interested in participating, and in what form?
(4) What steps can be taken?

In the course of the deliberations, some ASEAN delegates expressed concern that this Pacific cooperation concept might prove counterproductive to the strengthening and further development of ASEAN solidarity. Other delegates were concerned that the industrialized countries of the Pacific, specifically the United States and Japan, might take advantage of the concept to strengthen their domination of the region.

ASEAN itself was founded based upon a concept proposed by the Southeast Asian countries themselves and gradually achieved international recognition, and it is perhaps only natural that there may have been some reluctance among the ASEAN countries to go along too readily with this Pacific cooperation concept proposed by the industrialized Pacific countries of Japan, Australia, the United States, and the rest. Likewise the very vagueness of the concept as it was put forth may have caused concern that it might tie ASEAN hands. For example, Del Mund, who was then with the Philippine Foreign Ministry, expressed the concern that the formation of a Pacific Community might invite a flood of Japanese and American products in Asian markets, with the unintended result of killing off these Asian countries' fledgling industrialization efforts.

On this point, even though the report of the Japanese Pacific Cooperation Study Group and other documentation and materials distributed to Seminar delegates made it quite clear that the Pacific Community was not intended to be anything like the European Economic Community, the Seminar felt that the very term "Pacific Community" called up images of the European Community and lent itself to the misunderstanding that it was a similar sort of organizational structure which was envisioned. In order to avoid such misunderstanding, the Seminar decided in its final stages to discard the "Pacific Community" phrase and to use the term Pacific Regional Cooperation instead. Likewise, because it was felt that the term Pacific Rim would be understood as meaning only the countries which border on the Pacific and not including the island countries which are actually in the Pacific, it was decided not to use the word "rim."

On all of these semantic issues and more, the three-day seminar saw active discussions leading to the adoption of the chairman's report on the final day and its release at the public forum held the next day. The proposed procedure was that once Crawford's report on the seminar's recommendations was sent to the governments of the participating countries and received their approval, a committee of government and private-sector people was established to coordinate Pacific cooperation, with this committee selecting issues of importance to the Pacific region and assigning them to expert subgroups for study with the results of the studies to be ready for deliberation at the next Seminar two years hence. As further evidence of the Pacific cooperation concept's open nature, it was decided that membership in the expert subgroups should not be restricted to countries which had attended the first seminar but should be open to all of the countries of the Pacific which wished to participate.

In the spring of 1981, the year after the Canberra Seminar, Crawford visited the ASEAN countries. In May of that same year, as chairman of the Japanese National Committee for Pacific Cooperation, I wrote "A View on the Pacific Basin Cooperation Concept" addressing some of the concerns which were raised by the ASEAN delegates to the Canberra Seminar, and this was then distributed to the ASEAN countries. In this paper, I emphasized, inter alia, the following three points:

(1) The Pacific Basin Cooperation Concept is an idea to

secure and promote the present trend of interdependence among the countries of the region looking ahead to the twenty-first century.

(2) In order to implement the idea, it is desirable to create a network of nongovernmental forums with the blessings of the governments concerned.

(3) Our purpose is not to create an economic sphere of influence dominated by the "haves," or a politically-oriented exclusive regional bloc, but rather to promote cooperative relationships based on interdependence and mutual understanding among the countries of the region.[5]

During this period, interest in Pacific cooperation was gradually growing among the ASEAN countries. The second Pacific cooperation seminar was held in Bangkok in June 1982 at the initiative of Thailand's Deputy Premier Thanat Khoman, and the United Nations ESCAP office in Bangkok also cooperated with this by assisting in the preparation of seminar documents. The third seminar was later held in Bali, Indonesia, in November 1983. This series of seminars has since come to be called the Pacific Economic Cooperation Conference (PECC), and the fourth meeting is scheduled to be held in Seoul in April 1985. The general directions of Pacific cooperation have been structured in the three seminars which have been held so far, and it remains now to give this cooperation life.

First was the question of defining the Pacific countries. Taking Pacific countries as meaning all of the countries of Northeast Asia, Southeast Asia, Oceania, North America, and Latin America which in some way border on the Pacific would mean a vast number of countries with almost unimaginable linguistic, religious, historical, cultural, economic, political, and other differences. Too broad a definition could well diffuse the concept beyond usefulness. Accordingly, it is felt that the group should, for the time being, have the thirteen regular members of the six

---

[5] "A View on the Pacific Basin Cooperation Concept," Saburo Okita, *Pacific Cooperation Newsletter*, The Special Committee on Pacific Cooperation, Japan Institute of International Affairs, Vol. 1, No. 1, Spring 1982.

ASEAN countries (Brunei, Indonesia, Malaysia, the Philippines, Singapore, and Thailand), the five industrialized Pacific countries (Australia, Canada, Japan, New Zealand, and the United States), the Republic of Korea, and the South Pacific Forum as a single member representing the island countries of the South Pacific. However, it is understood that the other countries and communities of the Pacific are welcome to participate as observers.

Second, it has been decided to structure the PECC organization for Pacific cooperation as a tripartite organization of representatives from government, business, and academia, with these people, however, not representing their official positions but participating in their personal capacities. PECC is also to make policy recommendations to the governments of the member countries, and it is expected that the governments will support and take advantage of PECC for policy planning and promoting mutual understanding.

As Indonesian Coordinating Minister Ali Wardhana noted in his keynote speech to the 1983 Bali Conference:

> much of the impetus for a Pacific Community approach comes from the perceived need to improve consultation, regularize economic planning and reduce economic tensions. These three needs can be and indeed are discussed in dialogue between and among leaders of the Pacific Rim governments. But even with the most sincere intentions, we have seen the limits to which summitry conducted on an ad hoc basis can deal with such needs.

Wardhana went on to say:

> I see a certain value in having these discussions on an extra-governmental basis while at the same time agencies like ASEAN, UNCTAD, GATT and others confront the issues on a policy-making level. I am sure we have all had the experience of seeing that officials benefit from the frank and full discussions that occur at meetings such as these.[6]

---

[6] Issues for Pacific Economic Cooperation: A Report of the Third Pacific Economic Cooperation Conference, Bali, November 1983.

PECC is in close communication with the business-oriented PBEC and the academia-oriented PAFTAD. While the very diversity of the Pacific region makes the idea of an EEC-like organization impossible, it may be possible at some point to consider the establishment of a loosely structured organization for consultations among governments.

Third is PECC's actual operation. PECC is organized with national committees for each of the members and a standing committee of representatives from each of the national committees to take care of the organization's administration between conferences. The standing committee also overseas the work of the task forces established to deal with specific topics. At the 1982 Bangkok Conference, task forces were established (and coordinating countries appointed, as indicated in parentheses) to study the following four issues:

Trade in Agricultural and Renewable Resource Goods (Thailand and Canada)
Trade in Minerals and Energy (Australia)
Trade in Manufactured Goods (South Korea)
Direct Investment and Technology Transfer (Japan)

These task forces submitted their reports to the Bali Conference for discussion, and the standing committee appointed coordinating committee members to integrate the findings of the task forces and draw up action programs.

At the Bali Conference, task forces were assigned the following special topics and asked to prepare their reports to be submitted to the Seoul PECC meeting:

Task force (and coordinating organizations)	Special topic
(1) Trade in Agriculture and Renewable Resources (Canada)	Fisheries development
(2) Trade in Mineral and Energy (Australia, PBEC)	Consultative arrangements
(3) Trade in Manufactured Goods (Korea)	Industrial complementation and trade negotiations
(4) Direct Investment and Technology Transfer (U.S.A., Japan, Singapore)	Technology transfer through investment
(5) Capital Flows (Indonesia, Japan, U.S.A.)	Financial resources and services

Because PECC has government officials among its tripartite structure, it is able to maintain close liaisons with the governments of the member countries. Likewise, the governments are able, as the need arises, to ask PECC to take up specific policy studies.

One recent and noteworthy institutional development was the suggestion by Indonesian Foreign Minister Mochtar that the question of Pacific cooperation be included on the agenda of the ASEAN Ministerial Conference with the Dialogue Countries (the six ASEAN countries plus the five Pacific industrialized countries) held in July 1984 in Jakarta and the ready assent which this proposal drew from the foreign ministers of the participating countries. At this Ministerial Conference, it was agreed to take up long-term Pacific trends from the broad policy perspective and to work on the issue of human-resources development as an initial specific theme for cooperation.

The United States has also shown increasing interest in the Pacific, as evidenced in the statements by President Reagan, Secretary of State Shultz, and other government officials. In March 1984, Richard Fairbanks was appointed ambassador for pacific cooperation issues. Also, in line with the PECC agreement, the United States National Committee for Pacific Cooperation was formally inaugurated at the White House in September 1984 in the presence of President Reagan, Secretary of State Shultz, and other officials. In Canada, too, the establishment of the Asia Pacific Foundation was approved by Parliament in June 1984, and this Foundation has already started operation.

One of the factors heightening American and Canadian interest in the Pacific is the fact that their Pacific trade has exceeded their Atlantic trade, in 1981 for the United States and in 1982 for Canada.

These developments in Pacific cooperation are clearly very close to that outlined by Crawford in his speech before the 1980 Canberra Seminar, and this is further proof of Crawford's prescience and wisdom.

At the October 1981 nineteenth Australia-Japan Business Cooperation Committee meeting in Sydney, Crawford gave a speech on "Australia, Japan, and the Pacific Community in the Year

2000" in which he said that Australia's trade would increasingly be with the Pacific region:

> Already nearly two thirds of Australia's trade is with the free market economies of the Pacific Basin area. Incredible as it may seem, this proportion will almost certainly be much higher in twenty years' time. But even if the very high level of trade interdependence with the region that has already been established merely continues, it will provide the basis for a huge growth of trade in absolute terms over the coming decades. On the export side, by far the largest proportion of the increase in exports of resources and resource-intensive processed goods will find markets in the countries of the Pacific Basin area. On the import side, much of the "engine for growth" represented by growth in world trade will take place in the free market economies of Asia, including not least those in the ASEAN area.[7]

As Crawford pointed out, the Pacific region, and especially the Western Pacific, is one of the most dynamically developing economic regions going into the twenty-first century. In the twenty years from 1960 to 1980, economic growth rates in this area were 8.5 percent for the Republic of Korea, 9.6 percent for Taiwan, 10.0 percent for Hong Kong, 7.4 percent for Thailand, 5.8 percent for the Philippines, 5.8 percent for Indonesia, 8.2 percent for Malaysia, and 9.2 percent for Singapore.[8]

Although Japan's per-annum economic growth rate was halved in this period, from 10 percent in the 1960s to 5 percent in the 1970s, the Asian newly industrializing countries (NICs) and the ASEAN countries continued the acceleration in their growth rates despite the oil crises and the stagnation in the industrialized countries' economies. As a result, per-capita GNP figures were sharply improved—the 1982 figures for these countries' being $5,910 for Singapore, $5,340 for Hong Kong, $2,500 for Tai-

---

[7] *Australia-Japan and the Pacific Community in the Year 2000*, John Crawford, Australia-Japan Research Centre, Pacific Economic Papers, Number 89, Australian National University, January 1982, p. 19.

[8] *2000 Nen No Asia* (Asia in the Year 2000), Miyohei Shinohara et al., p. 1.

wan, $1,910 for the Republic of Korea, $1,860 for Malaysia, $820 for the Philippines, $790 for Thailand, and $580 for Indonesia. As a result, these countries are gradually closing the gap with the Pacific industrialized countries' per-capita incomes of $10,080 for Japan, $11,140 for Australia, and $7,920 for New Zealand.[9]

China has also achieved accelerating economic growth in recent years with its policy reforms and more open economic measures. In the three years from 1982 to 1984, China has achieved economic growth of roughly 8.7 percent per annum to contribute importantly to the economic dynamism of the Western Pacific.

While it is unlikely that Japan will again achieve the very high growth rates which were achieved in the 1960s, average annual growth of 4–5 percent is considered feasible. This 4–5-percent figure will be supported by the continued high savings rate, the positive social climate for technological innovation, and the strong growth in neighboring countries. Australia and New Zealand will also see their economies stimulated by this Western Pacific dynamism and by the fact that the two countries' economies are in a complementary relationship with the East and Southeast Asian countries in both resources and industrial structures. In the 1960s, strong Japanese economic growth was a factor stimulating the economic activity in the Pacific region, but in the 1980s and beyond it is expected that the dynamism of the Western Pacific region will generate brisk economic activity throughout the Pacific region.

If China can achieve its goal of quadrupling its economic output in the two decades to the year 2000, and if the countries of East and Southeast Asia can maintain GNP growth of 6 percent per annum, there will be a conspicuous increase in the importance of the Western Pacific in the world economy. In the United States and Canada, the Pacific coastal regions will find themselves growing faster than the rest of the country. As predicted by Crawford, the dynamism of the Pacific region is generating further development for Australia and the entire world economy. If the economic development of the developing countries of this region proceeds smoothly, there is a strong possibility that North-South

[9] World Development Report, 1984, and Taiwan Statistical Data Book, 1983.

relations in this Pacific region can move from a confrontational relationship to a relationship of cooperation and interdependence. If this can be done and the growth directed toward alleviating North-South relations in the region, the results should also be able to contribute to improved North-South relations on a global scale.

Crawford's vision of Pacific cooperation's development is likely to be realized in the years to come, and there could be no more fitting tribute to Crawford than to see his dream of Pacific cooperation for stable peace and prosperity come true.

The Japanese Diet and Foreign Policy

The Japanese political system today is fundamentally governed by the postwar Constitution of Japan that came into force forty years ago, on May 3, 1947. Drafted and adopted during the brief postwar period when a defeated Japan was administered by the victorious Allied (primarily American) military authorities, this Constitution was obviously influenced by the United States Constitution in some places, yet it is basically patterned after the parliamentary democracies of the United Kingdom and Europe, and its political arrangements are clearly different from the United States' presidential system with its tripartite division of powers and its checks and balances. As such, the postwar Constitution of Japan continued the tradition of parliamentary government that was begun with the adoption of the Meiji Constitution in 1889.

I

Just as in other countries where the majority party forms a Cabinet that then takes the helm of the ship of state, in Japan the Diet serves primarily to endorse domestic and foreign policy initiatives taken by the Cabinet, and the Diet rarely if ever initiates policies on its own that are distinct from or in conflict with those of the Cabinet. In this, the Japanese system differs from the American system of government in which President

This paper was prepared at the request of Jawaharlal Nehru University, New Delhi, in January 1987, and was published in "Foreign Policy and Legislatures: An Analysis of Seven Parliaments" (Abhinav Publications, New Delhi) in 1988. The paper was written jointly with Professor Akio Watanabe of the University of Tokyo.

and Congress, both elected to represent the will of the people, are equal partners in government, each with its own powers. Consequently, any analysis and assessment of the role of the Japanese Diet in the present system of government is better made in comparison with the British and other parliamentary forms of government than with the American system.

In these parliamentary countries, the Cabinet, deriving its legitimacy from the will of the majority (as expressed by the majority party in the parliament), works through the bureaucracy to formulate and execute the total range of domestic and foreign policies. In that the executive functions under the Cabinet, this system may also be termed cabinet government. In the Japanese Constitution of 1889, the Diet had relatively little authority and the Cabinet was conspicuously independent of the Diet as part of the long historical legacy in which the bureaucrats wielded power in the emperor's name. This influence is part of today's modern tradition.

Yet, there is one other feature characteristic of the modern Japanese system of government—the very strong influence of the ruling Liberal Democratic Party (LDP), which appears, at first blush, to contradict the explanation given above. Unlike the other industrial democracies, Japan has seen the evolution of a party system in which one strong party maintains continuity in power without transition to other parties, and this continuity of power has in turn contributed to making the ruling party, the LDP, a very strong policy force. Except for a brief period of about one and a half years (from May 1947 to October 1948) in which the Japan Socialist Party and the Democratic Party formed coalition governments, the conservative parties have maintained their hold on the reins of government throughout the postwar period, this trend reinforced with the merger of the two conservative parties in 1955 to form today's LDP. This single party has remained in power for over thirty years.

One of the consequences of this situation has been that ruling-party politicians have developed an improved grasp—relative to the bureaucracy—on the information and skills needed for policy formulation and execution. The LDP currently holds over 300 seats in the 512-seat House of Representatives, houses its party offices in a large building near the Diet Building itself, and maintains its Policy Affairs Research Council (about which more later) as a highly developed policy deliberation body. All of the legislation and treaties that the Cabinet submits to the Diet for deliberation and approval must be previously cleared by the ruling party's deliberative process, and conversely it may be said that any legislation or treaty that clears this hurdle is virtually assured of passage in the Diet, given that the ruling party has a clear majority and that the strict party discipline that exists all but rules out the possibility of dissident Diet members' voting in defiance of instructions. Seen in this light, Japan's current political system may best be termed one of party government.

Such is not, however, to imply that the ruling-party politicians completely dominate the bureaucracy. While the elected officials do have more authority by virtue of their popular election, the bureaucracy of non-elected officials (given the bureaucracy's entrenched position and vast size, and despite the recent efforts of politicians) still has a better grasp of the information and administrative machinery. Thus the relationship between politicians from the ruling party and the civil service officials is overall one of cooperative co-existence, albeit underlain by a subtle tug-of-war for power.

The question of what functions the Diet fulfills in the formulation and implementation of foreign policy must therefore be examined in the context of these basic features characterizing the Japanese system of government. In so doing, it would be wrong to limit our assessment to the Diet system per se, and the issue cannot be fully understood without also looking at the activities of the ruling party—an institution that some people have termed an extra-parliamentary parliament and others "the third house of the Diet" in reference to the fact that Japan's Diet is bicameral—and individual Diet members.

II

Because the Diet's most visible involvement in the making of Japanese foreign policy is in the deliberation on and approval of treaties, this is a fitting place to begin this study. Article 73 of the Constitution gives the Cabinet the authority to conclude treaties, yet contains the proviso that "it shall obtain prior or, depending on circumstances, subsequent approval of the Diet."

While it is theoretically possible to conceive of different meanings for the Constitution's "prior" approval, this is generally taken to mean not prior to the Cabinet's signing the treaty but prior to its ratification. In effect, the Japanese practice is that treaties and other international agreements signed by the Cabinet do not formally come into force until the exchange of the instruments of ratification following approval by the Diet. (Not all international agreements require ratification, and those agreements that go into effect without ratification do not require Diet approval.)

This said, it should be noted that Japan's postwar parliamentary history contains no instances in which a treaty or other international agreement submitted to the Diet for its approval had to be amended or rejected because it failed to win approval. On the issue of amendment, the accepted political interpretation is that the Diet is asked to decide not on the text of the treaty but only on whether or not to approve the treaty.[1] As a result, it is inconceivable that the Diet should amend a treaty signed by the Cabinet. Even on the issue of approval or non-approval, the Japanese system of parliamentary government ensures that approval will be forthcoming except in those exceptional cases when there are sharp differences of opinion within the ruling party.

In the twoscore years from the First Session of the Diet, convened in 1947, through the 107th Session of the Diet, adjourned in late 1986, a total of 615 treaties have been submitted to the Diet for approval. All of them have been approved.

Of course, not all treaties sail effortlessly through the Diet. In the Ninety-first Session of the Diet (December 21, 1979, through May 19, 1980), held when co-author Okita was Minister for Foreign Affairs, forty-two treaties were submitted to the Diet for approval and all were approved within that session. This set a new record for the most treaties submitted and ap-

---

[1] The actual text of the treaty is studied by the Cabinet Legislation Bureau before the Cabinet signs the treaty, and the Diet takes no part in this process.

proved in any one session of the Diet, yet the reason for this heavy concentration of treaty deliberations and approvals in this particular session was that Diet deliberations got sidetracked in several earlier sessions and most of the treaties were held over until this ninety-first session. Yet, even these delays in the Diet were not so much because the treaties themselves were controversial but rather because the balance of power between the Cabinet and the Diet was very evenly balanced and it was difficult to obtain Diet cooperation for government policies. At the time, the executive (Cabinet) experienced considerable difficulties in managing its relations with the Diet, both because the government and opposition parties held roughly the same number of seats in the Diet and because there were a number of political groups within the ruling party that were not favorably disposed to Prime Minister Ohira. Indicative of the relationship between the Diet and the Cabinet as it then existed is the fact that the budget proposal submitted by the Cabinet was rejected by the House of Representatives Standing Committee on the Budget (a very rare occurrence, and the only time this had happened since the Standing Committee on the Budget rejected the fiscal 1948 budget proposal submitted by the Socialist and Democratic coalition Cabinet) and only just barely passed by the full session of the House.

It does occasionally happen that the opposition parties refuse to deliberate on, or withhold their approval of a treaty, in effect holding the treaty hostage, as a means of frustrating and obstructing the government's other policies. However, not all delays are of this nature, and it also sometimes happens that approval is delayed or difficult to obtain because the text of the treaty is controversial. The best-known example in this category is the 1960 revision of the Security Treaty between Japan and the United States. In this instance, the opposition parties, egged on by the daily demonstrations massed outside the Diet Building and encouraged by the mass media's coverage, used all of the means at their disposal to try to block the treaty's approval. The government party finally approved the treaty at a special session of the House of Representatives Special Committee on the United States–Japan Treaty of Mutual Security and Cooperation at which the opposition parties were not present and this was sub-sequently approved by the House of Representatives again in the opposition parties' absence. It proved impossible, however, to convene the House of Councillors, and the decision of the House of Representatives stood as the decision of the Diet in accordance with Article 61 of the Constitution. Under this pro-vision, failure of the House of Councillors to take action within thirty days of receipt of the treaty from the House of Representa-tives results in the decision of the House of Representatives' being the decision of the Diet. There have been a few other cases, both before and after 1960, in which this provision was invoked and treaties approved with the approval of only the House of Rep-resentatives. Examples include the 1958 Agreement Between the Government of Japan and the Government of the United Kingdom of Great Britain and Northern Ireland for Cooperation in the Peaceful Uses of Atomic Energy, the 1958 Agreement for Cooperation Between the Government of Japan and the Govern-ment of the United States of America Concerning Civil Uses of Atomic Energy, and the 1974 Agreement Between Japan and the Republic of Korea Concerning the Establishment of a Bound-ary in the Northern Part of the Continental Shelf Adjacent to the Two Countries. This last is the outstanding example of a treaty that provoked a storm of political debate, and it took six sessions of the Diet spread over a three-year period to get it approved.

As noted above, the conclusion of treaties is a power accruing to the Cabinet, and as such, treaties differ from other legislation in that there can be no treaties submitted by individual Diet members for approval. In that sense, the Diet inevitably has to respond to Cabinet initiatives, but this passivity is somewhat mitigated and the Diet's role somewhat more active in the case of multilateral treaties. This is especially so when Diet members press the government to have Japan accede to multilateral treaties to the drafting of which Japan was not a party. Typical here are the ILO conventions. The issue of Japan's becoming a party to ILO Convention 87 guaranteeing freedom of association, for example, was submitted to the Diet in 1960 yet not passed until 1965. This issue was first championed by the labor unions, and it was union pressure that led the government finally to submit this Convention to the Diet for approval. Following that, it took another five years and shepherding by three different Cabinets before the Convention was approved, mainly because there was determined opposition within the LDP to any concessions to the labor unions or to the labor-supporting Socialist Party and the government had to be very wary of this opposition within the government party so as not to endanger the Cabinet's survival.

Even today, Japan is still not a party to many of the ILO conventions, and there are nearly forty unapproved agreements just among those that the government is considering ratifying. One of the ones that has been prominently discussed recently is Convention 156 providing for sexual equality in employment opportunities.[2] In addition, the Convention Relating to the Status of Refugees, the International Convention on the Elimination of All Forms of Racial Discrimination, and other multilateral treaties drafted and signed under the pressure of international public opinion are exposed to a greater or lesser degree of public scrutiny before being submitted to the Diet for approval. Although the Convention Relating to the Status of Refugees did receive Diet approval and Japanese ratification in 1981, the International Convention on the Elimination of All Forms of Racial Discrimination has yet to be ratified.

While all of the above multilateral treaties were drafted without the participation of the Japanese government, there are also a number of multilateral treaties that the Japanese government had a hand in drafting but that remain unratified. Including those that date back to prewar years, they number approximately twenty, although there are only half a dozen such major postwar treaties in this category. Among others, these include the Convention for the Protection of Cultural Property in the Event of Armed Conflict signed by Japan and forty-nine other countries

---

[2] According to the December 24, 1986, *Nihon Keizai Shinbun*, the four major Japanese labor organizations have recently pressed the Minister of Labor to work positively for ratification of this and other ILO conventions. Noting that Japan has ratified only 32 of the total 162 ILO conventions, and only 9 of the 17 conventions designated by the ILO as basic conventions, the labor organizations contend that this is hardly a record befitting a leading industrial country.

at the Hague in 1954 and the International Convention Against the Taking of Hostages.

There are a number of reasons why the government would sign a treaty yet not submit it to the Diet for approval, from technical reasons such as the need to coordinate domestic laws and regulations for consistency with the treaty's provisions to political reasons. The Treaty on the Non-proliferation of Nuclear Weapons approved by the Diet in 1976 is an example of a treaty whose submission for Diet approval was delayed for political reasons. While the government finally signed this treaty in 1970 after long and involved domestic political debate, Prime Minister Sato, who had signed the treaty, was unable to submit it to the Diet for approval.

In the case of the Treaty on the Non-proliferation of Nuclear Weapons, there was a broad stratum of opposition to ratification cutting across party lines in both the government party and the opposition parties. Generally, the government and government party tend to be less enthusiastic about promoting multilateral treaties, especially those proclaiming such general ideals as human rights, freedom, peace, and natural conservation, than they are about promoting treaties involving economic issues or other issues having a practical impact upon vested interests, and the pattern is generally one of the opposition parties' pressing for these multilateral treaties' approval by the Diet.

Even so, once the Cabinet has signed a treaty and submitted it to the Diet for approval prior to ratification, Diet approval can invariably be obtained unless there are extraordinary extenuating political circumstances. The Diet is unable to touch the actual text of the treaty, and in most cases the treaty passes even without any exhaustive deliberation on its implications. The exceptions are cases when the government and opposition parties are of nearly equal strength and the Cabinet is not absolutely sure that it has the majority to ensure Diet approval or when there are sharp divisions within the government party or the Cabinet itself. Yet, the possibility exists that Diet members themselves can take the initiative for the approval of multilateral treaties when the Cabinet or executive is not actively pushing for their approval.

III

From the government's perspective, it is most efficient to minimize Diet involvement in all stages of the treaty process. Yet, from the perspective of maintaining parliamentary government principles, the Diet's power to deliberate treaties should be respected to the maximum possible extent. This issue of how to balance these conflicting positions is a question common to the role of the Diet in foreign policy everywhere.

In Japan's case, the government's formal position was stated on February 20, 1974, in the House of Representatives Foreign Affairs Committee by then Minister for Foreign Affairs Ohira, who said, in response to questioning, that whether or not a treaty requires Diet approval is determined based upon three criteria: (1) whether or not the treaty requires the enactment of new legislation or the amendment of existing legislation, in which case Diet approval is obviously required from the perspective of not infringing upon the Diet's authority to enact legislation, this category generally being agreed to include treaties impinging on territorial issues or other issues of national sovereignty; (2) whether or not the treaty entails fiscal or financial disbursement, with the understanding that Diet approval is needed for the conclusion of any international treaty that entails disbursements above and beyond the normal budget as already approved by the Diet or by law, this also being in obvious deference to the Diet's power to pass on the government budget; and (3) whether or not the treaty is an international agreement that requires ratification before it comes into force, which treaties generally require not simply the signatory procedure but the weightier ratification procedure because of their involving important political issues.

While international commitments can go by many names, including treaties, administrative agreements, exchanges of notes, protocols, and more, the above three criteria apply to all international commitments regardless of name. Conversely, it may be said that the executive is able to conclude any international commitment that does not fall under one of the above criteria without Diet approval, even if the agreement is formally called a treaty. Thus the executive is able to act on its own to enter into international agreements when they are administrative agreements to a treaty that has already received Diet approval and are in accordance with legislation already on the books and within the budgetary provisions already enacted.

The incident that directly caused the government to formulate this official position was the Diet deliberations on the protocol revising the Agreement for Cooperation Between the Government of Japan and the Government of the United States of America Concerning Civil Uses of Atomic Energy in 1973. Because it was anticipated that there would later be an exchange of notes adjusting the maximum amount of enriched uranium supplied to Japan under Article 9 of this agreement, the question arose as to whether or not this exchange of notes could take place without any Diet approval or role. While such an administrative agreement would not itself require Diet approval under the criteria enumerated above, the government agreed that it would "submit information" to the Diet (specifically to the Foreign Affairs Committee) in the case of an administrative agreement subsequently altering the implementation and execution of a treaty even if that treaty had already been approved by the Diet.

Administrative agreements are thus a gray zone, and the government resorted to administrative agreements in the early years of Japan's postwar parliamentary history to get around the drawn-out deliberations that were anticipated in some instances. The most glaring example of this is the Status of Forces Agreement that was signed as an administrative protocol to the Security Treaty Between Japan and the United States of America concluded at the time of the San Francisco Peace Treaty of 1951 and which was treated as not requiring Diet deliberations and approval despite the issue's political importance. In 1960, when the treaty was revised and the Treaty of Mutual Security and Cooperation Between Japan and the United States of America signed, both the treaty and its accompanying agreement regarding facilities and areas and the status of United States armed forces in Japan were submitted to the Diet.

The government's position as elucidated in February 1974 provided a tentative end to the prolonged dispute between the Cabinet and the Diet over the extent of the Diet's treaty deliberation powers. At present, there are no direct challenges to this authority. However, the question of how much Diet involvement there should be in economic cooperation and other international commitments has the potential for becoming the focus of new controversy.

Because international commitments for economic cooperation and assistance entail fiscal disbursements, it may be logically argued that they should obviously be subject to Diet deliberation and approval in keeping with the second criterion in the government's position. However, such is not the case. Rather, funding for this overseas assistance is included along with funding for other purposes in the total funding for the ministries and agencies having jurisdiction over such overseas assistance—the Ministry of Foreign Affairs, Ministry of Finance, Ministry of International Trade and Industry, and Economic Planning Agency, among others—as drawn up by these ministries and agencies in their budget requests and subsequently whittled down and totaled up by the Ministry of Finance for submission to the Diet by the Cabinet as the national budget bill for the fiscal year. Thus the only opportunity the Diet has to debate the overseas assistance budget is when it debates the total budget bill. Once the budget has been passed by the Diet, budgetary disbursements are executed by the executive and the specific programs for assistance to specific countries are not submitted for Diet deliberation. (Of course, Diet approval would be needed were the executive to want to enter into a commitment for overseas assistance outside of the scope provided for in the budget as passed, but this is a purely hypothetical and theoretical construct.)

Because the government's budget bill is completed and finalized before it is submitted to the Diet, such that there is no leeway for amendment or revision in the Diet's deliberative process except in the most extraordinary circumstances, the question thus boils down to one of how much, if any, input individual Diet members can have prior to the bill's submission to the Diet. Both government and opposition Diet members attempt to lobby the various ministries and agencies in concert with groups of petitioners from their constituencies on most issues, but any attempt to exercise such pressure regarding the budget for overseas assistance would be very unusual in that overseas assistance does not work to any particular election district's advantage and no district has a special vested interest in its budget provisions.

More important here is the role of the LDP's policy-making machinery. The LDP Policy Affairs Research Council is divided into a number of divisions corresponding to the areas of interest of the various ministries and agencies. For example, the Foreign Affairs Division corresponds to the Ministry of Foreign Affairs, the Commerce and Industry Division to the Ministry of International Trade and Industry, and the Educational Affairs Division to the Ministry of Education. These divisions and their counterpart ministries and agencies then join together in the budget formulation process to ensure funding for their programs. For example, the Ministry of Foreign Affairs' budget requests are taken before the LDP Policy Affairs Research Council Foreign Affairs Division—frequently with joint participation by the Special Committee on External Economic Cooperation and a few other related groups—and discussed there. However, this discussion by LDP Diet members is not so much to conduct a rigorous examination of the ministry's budgetary requests as it is to support the ministry in its subsequent negotiations with the budget-controlling Ministry of Finance.

Responsibility for overseas economic assistance is shared by a total of eleven ministries and agencies including the Ministry of Foreign Affairs, the Ministry of International Trade and Industry, and the Economic Planning Agency, and the economic assistance budget is thus doled out among these ministries and agencies, being included, as noted earlier, in the total budgetary request for each ministry and agency. After being pared down in negotiations with the Ministry of Finance, this total request is then put together with the pared requests from other ministries and agencies and the draft national budget for the national government as a whole is again reviewed by the top executive leaders, leading LDP officials, and the Ministry of Finance leadership before emerging as the government–LDP budget proposal for submission to the Diet.

This government budget proposal is virtually a finished product by the time it. is submitted to the Diet for approval, and it would be very rare for the Diet to revise the budget bill. (In fact, the Diet has revised the budget bill only three times in postwar Japanese history.) The budget bill is submitted to the Standing Committee on the Budget in both the House of Representatives and the House of Councillors, but Diet members tend to use the debate on this bill not so much to discuss specific points of the budget per se but rather as a center-stage opportunity to state their positions on the whole range of political issues and to question the government on these issues. Even in the Diet's Foreign Affairs Committee and other committees (here too, there are committees corresponding to the executive's organizational structure), the tradition is not one of examining and debating specific budget items. In addition to these institutional factors, debate on specific budget items is inhibited by the fact that the budget proposals submitted for deliberation include only the grand total and the category subtotals (e.g., the budgets for the Overseas Economic Cooperation Fund and other executive bodies), and there is no information available on how much is to be disbursed to any specific country or for any specific project.

For all of these reasons, the Diet's role in formulating policy on overseas economic assistance is very marginal, and not even the ruling party's policy-making machinery plays that much of a role, being only appendages to the responsible ministries and agencies. While there are some people who argue that the system needs to be changed to require Diet approval of the specific economic assistance agreements as one way of rectifying this situation, this view does not have wide support at this time.

Yet, such is not to say that the Diet is totally uninterested in economic assistance issues. Albeit after the fact, the Diet does question the government in considerable detail on how effectively Japanese assistance is being used, so meticulously in fact that one Ministry of Foreign Affairs official has speculated that Japanese assistance is probably the more economically effective for it.

Until recently, economic effectiveness—meaning not whether or not the aid will work to Japan's benefit and the benefit of specific Japanese companies but rather whether the aid will be effective from the point of view of promoting economic development in the recipient country or whether it will go to waste—was the basic criterion for Japanese economic assistance. Yet, in recent years there has been increasing pressure on Japan to extend foreign assistance as a means of providing relief (i.e., for humanitarian considerations), for political and cultural reasons, and for other ends that do not have strictly economic justifications. However, public opinion in Japan, including the Diet, has not been very favorably disposed to such forms of assistance, since they are often seen as a waste of money in strictly economic terms.

So far, public opinion has been supportive of increases in the budget for economic assistance, and economic assistance has been among the few items that have consistently been achieving considerable increases even as the total level of government expenditures was being held to zero or near-zero increases. However, as the total spent on economic assistance has grown, and as this assistance has become increasingly involved in non-economic realms, it may be expected that Diet supervision will become stricter in the years ahead. Whatever the ultimate outcome, it is clear that public opinion, reflected both within the Diet and at large, is a major albeit invisible factor affecting the formulation of foreign assistance policy.

IV

Japan does not have a tradition of the Diet's enacting legislation to guide government policy formulation. In the United States, Congress tries to influence the executive's foreign policy by enacting laws such as the Taiwan Relations Act or to limit the president's foreign policy negotiating leeway by enacting laws such as the Trade Expansion Act, but such things do not happen in Japan.

Even so, it frequently happens that the Diet passes resolutions designed to nudge the government in the direction of certain foreign policy positions or to serve notice that certain positions are unacceptable. A few examples should suffice to make this point.

The restoration of territorial sovereignty is the most common subject of such Diet resolutions. When the Ryukyus were under American military jurisdiction, there were repeated Diet resolutions calling for their restoration to Japan, a goal that was finally achieved when residual sovereignty became reversion in 1971. While there is no telling how much these resolutions did to buttress the government's negotiating position, they were dramatic expression of a consistently strong public opinion in favor of reversion. Likewise, the Diet has passed repeated resolutions calling for the return of the small Northern Territories off Hokkaido that are now an issue of contention between Japan and the Soviet Union. For the Japanese government to faithfully observe the letter of these resolutions in its negotiations with the Soviet Union would commit the government to this position and limit its flexibility (in that the resolutions demand the return of all four islands and island groups and do not permit any concessions on this demand). Since, of course, no resolution could win Diet approval that did not first have the approval of the majority party, it may be said that the territorial position expressed in these resolutions is also the position of the government itself. As such, the other side in such negotiations may reasonably be expected to assume from these repeated resolutions that there has been no change in the Japanese government's position.

The most sensitive issue for Japanese public opinion is that of possible involvement in overseas military conflicts, because this has a direct bearing on the question of how to maintain Japan's reputation as a peace-loving country. The Diet has frequently passed resolutions condemning nuclear testing by India and other powers and calling for a comprehensive nuclear test ban. Referring to Japan itself, the House of Representatives adopted the three non-nuclear principles of non-possession, non-manufacture, and non-introduction in November 1967. Other well-known resolutions in this area are the House of Councillors' June 1954 resolution against sending Self-Defense Forces personnel overseas and the House of Representatives' March 1981 resolution against weapons exports. This last is especially interesting in that it was a multi-stage progess. Under questioning in the House Standing Committee on the Budget, Prime Minister Sato stated on April 21, 1967, that Japan would not export weapons to any communist country, to any country subject to a United Nations resolution embargoing weapons exports to that country (e.g., the Republic of South Africa), or to any country which is or is feared likely to become a party to an international conflict. Some years later, under Prime Minister Takeo Miki, the Cabinet formally approved a policy statement on weapons exports that included the three provisions set forth by Prime Minister Sato plus a statement that Japan would be most reluctant, in keeping with its peace Constitution and the provisions of the Foreign Exchange and Foreign Trade Control Law, to export weapons to any country at all, and it was this February 21, 1976, Cabinet policy statement that was the basis for the 1981 House resolution against weapons exports.

There is, however, some question as to how binding these Diet resolutions are. In the strict legal sense, it may be said that they are not binding. Nevertheless, it would be difficult for the government to act in flagrant violation of the expressed will of the Diet as "the highest organ of state power" (Article 41 of the Constitution). In that sense, it may be said that Diet resolutions are politically binding. This is especially so in that the resolutions are often adopted by unanimous acclamation (or at times with only the Communist Party in opposition or abstention), meaning that it would be very difficult to pass a new resolution amending or disowning a resolution once it is passed.

In fact, however, many of these Diet resolutions originated in government policy declarations to the Diet. The three principles restricting weapons exports, for example, were adopted by the government on its own initiative to provide guidelines for the application of the Export Trade Control Order to control the export of weapons. They were later extended to a Diet resolution when the question arose in the Diet as to whether or not a particular private-sector company's exports fell into the weapons category and the resolution was passed by way of pressing for the rigorous application of these principles by the government.

The three non-nuclear principles are a somewhat similar case. These three principles were originally adopted by the government as internal policy guidelines, and they were passed as a Diet resolution only later as a concession to the opposition parties (which had been pressing for the passage of such a resolution) in order to win these parties' support for the agreement with the United States governing the reversion of the Ryukyus when that agreement was submitted for Diet approval.

As seen in these two examples, the politics of passing Diet resolutions is typical of the postwar Diet deliberations over Japanese foreign policy. While Diet debate takes place both in standing and special committees and in the full session, the Foreign Affairs Committee, for example, meets only twice a week, once to discuss treaty approvals and once to question the government about its positions on foreign policy issues of general interest. In addition, foreign policy issues are frequently taken up in the Standing Committee on the Budget. Question time in each House is allotted to each party in proportion to the number of seats it has in that House, such that most of this question time is allocated to the ruling party by virtue of its majority. However, LDP Diet members do not have to ask questions in the Diet, since they have ample opportunity to ask questions and to get explanations from the government in the party's own policy-making bodies and elsewhere, which forums often yield more candid exchanges of views than those in the Diet. For ruling-party Diet members, the Diet is thus not so much an opportunity to criticize the government and expose policy fallacies as it is one to elaborate on these policies. Thus the debate in the Diet—be it in committee sessions or in plenary sessions—is primarily that between the government and the opposition. In light of this, current practice in the House of Representatives Foreign Affairs Committee is for ruling-party Diet members to yield some of their allotted time to opposition Diet members, probably in the hope that giving these people disproportionate time to ask questions will, if not satisfy them, at least mitigate their dissatisfaction.

There is one very distinct pattern that emerges from this Diet debate between the government and the opposition parties: that of the opposition's pressing the government and questioning minutely as to whether or not a policy statement or policy action might not be inconsistent with a previous government policy statement or stated legal or treaty interpretation. Thus Cabinet ministers find themselves under constant scrutiny as to whether or not their current statements are consistent with statements made in the Diet by previous Cabinet ministers many years earlier. It may seem odd that the current Cabinet and current ministers are constrained by statements made by previous Cabinets and previous ministers, but this is an accepted part of modern

Japanese politics in that the same party has held the reins of power for an extended period and that the government is thus expected to exhibit policy continuity despite changes in the composition of its Cabinets. This expectation of policy continuity, changes in cabinet lineups notwithstanding, is further buttressed by the traditionally strong policy role played by the standing bureaucracy.

Even if a Cabinet or a Cabinet minister has a specific policy or legal interpretation, it is to the government's advantage to avoid having this policy or interpretation embedded in a Diet resolution and to leave as much maneuverability as possible for responding to new situations and circumstances as they arise. The Diet resolution on the three non-nuclear principles is the prime example here. At the time, Prime Minister Eisaku Sato and his Cabinet came down hard against the passage of a Diet resolution embodying these principles even though the opposition proposed such a resolution many times. However, the Cabinet later withdrew its opposition and agreed to the passage of a Diet resolution on the three non-nuclear principles in order to win opposition cooperation and to get the agreement with the United States on Ryukyu reversion approved by the Diet on schedule.

Because Diet resolutions are thus the product of political dealing between the LDP and the opposition parties, even though they often originate in government policy positions, they are also in part "won" by the opposition from the government and LDP. So long as the government is unable to ignore these political dynamics within the Diet, it is possible for the Diet to influence government policy formulation through subtle means.

V

Given this situation, what are we to make of the role of the Diet in Japanese government foreign policy formation?

Setting aside political systems such as that in the United States for the time being, the general practice in countries with parliamentary forms of government is for the parliament (the Diet in Japan's case) to be the final endorser of policies formulated and adopted by the Cabinet. Very seldom does the parliament itself initiate policy formation, be it concerning domestic policies or foreign policies. While provision does exist for individual Diet members to submit legislation concerning domestic political issues, far and away the majority of all bills originate with the government. On foreign policy, given that the executive is invested with the authority to conclude international agreements (treaties), it is logical that all of these bills and other initiatives should originate with the Cabinet.

In addition to the fact that the Diet itself cannot sign an international agreement, it has also been pointed out that the fact that foreign policy does not directly impinge upon the vasted interests of any major constituencies or constituents means that this is not a prime subject of interest for Diet members, and this is another factor tending to make the Diet more passive about foreign policy issues. The third reason for this relative lack of Diet involvement in foreign policy is that foreign policy, insofar as it concerns national security and the ultimate national interest, lends itself to suprapartisan consensus and hence is not seen as a fit subject for Diet debate.

Most people—Diet members included—would respond negatively or only vaguely if asked about their perceptions of the Diet's role in the formulation of Japanese foreign policy. As if to demonstrate this, people who leave the Ministry of Foreign Affairs to go into politics have less of a chance of being elected than candidates with professional backgrounds in the other ministries and agencies. And once elected, Diet members compete for assignment, if not to the prestigious Standing Committee on the Budget, then at least to Finance, Commerce and Industry, Agriculture, Forestry and Fishery, and other standing committees with strong ties to domestic special-interest groups, and assignment to the Foreign Affairs Committee is not a particularly coveted post.

As such, it may be felt that the Diet's role is insignificant, at least insofar as it concerns the making and execution of Japanese foreign policy. However, the authors feel that the Diet is both potentially and actually a more significant factor in the formulation of Japanese foreign policy than most people realize.

The first reason for this is that, even though it is difficult for the Diet to take the initiative in the conclusion of international agreements and other treaties, it is possible for Diet members to make their views known to treaty negotiators not only in the obvious post-signatory process of deliberations relevant to treaty approval but also in the pre-signatory negotiating stage through their questions and comments in the Diet. At the very least, the Diet is fully able to highlight the issues involved. Moreover, even after the treaty is signed and ratified, it still has to be put into effect and there is considerable room for Diet deliberations to affect the way the treaty is executed and enforced. Specific examples here include the question of how "Far East" is to be defined in Article VI setting forth the scope of the United States–Japan Treaty of Mutual Security and Cooperation and the interpretation of which matters regarding the American military's use of facilities in Japan shall be subject to prior consultation under the Exchange of Notes pursuant to the same Article VI. Until recently, these were among the opposition parties' favorite topics of discussion in the Diet.

The second reason is that, as clearly demonstrated by the ILO conventions, it is possible for the Diet rather than the government to take the initiative in pressing for the ratification of multilateral treaties and other international agreements. In this way, domestic public opinion, backed by the force of international public opinion, is able to push the government to take certain actions and move in certain ways. While this is not foreign policy in the traditional sense of the term, the increasing interdependence among nations means that there is an increasing tendency for people to focus on whether or not domestic practices and activities are compatible with internationally accepted practices and ideals. Likewise, the tendency is also for increasing attention to be paid to the shared assets of all mankind (such as peacekeeping, disarmament, human rights, natural conservation, the preservation of cultural assets, and other concerns transcending national borders), which tendency may well work to enhance the Diet's role in this aspect of foreign policy.

The third reason is that foreign assistance, insofar as it entails considerable fiscal disbursements, can reasonably be expected to be a subject of some interest to the Diet. So far, the Diet has not demonstrated any great interest in this issue, but this is probably because the scale of foreign assistance disbursements was relatively small (and was distributed among the budgetary requests of a number of different ministries and agencies, such that it was not seen as a single lump sum) and because there has been a broad public consensus that it is dangerous to increase defense spending but desirable to step up economic assistance to the developing countries. However, there is a very real possibility that foreign assistance may increasingly be a focus of serious Diet debate, both because it is questionable whether or not the system can tolerate continuing increases in foreign assistance within a general context of budgetary austerity and because the actual forms this policy takes are gradually moving from the less controversial emphasis on economic development to non-economic realms.

Finally, the authors would like to say a word or two about some of the issues in external economic policy, an area which it has been impossible to treat at any satisfactory length in this paper. There is a crying need to have serious treatment and discussion of the role that individual Diet members and the Diet as a whole play or potentially play in the area of economic friction. Here, however, the authors will only deal very briefly with a few of the main features. While there is increasing pressure for Japan to further open its markets, there is in Japan, as in any other country, opposition to this from constituencies or other vested-interest groups that would be adversely affected by market opening. While a broad consensus is finally gelling on both the need and the desirability of further opening the Japanese market, there is still strong opposition and resistance on specific policies to implement that opening, and it is unlikely that there will be any sudden, wholesale shift to market-opening. As in any country, it is the Diet members who depend upon particular vested-interest groups or constituencies for their voter and financial support who are the mainstay of the protectionist forces. Unlike in the United States Congress, however, Diet members are very unlikely to propose, much less pass, protectionist legislation or resolutions directly embodying the positions of these special-interest groups.[3]

---

[3] According to the *Asahi Shimbun* (December 30, 1986), four opposition parties (the Socialist, Komei, Democratic Socialist, and Communist parties) recently submitted a joint bill for the protection of the Japanese fishery industry. Declaring that the United States, the Soviet Union, and other countries have unjustly restricted Japanese international fishing activities, this bill calls for retaliatory limitations on or an em-

For better or worse, the pattern in the Japanese system of interest aggregation and interest articulation is for these various special-interest groups to be represented within the different stages of the ruling party's policy-making machinery and then homogenized with other interests for inclusion in government policy. Given this, the determining factor in the formulation of Japanese external economic policy is that of how well the ruling LDP's policy-making machinery can control the interplay of policies advocated by specific special-interest groups (such as rice farmers or the agricultural cooperative) and their specific advocacy ministries and agencies (in this case the Ministry of Agriculture, Forestry, and Fisheries) and coordinate these special interests and the accompanying bureaucratic clash in the interests of the whole. It is, in effect, a question of political leadership.

---

bargo against imports of fishery products from these countries. The LDP also considered submitting a similar bill at one time, but decided against it. Although there is no chance of this opposition bill's being enacted so long as the LDP holds a majority in the Diet, it is nonetheless a symbolic expression of opinion. While this does not represent the sort of protectionist legislation opposing market opening that is discussed in this paragraph, it is clearly an attempt to protect and promote fisheries interests in a climate of increasingly harsh international competition. This bill may also signify a new trend in the Diet in that the opposition took up a protectionist cause and that the Communist Party was among its co-sponsors.

PART III
Problems in
Economic Development

Economic Development in the Third World and International Cooperation

Twenty-five economists from fourteen countries recently held a meeting at the Institute of International Economics in Washington, D.C., and produced a report *Promoting World Recovery* (December 1982). The group emphasized the need for conscious efforts to promote economic recovery. The report started with the following paragraphs:

The world is in an economic crisis. There is scant prospect of any prompt spontaneous recovery from the present deep recession. Until recovery occurs there is a continuing danger of an outbreak of trade warfare and competitive devaluation, or of financial collapse, that could destroy the interdependent world economic system that emerged in the postwar years.

The decline in inflation does not itself promise to produce a recovery, but it does provide scope for policy to be shifted in an expansionary direction so as to promote recovery. Such a policy adjustment should be undertaken promptly. It should be internationally coordinated, for there is little prospect that an adequate global stimulus could result from a series of isolated national actions, and considerable risk that isolated "locomotives" might find themselves subject to excessive depreciation that rekindle inflation. In particular, neither can the world simply wait for the United States, nor can the United States be certain of achieving adequate recovery on its own.

This paper for the Non-aligned World Conference in New Delhi was presented in January 1983.

In recent years Keynesian policies for stimulating demand have been unpopular in most industrial countries because they were interpreted as one major cause of the prolonged stagflation. In the face of serious recession and very high levels of unemployment, however, the economic policy emphasis is likely to shift from fighting inflation to fighting recession, although the fears of renewed inflation will be kept very much in mind by policymakers.

The nations of the South have an almost endless list of areas requiring development, including expanding food production, developing energy resources, building improved infrastructures for transport and communications, and halting the erosion of tropical forests. Promoting these ends will require both capital and technology. In the nations of the North, labor and production facilities are operating at far less than capacity, and there has been a noticeable falloff in effective demand. Yet, both the developing countries and the industrialized countries need to raise their domestic savings rates and to direct the capital to productive investment. Moreover, the balanced development of the world economy demands that as much of this investment as possible be directed to expanding production and income in the developing countries.

Food

A number of developing countries have recently had remarkable success in expanding foodstuff production. Several years ago, Dr. Kunio Takase and I co-authored a report on a plan for doubling rice production in Asia.[1] In this report, we pointed out that a controlled water supply for paddy fields was one of the key factors for raising the rice yield in the monsoon areas. High-yield varieties of rice and the use of fertilizers are more effective if water supplies can be properly controlled. There has been a remarkable increase in rice yields in some countries, including Indonesia and the Philippines, which are moving from being rice-importing to

[1] "Doubling Rice Production in Asia," in Saburo Okita, *The Developing Economies and Japan*, University of Tokyo Press, 1980.

being rice-exporting nations. Technical progress and infrastructure investment, partly assisted by the World Bank and bilateral aid programs, has enabled India to double food production in a quarter-century, as mentioned earlier. Yet, the increasing population and rising income will add to the demand for grain for both human and animal consumption. It has been Japan's historical experience that demand for animal feed grains can increase almost explosively as people start consuming animal protein. In fact, Japanese imports of such feed grains increased from practically nothing twenty years ago to 20 million tons per annum today. On the other hand, many of the poorer countries, particularly in Africa, are suffering from food shortages. The apparent surplus in or self-sufficiency of some Asian countries may partly be due to lack of effective demand because of the low average income. Recent improvements in food supply in some countries may, therefore, be temporary, and continuing efforts for increased food production in the developing countries will be required. Even if the developed countries are able to expand their food production, the food-needy countries lack the necessary foreign exchange to import this food. What matters most is that the developing countries strengthen their own food production capability.

Forests and the Environment

As for the forestry problem, rapidly diminishing tropical forest areas are a matter of serious concern. Although there are differences among the various estimates, such as the United States government's 1979 "Global 2000," the FAO's 1981 "Assessment of Tropical Forest Resources," and ESCAP's 1981 Environment Study, they are all agreed that the tropical forests will quickly be depleted if current trends continue. The increasing demand for food makes it necessary to cut trees and convert forests into farmland. The high cost of energy makes people dependent on fuel wood and charcoal. Timber exports to earn foreign exchange are another reason for cutting trees. The tradition of migratory cultivation in some of the developing countries is another factor reducing forest area. Moreover, in many of the developing countries, the current laws and regulations on forest management are those of a colonial era and not sufficiently adjusted to local conditions and needs. Rapidly diminishing tropical forests will result in eroding fertile soil, damaging water conservation, reducing the absorption of carbon dioxide by trees, rapidly reducing the number of animal and plant species, and so forth. The consequences will not be confined to the tropical countries alone, but will have global climatic and other far-reaching effects on the countries of the North as well. Global cooperation to prevent the further diminishing of tropical forests is called for.

A Japanese government Ad Hoc Group on Global Environmental Problems produced a report entitled *Basic Directions in Coping with Global Environmental Problems* in December 1980. It contains the following paragraph:

> Although it is of course necessary that each country steadily implement its domestic environmental policies, it must be recognized that problems of a global scale cannot be solved by the mere accumulation of domestic environmental policies by individual countries. In addition, since global environmental problems have an impact on the great majority of the world's people, it ultimately is in the interests of all countries albeit differently situated to preserve the earth's environment. In view of these considerations as well as the urgency of the problems already mentioned, it is necessary to cope with these problems as soon as possible on a global scale. This will involve international understanding and cooperation.

This report also recommended, among other items, that "Development aid programs should be reviewed from the viewpoint of global environmental preservation, and adjustments made where necessary."

Finance

There must be a complementary relationship to mobilize the underused labor and equipment of the North for meeting the development needs of the South. When the developing countries seek to procure the capital necessary for development, there is a gap between the terms demanded by the lending countries and the terms acceptable to the borrowing countries. Part of the resource transfer from the North to the South can be purely commercial loans or investments. But a large number of developing countries want concessional loans or grants. Loans for infrastructure building such as irrigation, afforestation, and road and harbor construction would require long-term, low-interest finance. Although there are good possibilities of effective lending and investment through private channels, there is an undeniable need for concessional transfers. These could be supplied in the form of mixed or blended loans, and terms of lending could be differentiated according to the borrowers' repayment ability. It has been recognized that, together with the bilateral transfers through private channels, the essential role of international financing institutions like the International Monetary Fund and World Bank is to deal with short-, medium-, and long-term financial requirements of developing countries.

The IIE report *Promoting World Recovery* recommended that "a reasonable level of commercial bank lending to developing countries needs to be sustained, and part of the remaining gap should be filled by increased lending by the International Monetary Fund and the World Bank."

If the present stagnation of the world economy continues with no recovery in sight for some time to come, the need may arise for convening a second Bretton Woods Conference to confer on basic policies for the revitalization of the world economy. The summary report of the NSRT (North-South Round Table) recommended reforms in the IMF and World Bank, and called for the convening of a second Bretton Woods Conference after the intellectual spadework is done by experts.

One of Japan's business leaders, Mr. Masaki Nakajima, former president of Mitsubishi Research Institute, has proposed that a Global Infrastructure Fund (GIF) be set up to spur the world economy out of its present stagnation through long-term, large-scale infrastructure construction projects. Global projects Mr. Nakajima has proposed include a second Panama Canal, the greening of the Sahara desert, and massive hydroelectric and irrigation projects in the Indian subcontinent, Africa, and Latin America. He estimates the total cost of such projects over twenty years would be about $500 billion, which is less than the world's current annual military expenditures. This GIF idea may sound somewhat unrealistic given the pessimistic mood of the world, but such a scheme would address itself as a challenge to mankind to overcome this deep recession and achieve worldwide prosperity.

Trade

The world economy is now undergoing a far-reaching and dynamic process of international division of labor. Comparative advantages in world trade are changing rapidly and demanding structural adjustments in both developed and developing economies. Some older industrial countries want to maintain their status quo, while others welcome change. This causes trade friction among industrialized countries themselves and between developed and developing countries, particularly the NICs. With the continuing recession and very high unemployment, protectionism is gaining strength in many of the developed countries. Such friction and protectionism can be mitigated if reasonable growth is restored to the world economy. A mixed policy of free competition based on market mechanisms and structural adjustment based on some sort of global planning may be called for in light of the lower rate of growth of the industrial economies and the developing economies' need for accelerating growth.

Technology

Technology is the basis for economic progress. It is also a basic factor for reducing a nation's dependence on countries which possess advanced technology. Technological progress cannot be attained overnight. It is a result of patient efforts in education, training, and research. Countries can import a factory or equipment incorporating modern technology, but unless they develop an indigenous capability in the equipment's maintenance, repair, and improvement, this technology will never become their own.

The history of Japan's economic modernization and development of technology clearly indicates the importance of the human factor. In order to avoid creating foreign enclaves by importing plants and equipment, it is sometimes desirable to "depack" technology. This will enable the imported technology to spread widely into the national economy. The development of small industry is an essential factor for sound industrialization. Japanese industry's current strength depends very much on the numerous small enterprises which work as subcontractors for large companies or compete independently in the marketplace.

One crucially important factor for the future world economy is the development of microelectronics. While extensive automation may compete with cheap and abundant labor in the developing countries, microelectronics may nonetheless create various possibilities for the developing countries to facilitate the transfer of technology by providing inexpensive audio-visual education and training facilities. Software technology may also be furthered in developing countries because of their potentially large number of "good brains." It is probably necessary for experts from both developed and developing countries to cooperate in microelectronics research in order to work out a prognosis for making this new technology beneficial to developing nations.

Differentiated Strategy for Development

Growing diversity among the developing countries is another important aspect of the world economy. The United Nations Committee for Development Planning (UNCDP) discussed this topic in preparing proposals for the Development Decade of the 1980s. A UN publication, *Development in the 1980s: Approach to a New Strategy*, published in 1978, contains the UNCDP's conclusions. The chapter entitled "Strategies Specific to Different Groups of Countries" listed the following four groups of countries:

(a)   oil-exporting countries,
(b)   countries depending heavily on exports of other primary products,

(c)   rapidly industrializing countries, and

(d)   low-income developing countries.

These groups, while to some extent overlapping, nevertheless permit tentative approaches to a differentiated strategy. As they are likely to introduce some realism in the debate of North-South problems, I am quoting here at some length the differentiated strategies for each of the above four groups from the UN report:

The oil-exporting countries, because they still have under developed aspects, need inputs of technology and expertise from the advanced economies and from other developing economies with such resources. As for the oil-exporting countries with substantial surpluses, one will need to explore how their accumulated capital can be better used for the sake of world development, particularly of the economies of developing countries. Since their capital represents a conversion of non-renewable resources into long-term investment, it is obviously vital for these countries to have hedges against the depreciation of currencies and to use most of their capital profitably. One of the desirable directions for the employment of oil capital—in addition to supplementing the flow of concessional assistance—may be to use more of it for financing the development of rapidly industrializing developing countries at commercial or near-commercial rates.

For other developing countries highly dependent on the exports of primary commodities, commodity agreements and other related measures are desirable in order to stabilize their econom [ies]. There will also be a possibility of transfer of resources through improving the terms of trade in favor of exporting countries. But in the latter case it is easy to oversimplify the resulting benefits and costs for (a) resource-rich rich countries, (b) resource-rich poor countries, (c) resource-poor rich countries, and (d) resource-poor poor countries. In order to avoid an arbitrary transfer of resources from relatively poor to relatively rich groups of countries, the selection of commodities which are candidates for commodtiv stabilization requires careful consideration. Accordingly, along with the conclusion of commodity agreements, a wider use of compensatory financing mechanisms deserves attention. To assist their processing of raw materials before export, producing countries particularly need modification in the escalating tariff structures still found in many importing countries.

As regards the rapidly industrializing developing countries with high rates of economic growth and export expansion, the conditions necessary for their further economic progress are: (a) continuation of a liberal world trade system; (b) access to the markets of both developed and developing countries; and (c) access to the world capital markets on commercial or better than commercial terms. Developed countries are increasingly feeling the pressure of exports from these developing countries as well as the exports of more sophisticated industrial products from some of their own newer members. The older industrial countries have been slow to make changes. Adjustment is difficult because of their domestic political and social problems. However, if these countries move towards a hardened stand of protectionism the result could be a stagnation of the world economy, with adverse impacts on the developing countries as well. As a matter of practical concern the countries exporting manufactures may at times be obliged to accept export restraints. But this can only be justified as a temporary solution and if it is used to make adjustment policy more feasible for the developed industrial countries.

As for the low-income countries, their problems are central to a global endeavor for accelerated progress. The elimination of mass poverty from the face of the earth is the joint responsibility of all nations, rich and poor alike. This is implicit in giving the highest priority to the satisfaction of basic human needs, such as adequate nutrition, health services and basic education, by both domestic and international measures. But international aid to the poor countries should also aim at making them self-sustain [able] by helping to finance major improvements in [their] economic infrastructure which are a precondition of rapid agricultural and industrial expansion in such countries. Poverty is not confined to low-income countries but international efforts will have to be very largely concentrated on the problems of low *per capita* income countries. Developing countries with higher *per capita* incomes should be able to go further towards meeting such needs from domestic resources. Although the content of basic human needs will differ from country to country, there should be an effort towards quantifying such needs.

The above ideas discussed at the UNCDP sessions were not readily welcomed by the government-based preparatory committee for the International Development Strategy on the ground that such a grouping or differentiation of the developing countries would undermine the solidarity of developing countries as a whole. Consequently, the idea of grouping was not incorporated explicitly in the Development Strategy for the 1980s adopted by the UN General Assembly.

Slow Growth of Developed Economies

Although the recovery of the world economy will come sooner or later, the growth rate of the developed economies is likely to be lower than in the past because of structural factors. Therefore, it will be necessary to search for a set of policies which will make it possible to maintain a reasonable level of employment with a slower rate of economic growth. Otherwise there will be a continuing danger of protectionist trade policies being adopted in the industrial economies.

On the other hand, the developing countries will have to make their economies more resistant to the slower rate of growth in the industrial economies by strengthening self-generated growth. This will require structural changes in their economies and closer cooperation among developing countries.

There are various factors behind the slowdown of the industrial economies. Some of the salient factors are: (a) as income rises, demand for goods tends to diminish while demand for services increases, and this leads to a slower growth rate for material production; (b) as income rises there seems to be a diminishing return of additional production on welfare; (c) progress in social security measures tends to increase consumption and reduce savings with the result of a lower rate of investment and growth; (d) affluence tends to weaken social discipline and the work ethic; (e) the changing age structure of the population towards a larger share of the elderly leads to a less dynamic society and a slower rate of productivity growth; and (f) growing awareness of the "limits to growth" weakens the incentive for economic growth.

The Limits to Growth: Report for the Club of Rome's Project on the Predicament of Mankind, prepared by Dr. Dennis Meadows and his group and published in 1971, contains as an annex a commentary by the Club of Rome's Executive Committee that includes the following paragraphs:

> We unequivocally support the contention that a brake imposed on world demographic and economic growth spirals must not lead to a freezing of the status quo of economic development of the world's nations.
>
> If such a proposal were advanced by the rich nations, it would be taken as a final act of neocolonialism. The achievement of a harmonious state of global economic, social, and ecological equilibrium must be a joint venture based on joint conviction, with benefits for all. The greatest leadership will be demanded from the economically developed countries, for the first step toward such a goal would be for them to encourage a deceleration in the growth of their own material output while, at the same time, assisting the developing nations in their efforts to advance their economies more rapidly.

Conclusion

Human society as a whole is moving toward progress. There are many dangers, however, in the coming decades. Most serious is the danger of global war involving the superpowers. This must be prevented at all costs. The nonaligned world has a crucial role to play in staving off such a catastrophe by exerting influence on both of the superpowers.

The world economy is undergoing far-reaching structural change. Some countries may gradually lose their shares of world economic output while others may gain. This is part of the process of the historical evolution of the world economy. Yet, the progress of modern technology brings countries closer and closer, and all nations have come to realize that we live on a small planet. Economic progress can benefit all peoples in this interdependent world if properly shared among nations. A cooperative approach to global issues will also gain in importance in the course of time, although the basic foundation for economic progress is the national determination to develop the economy. At the same time, the regional approach, particularly cooperation among the countries of the South, will enhance their economic viability even when growth slows in the North. Here again the role of the nonaligned nations will be crucial.

Stages of Economic Development and Industrial Relations

In speaking to you today on the stages of economic development and industrial relations, I would like to start with a look at the changes which the successive oil crises have wrought in the world economy over the past decade.

The sharp increases in the price of oil instituted by the Organization of Petroleum Exporting Countries (OPEC) in the fall of 1973 sparked a crisis which ultimately engulfed the entire world. In the ten years since, the world economy has suffered confusion and turmoil marked by two drastic increases in oil prices.

In a way, the global ramifications of these soaring oil prices have served to throw into sharp relief the increasingly interdependent shape of the world economy in resources, technology, trade, financing, currency, and a host of other aspects.

It was shortly before the first oil crisis that the new economic policies announced by President Nixon in August 1971 spelled an end to fixed currency exchange rates and set currencies adrift on a floating system. It was against this tumultuous background that OPEC announced it was raising oil prices. The OPEC move served to exacerbate the tremors already evident in the world economy, and severe chaos beset all nations, East and West, North and South.

Indeed, confusion continues to reverberate throughout the world economy even today. The beast of inflation has been tamed somewhat, but the other enemies remain: unemployment, mount-

This paper was presented at the Sixth World Congress of the International Industrial Relations Association, in Kyoto, on March 29, 1983.

ing fiscal deficits, prolonged global recession, contraction in world trade, mounting external debts for the non–oil-producing developing countries, and the global banking crisis.

By any measure, things are the worst they have been since the end of World War II. In 1982, for example, world trade showed its first minus growth in the postwar period. Unemployment figures are nearly as high as they were during the Great Depression of the 1930s. The external debt obligations of the developing countries now exceed any reasonable debt service ratio, throwing the world banking system into increasing fear of a default. Moreover, these various economic woes, bad enough individually, tend to reinforce and amplify each other to make things even worse.

Faced with the triple threat of inflation, unemployment, and government deficits, the industrialized nations find themselves unable to mount effective policies in the fiscal and financial spheres. Buffeted by the oil crisis, it has been all each country can do to maintain a steady hand on the domestic economic helm, and no one has had much time or energy for international economic considerations. As a result, there has been an unmistakable deterioration of faith in world economic development. Nothing illustrates this loss of faith better than the recent rash of protectionist measures.

Yet, in retrospect it seems a wonder that the world economy has stood up to this decade of turmoil as well as it has. Despite their various domestic economic difficulties, the industrialized countries have made and are making every possible effort to cooperate in currency exchange, financing, and trade. Let me briefly review the record of international financial cooperation by way of illustration.

In the fall of 1973, the first oil crisis generated a major shift in the structure of the international trade accounts. This is illustrated, on the one hand, by the $60 billion current surplus which erupted in the oil-producing countries' 1974 balances of payments and, on the other hand, by the deficits of $30 billion for the industrialized countries and $25 billion for the non–oil-producing developing countries. It was a major revolution in the international balance-of-payments structure. A similarly abrupt shift in the balance-of-payments structure was seen after the second oil crisis.

In response, the international banking system displayed a remarkable flexibility and adaptability in recycling assets. Indeed, the fact that the non–oil-producing developing countries are now burdened with such heavy debt obligations that their very weight threatens to bring down the international banking structure is ironic testimony to the efficiency with which the international banking system worked to channel the massive amounts of money from the oil-producing countries to the developing countries in this time of weakening trade.

Happily, there have been signs that inflation is on the wane in the industrialized countries in the summer of 1982, some four years after the second oil crisis. Indeed, this is the first good news the world economy has had in the nine years since the 1973 oil crisis.

As inflation recedes, this loosens one of the major constraints which have been tying the governments' fiscal and financial hands.

The industrialized countries are watching to see what U.S. interest rates will do, and, now that there is less threat of inflation, everyone is looking for the chance to lower interest rates, so as to stimulate the economy and ring down the curtain on this long recession in the wake of the oil crisis.

One other hopeful sign has appeared on the horizon. This is the decline in oil prices, the first real decline in ten years.

Ten years ago, high oil prices led to the double problem of inflation and stagnation, creating that new phenomenon dubbed stagflation. Today, stagflation has circled the globe and returned to its birthplace in the form of lower oil demand and lower oil prices. In the popular press, this is being referred to as a reverse oil shock. The blockbuster which the oil-producing countries launched ten years ago has now come back to haunt its makers.

Given these lower oil prices, plus the fact that the industrialized countries had managed to bring inflation under control even before oil prices came down, it appears that the world has finally secured a firm foothold for working its way out of the oil crisis.

What does the future hold for the world economy?

The 1971 Nixon destabilization of currency exchange rates more than a quarter of a century after Bretton Woods, the 1973 oil crisis two years later, and the difficulties which the world economy has faced in the decade since then have posed a major challenge to human wisdom. The challenge, as I see it, is one of how we can change the postwar world economic structure in a positive way for future development.

The postwar world economy enjoyed unprecedented prosperity and development in the 1950s and 1960s. Yet, its very success rendered the basic structures which sustained this growth unable to respond adequately in the rapidly larger and more interdependent world.

It is thus possible to see the oil crisis as having arisen when the world economy ran up against its resource constraints. Likewise, the credit and currency crises may be seen as calls for new structures able to accommodate the growth which has taken place.

Next, I would like to sketch the course taken by the industrialized countries' economies in the wake of the oil crisis and, with reference to the wage-price spiral in these countries, to give some thought to industrial relations.

In considering industrial relations, it is important to look at the three players of labor, the corporation in which labor and management interact, and the government as the public entity which, transcending the corporation, manages the allocation of resources and income redistribution for the society as a whole. All three of these players, as well as the interactions among them, change with the historical process of industrialization.

In the industrialized countries which have come furthest along this development path, there have been definite changes in industrial relations as labor has gained and consolidated the right to collective bargaining and social influence.

Seen in the historic perspective, the trend is for labor to acquire collective bargaining strength and political power in both corporate management and macroeconomic policy in the industrialized countries as industrial relations approach maturity.

It is possible with the help of economic indicators to trace how industrial relations in the industrialized countries responded to the impact of this external change embodied in the OPEC oil-price hikes.

Looking at prices in the industrialized countries as reflected in the consumer prices indices, prices were relatively stable in the 1960s yet rose sharply after the 1973 oil crisis watershed. Higher prices for crude oil necessarily pushed up energy prices and petrochemical product prices. Moreover, because these are basic commodities, their higher prices soon had a ripple effect across the total spectrum of goods and services.

It is instructive here to compare price trends in the two periods of the 1960s and the crisis-ridden 1973–81 period. Between the two periods, consumer prices tended to be double or even quadruple: in the United States going to 9–10 percent from 2–3 percent, in the United Kingdom to 15-percent-plus from 4-percent-plus, in West Germany to nearly 5 percent from 2-percent-plus, and in Japan to 9-percent-plus from around 6 percent.

Such is not, however, to imply that all of these higher inflation rates have been caused by higher oil prices. Along with higher oil prices, the acceleration of wage increase rates has been another factor accounting for inflation's acceleration. For example, comparing wage increases in the four years before 1973 with those in the four years after 1973, we see increases in the United States going to 8-percent-plus from 6-percent-plus, in the United Kingdom to 16-percent-plus from 12-percent-plus, in West Germany to 8-percent-plus from 7-percent-plus, and in Japan to 15-percent-plus from 10-percent-plus.

As I mentioned earlier, the oil crisis also caused changes in the global international balance-of-payments structure. With the first oil crisis, the oil-producing countries accumulated a massive $60 billion current-account surplus while the industrialized countries ran a total deficit of $30 billion. This very rapid transfer of income meant that the oil-producing countries suddenly became very rich and the industrialized countries saw their income positions deteriorate.

Because the oil-importing countries saw the oil-exporting countries take an added share of production equivalent to the increase in oil prices, this income decline spread throughout their total national economies. Yet, in the industrialized countries labor balked at accepting its share of this decline and fought hard to keep up with rising prices. The result was to put corporate profits under that much more pressure. At the same time, a wage-price spiral developed.

The current world economic difficulties have been triggered by the sharply higher oil prices. However, the policy decision in the industrialized countries to raise wages in the midst of this difficulty has undeniably compounded the difficulties.

This realization brings us to our discussion of industrial relations.

There is a basic conflict in industrial relations between labor and management over such issues as income distribution and working hours. At the same time, overall sound social development through increasing consumption and stabilizing and enriching livelihoods demands that labor increase its share of the pie through increased bargaining power. However, in the ten years of the oil crisis, industrial relations have generated a wage-price spiral and aggravated the world economic problems.

The experience of the oil shock shows how important it is that labor and management cooperate when the economy is subject to a major external force. We need a new framework for industrial relations combining conflict and cooperation between labor and management in the mature industrialized economies. Moreover, I feel that our public institutions, which means our governments, must also make policy efforts for the creation of such a framework.

Industrial relations in the industrialized countries are strategically important in the context of global economic development. The industrialized countries must actively promote industrial restructuring in response to technological innovation if they are to hope to be able to promote international economic specialization and growth in the developing countries.

The cooperative aspect of industrial relations in the industrialized countries is extremely important to making such development possible in the world economy. Along with confrontation to secure an acceptable distribution of income, it is also very important that labor cooperate to encourage management to develop a positive program of investment for future development. In effect, management should be granted a certain profit level so that it can invest in the hope of a later payoff. If management will seek to expand the size of the future pie through active investment and technological innovation to improve productivity, labor should respond with cooperation in job reallocation and retraining. Indeed, the challenge for industrial relations today is that of how to promote cooperation between labor and management in these fields.

Finally, I would like to speak on the Japanese experience in industrial relations.

In order to put Japanese industrial-relations performance in the global context, it may be good first to go back and to look at how the world's different economies reacted to the oil crisis.

The United States, United Kingdom, West Germany, and Japan all experienced a wage-price spiral in the wake of the oil crisis, with both wages and prices rising faster after the oil crisis than they had before. Yet national differences show up if we divide the total period into its first half (1973–77, after the first oil crisis) and second half (1977–81).

Looking at consumer prices, consumer price increases in the United States were 8-percent-plus in the first half and 10-percent-plus in the second half, indicating that inflation accelerated in the second half. By contrast, consumer prices rose slower in the second half in the United Kingdom (18-percent-plus vs. 12-percent-plus), West Germany (5-percent-plus vs. 4-percent-plus), and Japan (13-percent-plus vs. 5-percent-plus). The same trends are also evident in wages. In the United States, wages rose 8-percent-plus in both halves, yet in the other three countries they rose less in the second half than in the first half.

In Japan, wages in the manufacturing sector rose a total of 73 percent in the four years from 1973 to 77. By contrast, the increase in the second four years, 1977–81, was only 29 percent (averaging 6.7 percent per annum). The fact that the wage-price spiral was conspicuously less in the second half of this oil-crisis decade is indicative of the high level of adaptability Japanese industrial relations have in setting wages.

When it is realized that this adaptability has contributed to raising Japan's export competitiveness, the argument that today's trade friction is in large part due to the differentials in industrial-relations adaptability takes on a certain persuasiveness. Why, then, do Japanese industrial relations have this high level of adaptability? This can be understood in part by looking at the origins of industrial relations in Japan.

Because industrialization started much later in Japan than in the West, virtually the entire history of Japanese industrial relations has coalesced in less than one hundred years.

In the early years, Japan adopted the best systems that the West had to offer and brought them in wholesale as state-run enterprises. Textiles were at the forefront of this initial industrialization. In 1872, a textile plant was imported from France and started as a model factory operated by the state with the help of French advisers. Modernization in the heavy industrial structure did not make meaningful progress until the Russo-Japanese war of 1905. It was not until after World War I that the foundations were consolidated for the chemicals industry. Internationally, in fact, it was not until 1911—only seventy-two years ago—that Japan regained sovereignty over its own tariff rates.

By the 1920s, Japan had built the basic complement of modern industries and was poised to begin industrialization in earnest; yet, even then most of the industry was still pre-modern. The reality was that of an industrial structure in which over half of the labor force was employed in the primary sector with only a few large companies in the forefront of modernization. Even in these modern industries, industrial relations were still governed by subcontracting teams with each team's leader (*oyakata*) responsible for the people in his group.

After World War I, however, the wave of democratic thinking which swept the society enabled the labor movement to pick up momentum despite the lack of legal grounding. In 1919, the Friendly Society Greater Japan General Federation of Labor (Dai-Nihon Rodo Sodomei Yūai-kai) boasted 120 locals with a total membership of 30,000. Labor disputes arose in some of the modernized industries, and management was faced with the need to formulate industrial-relations policies. It was in this context that the modernized public- and private-sector industries came up with the concepts of linking remuneration to length of service and implicitly expecting/promising long-term employment.

Why were these key characteristics for modern Japanese industrial relations born in these industries? Generally, this is thought to be because of the need to promote industrial modernization with modern technology and facilities from the West. This need, which divorced industrialization from the traditional modes of management and craftsmanship, imposed a corollary need for management to procure skilled workers on its own. As a result, management employed large numbers of new school graduates who had never worked anywhere else before and provided them with on-the-job training to create a labor force of skilled workers. In order to keep these in-house–trained skilled workers on the job for an extended period of time, companies devised the seniority-based remuneration system of increasing rewards commensurate with the person's skills and position and the practice of encouraging people to work for the same companies until retirement.

In 1920, shortly after World War I, the total Japanese labor force of 27 million was employed 54 percent (over 14 million) in the primary sector and 21 percent (close to 6 million) in the secondary sector. Of this secondary-sector 21 percent, some 4 million (or 16 percent of the total labor force) were in manufacturing. It was not until 1927 that secondary-sector income caught up with primary-sector income in the national income statistics. Moreover, the bulk of these secondary-sector employees were self- or family-employed in less-than-modern industrial conditions.

The labor movement was neither recognized nor protected by law until after the end of World War II, but, at least in the modern industries, the democracy which swept over Japan just as these industries were undertaking full-fledged modernization lent labor's demands broad social support. It was then, as industrialization was poised for takeoff, that the managers of the large corporations which were modernizing took the initiative to introduce seniority-based renumeration and lifelong employment. Moreover, these systems were applied first to the white-collar workers and only later to the blue-collar employees.

There were efforts by some bureaucrats who had studied the situation in the West to gain passage of a law legalizing labor unions before the war, but these efforts failed to gain business support and died aborning as Japan went onto a wartime footing in the 1930s, leaving Japanese industrial relations in a still immature legal stage.

This was the situation as Japan entered and finally lost World War II.

If we look at Japanese industrial relations in the context of enhanced bargaining power and greater political influence for labor, it is clear that Japan's defeat in World War II was a decisive event. Indeed, Japan's modern industrial relations were largely shaped by the various democratization policies pursued by the Allied nations in the wake of Japan's wartime defeat.

Today, it is generally accepted that the three distinguishing factors characterizing Japanese industrial relations are seniority-based renumeration, the practice of lifelong employment, and enterprise unions.

It was the various postwar democratization reforms that laid the legal foundations for the organized labor movement and collective bargaining. With these reforms, the prewar system of having management unilaterally set working conditions was modified to have working conditions subject to negotiation between labor and management. This was a truly epochal change.

Such is not, however, to imply that this transformation was easy. Rather, today's Japanese industrial relations were born in a time of immediate postwar economic turmoil and fierce labor struggles as part of the storm of democratization.

The ferocity of these labor struggles may be seen in the figures for man-days lost per hundred employees per year. In the 1970s, this was a very low 11, yet in the second half of the 1940s, the half-decade immediately after the war's end, it was 46, and in the first half of the 1950s it was 45. These figures are inconceivable in today's Japan.

Even those large companies and public enterprises which enjoy such peaceful industrial relations today underwent fierce labor struggles over the total range of conditions, including worker control of production, until the mid-1960s.

To list just a few of the major disputes, there was the 56-day

Toshiba strike of 1946, the anti-dismissal disputes at Hitachi throughout the late 1940s, the Japanese National Railways and postal worker strikes, the 63-day 1952 and 113-day 1953 coal strikes, the 1953 Nissan strike, and the 1957 steel strike. Within this climate of tumultuous industrial relations, a number of younger union leaders realized that it would be impossible to achieve economic development and improved standards of living, given Japanese industry's weak foundations and perilous future, unless a new form of industrial relations could be constituted. Seized by a sense of crisis, they began to work seriously for the establishment of new industrial relations in such heavy industrial sectors as steel, automobiles, and shipbuilding. What they proposed was a stance of constructive cooperation with management for the future.

In response to this labor initiative, management adopted a cooperative tone, and the new attitudes taken by both labor and management thus served to modify the fiercely antagonistic relations which had previously existed between labor and management. Even though this drew opposition from the established labor leaders, who wanted to engage in even more radical strategies; management responded resolutely; and a qualitative change gradually took place in the union movement. This change, shown in the leadership transformation in the steel unions around 1960s, made it possible to create Japanese industrial relations in their modern form.

While there is still the final cutoff of retirement, Japan's seniority-based rewards and lifelong employment have made it easy for workers to plan their lives and to set realistic goals. For management, this accommodation by labor implies an obligation to keep up with the changing pace of innovation and market conditions and to manage the company for stable expansion so as to provide stable employment expansion.

Management cannot withdraw from an industry simply because it seems to be slipping in the rough and tumble of industrial restructuring. Each company must constantly have an entrée to new industrial sectors and markets for the future. This management stance is in large part responsible for Japanese industrial competitiveness and the ability to pounce on new markets.

Because labor appreciates the benefits of seniority-based rewards and lifelong employment, labor tries to take a flexible attitude toward reassignments or retraining to other jobs or workplaces as management tries to respond dynamically to the changes in the market and to the rapid pace of technological innovation. This workers do because they believe it is in their own interests.

It was in the fire of turmoil and trial within the postwar history of rapid heavy industrialization and economic recovery that the Japanese system of enterprise unions was consolidated. Although enterprise-wide and limited to only one enterprise, it would be wrong to brand these unions "company unions." Rather, they have arisen from the rigorous economic logic of corporate identification sustaining Japan's economic development through international competition within the harsh postwar international environment.

Japanese industrial relations thus posit one answer to the question of how to devise mechanisms to simultaneously optimize the short-term adjustments between labor and management over income distribution and the long-term adjustments over the allocation of resources to nourish the corporation's development.

Within this history of belated prewar industrial development and postwar democratization and rapid industrial development, Japanese industrial relations have managed to overcome sterile class antagonism and to devise mechanisms to mediate between the different interests.

At the same time, it is also a historical fact that the tumultuous initial postwar period in Japanese industrial relations which was characterized by class antagonisms was a major factor in building today's pattern of rational conciliation between conflicting interests.

In addition to collective bargaining, modern Japan's industrial relations contain three major information-sharing systems: the joint consultation system, the role of first supervisors, and QC circle activities. Indeed, collective bargaining at the top functions as well as it does because it is supported by dialogue and concert at these three subsidiary levels.

I began with a review of the experience of the decade of oil crisis. This shared experience has posed, and continues to pose, the very important question of how we can build mechanisms combining conflict and cooperation in the economies not only of the individual countries but of the world as a whole.

While collective bargaining by labor and the political clout of OPEC have achieved major success in gaining for themselves a larger share of the total pie through confrontation, they have not been entirely successful. The labor movement, because it lacked cooperative mechanisms, accelerated the wage-price spiral, aggravated the recession, and thus gave unions ultimately less to bargain collectively about. For OPEC, higher prices have come back boomerang-like to haunt OPEC with lower prices and slack demand.

Looking at East-West relations and North-South relations within the global economic context of mature industrial relations in the industrialized countries and heightening interdependence among all countries in the thirty-eight years since the end of World War II, it should be noted that it is to no one's benefit and to everyone's detriment to deal with these issues with over-simplistic confrontation over resource distribution or in a stylized dance of victim and victimizer.

We have at hand today an international economic system allowing for nonmilitary competition, and its development demands that we discover interfaces between the apparently contradictory aspects of conflict and cooperation, not only within our separate countries, but within the world at large. This is our task for the future, and the only way in which we can ensure that the heavy price paid in the oil crisis was not paid in vain.

Within this, Japanese industrial relations offer many useful suggestions on how mechanisms incorporating cooperative relations can be brought in and the levels of negotiations broadened between two sides which have usually tended toward an antagonistic relationship.

Economic development is sustained by market mechanisms and ambition to invest for the future. So long as the parameters are right, market mechanisms make it possible to find paths to economic development through competition in pursuit of profit. The question then is what kind of system we can build into this economic development system for negotiations to decide the allocation of resources for the future and the allocation of income for the present.

Now, ten years after the outbreak of the first oil crisis, it is vitally important that, rather than worrying about assigning the blame for the oil crisis and ensuing recession, we begin work as soon as possible in a cooperative effort to build new systems for the future both within our individual nations and internationally.

Flexibility and Efficiency
in the Private Sector

For the OECD member countries to live with change, it is necessary that the policies be consistent with the democratic political system and, at the same time, with the requirements of a mature industrial society, a stage which most of the OECD countries have now attained. Coercive measures or regimented systems must be avoided. Policies based on the market mechanism will be conducive to meeting these just-mentioned necessities. The dynamism of the market economy is best realized by establishing a "virtuous circle" of non-inflationary sustainable growth, technical innovation, active investment, and creation of job opportunities. It is important to note that friction arising from the process of structural change and technological innovation can best be resolved in the long run by enhancing flexibility and by adequate economic growth.

This year, the twentieth anniversary of Japan's accession to the OECD will be celebrated. Since starting as a poor agricultural economy more than a century ago, Japan has experienced various stages of development. As a latecomer to the industrial world, its earlier period was characterized by policies designed to enable Japan to "catch up with the advanced countries." After the Second World War, Japan attained a remarkable growth rate of over 10 percent per annum during the years from the late 1950s up to the early 1970s. The National Income Doubling Plan was formulated in 1960 and its target was attained in seven years instead of ten years as set out in the plan.

This chapter is the text of a statement presented at the Ministerial Conference of the OECD in Paris, on February 13, 1984.

199

About fifteen years ago, when Dr. Thorkil Kristensen left his position as secretary-general of OECD, a series of essays was published in book form in his honor. Among the economists and diplomats from member countries who contributed to this book, I wrote a chapter entitled "Virtuous Circle of Accelerated Growth" in which I analyzed the mechanism of high growth and predicted the emergence of rapidly growing economies, which were later termed the NICs (newly industrializing countries) by the OECD.

In the decade from the early 1970s to the early 1980s, the OECD economies have experienced two oil shocks and prolonged recessions. Japan's growth rate declined to 5 percent per annum during the 1970s and in recent years has dropped to around 3–4 percent. At the same time, Japan is reaching the state of a mature industrial society. General policy orientation has also shifted to meet this change. In many ways, Japan is now sharing the problems of other OECD countries. Sometimes outside observers emphasize the difference between Japan and other industrial countries, but from our point of view our economy and society is characterized by many more similarities with other OECD countries than differences, since our system is fundamentally based on a market economy and private enterprise system.

It may be said, however, that Japan's economic performance in recent years has been relatively good compared with that of other OECD countries. Here I may point out some of the causes of this relative success.

Flexibility and competition

It is generally recognized that there has been strong competition in Japanese society and such competition has motivated entrepreneurs' positive attitude toward investment and the introduction of new technologies. This, coupled with the general social flexibility, has resulted in a positive response to change.

Industrial adjustment

The basic approach of the government is to introduce measures designed to help ensure dynamic development and adjustment to change of the private sector by maximizing its vitality under the free-market mechanism and open-market system, although agriculture is not yet quite in line with this basic approach due to various political and social constraints.

Policies for declining industries are to facilitate positive adjustment without recourse to protectionist measures. In other words, policies are directed to the scaling down, in an orderly way, of industries which are losing comparative advantage, and are designed to encourage measures to revitalize their activities where viable.

In the case of the aluminium industry, for example, based on the guidelines recommended by the government, its production capacity was reduced from 1,640,000 tons per year in 1978 to 740,000 tons in 1982, and actual production has declined from 1,040,000 tons to 300,000 tons. During the same period, imports of aluminium increased from 760,000 tons to 1,350,000 tons, thus raising the import dependency ratio from 43 percent to 82 percent.

The shipbuilding industry is another example, cutting down its capacity from 9,800,000 cgrt (compensated gross registered tons), in 1977 to 6,200,000 cgrt in 1979, while actual production declined by about 40 percent during the same period. In this case, the share of Japanese shipbuilding in total sales of shipbuilding companies declined from 42 percent to 28 percent during the same period.

Policies for new technology are to promote technology development in the areas where the private sector alone is not capable of carrying out research and development. Mainly in basic research areas with high cost, high risk, and long lead time, the government sometimes takes direct measures such as the support of a portion of research funds, although the government's share in the total R&D expenditure is smaller than that of other major OECD countries.

Another measure to promote industrial progress is to provide visions of emerging trends of industrial structure which are intended to give useful and credible indications to entrepreneurs in making their decisions. This is not "central planning" because adoption or utilization of visions is left to the discretion of each enterprise. The government also provides inducements by preparing a favorable environment to help industries' own efforts, although legal, financial, and taxation measures to that end are limited in scope.

Labor-management relationship

Mutual confidence between labor and management is relatively strong in Japan. Employers generally regard workers as partners in their enterprise and avoid dismissal of a redundant labor force through internal transfer to new areas of activities, as discussed at last week's OECD Inter-Governmental Conference on Employment Growth.

On the labor side, workers are generally receptive to technological innovation and structural change. Japan's high level of education and stable labor-management relations contribute to this situation. There is also a widespread practice of encouraging participation of labor in entrepreneurs' decision-making, including quality control in factories, development of new products, and so forth.

Wage levels are agreed upon in a flexible manner by taking due account of the business performance of enterprise as well as the general economic condition.

The current cooperative relationship, based on mutual confidence, has been established based on the severe lessons learned from past experiences of conflicts between labor and management, particularly in the early postwar years. Both sides have come to realize that conflict does not lead to business development and stability of employment, and that cooperative relations are most beneficial to themselves. Such mutual confidence contributes greatly to the enterprises' flexible response to change. The basic approach of the government employment policy is to provide guidance and support for the private sector's efforts to respond positively to change.

Future problems

Japan is now facing emerging problems. Some of them are illustrated in the study by the Long-Range Prospect Committee of the government, which produced in the summer of 1982 a report entitled "Japan in the Year 2000." I worked as chairman of this committee.

Some of the salient issues touched upon were:

Rapid process of aging of population. Aged population of 65 and above accounted for 5 percent in 1960 and 10 percent in 1983, and will reach 16 percent in 2000 and 19 percent in 2010. This means that in the not too distant future, Japan will have the oldest age structure among OECD countries.

Technology. Japan, now one of the leading countries in the field of high technology, has a difficult task in developing new technological frontiers.

Internationalization. Japan has to live in a new and broader environment, responsive to the changing world economy, and must interact in harmony with the other nations of the world.

Pacific Development and Its Implications for the World Economy

As the world economy gradually recovers from the aftereffects of the second oil crisis, the Pacific region's dynamic economic development has attracted special attention in recent years. Within the region, the United States economy has recovered rapidly to chalk up an impressive 6.9-percent growth rate for 1984 and to lay the foundations for what is expected to be 4 percent growth in 1985. This has stimulated similar recoveries within the Pacific region and, for that matter, the whole world. Australia, Japan, and Canada, for example, grew 6.3 percent, 5.8 percent, and 4.7 percent respectively in 1984—considerably better than Europe's 2 percent and a clear indication of the dynamism of the Pacific region's industrialized nations.

The developing nations of the Western Pacific region also achieved conspicuous economic progress. The 1979 oil crisis forced many nations to make drastic adjustments in their economies. While this process is still under way in some nations, most have successfully adapted their economies to the new situation. The Pacific region as a whole has regained its economic dynamism in recent years. In addition to the newly industrializing countries (NICs) of Asia and the ASEAN nations, China has been showing remarkable growth and is making further efforts to open its economy.

World economic growth centered on the industrialized nations in the period between the end of the Second World War and the 1960s. The EEC's intra- and extra-regional trade was at its peak,

This chapter is the text of an address to the Fourth Pacific Economic Cooperation Conference, in Seoul, on April 29, 1985.

and the growth in the United States was reflected in the Atlantic region, which acted as the support for worldwide economic growth, trade expansion, and regional development. With the turn of the decade, however, the industrialized nations' economic growth slowed down drastically, and the world economy's center of gravity shifted to the oil-producing nations and the developing and newly industrializing nations of Latin America and Asia as these countries' trade expansion and economic growth made remarkable strides.

The oil crises forced another shifting of roles. The world cut back on its oil consumption, disrupting the international balances of payments of many of the oil-producing countries. Several Latin American nations found themselves saddled with the heavy cumulative debts that plague them even today. The Western Pacific nations survived the second oil crisis somewhat better, and since 1983 have embarked on a new period of rapid growth. The continuing economic recovery in the United States, Japan, Canada, and Australia suggests that the Pacific region will be the main driving force in the world economy in the 1980s. The Pacific region has made a major contribution to world economic growth and trade expansion between 1983 and 1985, opening up the possibility of continued global economic progress premised on the dual support of the Pacific and Atlantic regions.

The Elements of Growth

National efforts and policy achievements

What is behind the Pacific region's recent development? First and foremost are effective government policies buttressed by close cooperative efforts by government, industry, and academia. Of course, government policies vary from country to country, but the following similarities can be discerned within the Pacific region.

First are the export-oriented development policies. Whether a nation chooses to opt for import substitution or export promotion in its industrial development depends on the size of its economy, its access to natural resources, and its stage of development.

The Asian NICs and the ASEAN nations have consistently emphasized export promotion. There are several things to be said for concentrating on exports. For one, the process of tighter integration with the rest of the world economy exposes domestic industry to world-class competition and thus both fosters industries which are globally competitive and imposes cost consciousness on economic planning and policy choices. Another advantage is that it draws on market mechanisms to encourage private-sector vitality. And yet another is that exports earn foreign currency and thus mitigate foreign-exchange reserve limitations on development.

The Republic of Korea and the other Asian NICs have kept a careful watch on overseas market trends and developed their exports accordingly. The result has been rapid but primarily export-dependent industrialization. South Korea, Taiwan, Hong Kong, Singapore, and Malaysia have relied heavily on exports since the 1960s.

A second point of similarity is a high rate of investment, specifically investment backed by dramatically higher domestic savings rates. In general, a country whose savings and investment exceed 20 percent of its GNP can be said to have attained self-sustaining development. In 1960, Taiwan was the only nation among the Asian NICs and the ASEAN countries to have a 20-percent-plus investment rate. By 1982, however, all of these countries except Indonesia had exceeded the 20 percent figure. With their savings rates increasing faster than their GNP growth, and with additional financing from abroad, the Asian NICs and ASEAN countries have been able to invest heavily.

The result has been steady and rapid increases in the ratio of investment to gross domestic product (GDP) in the years between 1960 and 1982. In the Republic of Korea, for example, this grew to 26 percent in 1982 from 11 percent in 1960. Other figures are Hong Kong to 29 percent from 18 percent; Malaysia to 34 percent from 14 percent; the Philippines to 29 percent from 16 percent; Singapore to 46 percent from 11 percent; Taiwan to 26 percent from 20 percent; and Thailand to 21 percent from 16 percent.

Korea and the Philippines have been filling in the gap between domestic savings and investment demand with heavy influxes of foreign investment, while Taiwan and Thailand have relied primarily on domestic savings. As a result of this strong pace of industrial investment, the industrial sector has grown to fully 30 percent of GDP for most of the Asian NICs and ASEAN countries.

The third similarity common to this region is that of an aggressive and active private sector operating within what is basically a market economy system. Because price mechanisms do not function effectively within a rigidly planned economy, planned economies too often lead to uneconomical investment and inefficient management. At the Asian Development Bank's international symposium on privatization which took place this January, for example, there were numerous case studies presented on public-sector inefficiency. In both the developing and the industrialized countries alike, there is a need for privatization and deregulation to promote more efficient operation. It should be noted, however, that privatization has the two sides of privatizing ownership and privatizing management, and every care must be taken that privatizing ownership does not create or perpetuate social inequities. Even in socialist China, the trend of late is to retain public ownership and achieve efficiency and growth through allowing management greater latitude and at the same time adopting market mechanisms to govern the flow of goods. Although the Japanese economy is basically one of private ownership, there has been a division of ownership and management, and ownership has somewhat taken on the nature of a public trust. This is, I believe, one of the leading factors responsible for the economic dynamism of the Pacific region.

The fourth reason for the success of the Western Pacific economies must be the improvements made in agriculture. Back in 1976, when I was president of the Japanese government's Overseas Economic Cooperation Fund, the OECF's Dr. Kunio Takase and I cooperated on drawing up a document entitled "Doubling Rice Production in Asia." In this paper, we argued that the Asian countries should seek to double their rice production in fifteen years by developing better irrigation systems to enable them to use high-yield strains and fertilizer more effectively. I am pleased to see that the results of Asian efforts have been largely in line with that idea. According to the World Bank's 1984 *World Development*

Report, per-capita food production in Asia has grown rapidly. Taking the 1969–71 figures as 100, the 1980–82 figures were 117 in Indonesia, 125 in the Republic of Korea, 150 in Malaysia, 124 in the Philippines, and 138 in Thailand. These figures provide a striking contrast to the situation in Africa, where per-capita foodstuff production has declined 1.1 percent per annum for a more than 10 percent decline over the decade of the 1970s. The fact that agriculture had developed hand in hand with industrialization in the East and Southeast Asian countries has been a major factor contributing to economic growth.

Fifth is the success of the various countries' economic adjustment policies. All of the industrialized countries suffered recession throughout the oil-crisis-plagued decade of the 1970s and the first three years of the 1980s. Yet, despite this situation, the countries of East and Southeast Asia adopted economic policies which enabled them to stem inflation and to roll with the external dislocations. These policies enabled these countries, with only one or two exceptions, to weather the world economic storm without incurring the kind of massive cumulative indebtedness seen in Latin America, to achieve 3–4-percent growth even as the OECD countries overall were showing zero growth, and hence to be poised for nearly double-digit growth once the world economy got back on its feet.

This same mix of determined growth and successful policies applies to China as well. With its adjustment policies from 1979 through 1981, China has checked inflationary pressures by winnowing its large-scale projects and tightening up on government spending to restore fiscal balance. The introduction of private incentives for agricultural produce, the expansion of enterprise management discretion, the adoption of market mechanisms, the establishment of Special Economic Zones to attract foreign investment, and other moves to bring the Chinese economy into closer contact with the outside world have enabled China to revitalize its economy and to rapidly expand its agricultural and industrial production. In 1982, China's national income was up 8.6 percent, in 1983 9.1 percent, and in 1984 12.0 percent. Similarly, trade bounced back from its 2.7-percent slump in 1982 to record 17.9-percent growth in 1983 and 47.1-percent growth in

1984. China has thus become one of the powerhouses further stimulating economic dynamism in the Western Pacific.

"Flying-geese" development in the Pacific region

While development in the Pacific region has been propelled by the efforts of the Pacific countries, it is also significant that there existed in the Pacific a climate of international cooperation conducive to the effective implementation of these national efforts.

The division of labor in the Pacific region has aptly been called the "flying-geese" pattern of development. (This term was coined in the 1930s by the Japanese economist Kaname Akamatsu—the same man who originated the concept of dynamic change in the international division of labor.) Traditionally, there have been two patterns or types of international division of labor: the vertical division of labor such as prevailed in the nineteenth century to define relations between the industrialized country and the resource-supplying country or between the suzerain and the colony; and the horizontal division of labor typified by the EEC with its trade in manufactures among industrialized countries, often among countries at the same stage of development and sharing a common culture. By contrast with both of these types, the "flying-geese" pattern represents a special kind of dynamism. In the Pacific region, for example, the United States developed first as the lead country. Beginning in the late nineteenth century, Japan began to play catchup development in the non-durable consumer goods, durable consumer goods, and capital goods sectors, in that order. Now the Asian NICs and the ASEAN countries are following in Japan's footsteps.

Because there is such great variety in the Asian nations' stages of development, natural resource endowments, and cultural, religious, and historical heritages, economic integration on the EEC model is clearly out of the question. Yet, it is precisely this diversity which works to facilitate the flying-geese pattern of shared development as each is able to take advantage of its distinctiveness to develop with a supportive division of labor. And this flying-geese pattern in the international division of labor has in turn given rise to North-South relations between the industrialized and the developing countries free from their traditional rigidities. In this regard, it may be well to look briefly at the situations in some of the leading countries of the region.

Starting with the United States, one of this country's most important contributions to the cooperative international division of labor is its market. While there is no need to remind you how important America's import expansion was in powering the world economy in 1983–84, it should be noted that the American market is the largest, most diverse, and most accessible overseas market anywhere in the world. Little wonder that companies and traders all over the world have their sights set on the United States market. At the same time, American capital, technology, and managerial know-how have made important contributions to Pacific development—all of this in addition to America's obvious importance in maintaining the peace.

Japan is a very important market for foodstuffs, commodities, and resources in general. However, it is still seen as closed to manufactured goods by many people. In neither scale nor diversity is the Japanese market able to rival the American market. Japan's contribution is to provide high-quality, low-cost machinery and industrial materials, and Japan has contributed much to enhancing the competitiveness of industries in the NICs and ASEAN countries. More recently, Japan has also been increasingly forthcoming with industrial cooperation, capital exports, development assistance, and other efforts to contribute to Pacific industrialization. Yet, perhaps Japan's most important contribution was to show by its own example that it is possible for an Asian country to achieve industrialization on the Western model.

The contribution of the Asian NICs is in industrialization through their export strategies. Although Japanese and American capital once invested heavily in locating their labor-intensive industries in Asia, the Asian NICs are now rapidly expanding their production of consumer durables and capital goods. These countries are also developing into major import markets, and contributing to the expansion of intra-regional trade. Singapore and Hong Kong have also contributed much as Asia's two most important capital markets. Recently, Korea and Taiwan have begun to assist the other developing countries with direct investment, technology tie-ups, and other forms of assistance. To give you some idea of how quickly these countries are growing, the total combined exports and imports trade for Korea, Taiwan, and Hong Kong in 1983 came to $147.5 billion—54 percent of the Japanese figure and fully 31 percent of the United States' total two-way trade.

The ASEAN countries are blessed with plentiful labor and abundant natural resources. Indonesia, Malaysia, and Brunei are all oil exporters. The labor-intensive industries are shifting from the Asian NICs to the ASEAN countries. Not surprisingly, there is increasing momentum in all of these countries to do more processing of raw materials before they are exported. Many of these countries have also achieved remarkable progress in expanding their agricultural output. ASEAN two-way trade was worth $152.5 billion in 1983—55 percent of the Japanese figure and 32 percent of the American figure. Put together, the ASEAN countries and the Asian NICs combined had a higher trade volume than Japan did in 1983.

Canada, Australia, and New Zealand are both industrialized countries and important sources of foodstuffs, livestock, coal, and other mineral resources. As a result, they have complementary trade relations with Japan, Korea, Taiwan, and the other process-and-export countries of the region. At the same time, Canada, Australia, and New Zealand are increasingly thinking of themselves as Pacific countries, and there has been a conspicuous effort made to step up their economic, cultural, and other ties with the rest of the region.

In addition to the trends in the various countries of the region for a dynamic international division of labor, the region is also developing a multifaceted infrastructure for trade. Where the Pacific was once an obstacle to trade and communication among our nations, recent advances in transport and telecommunications have transformed this barrier into a facilitator. The trade between Japan and Australia in coal and iron ore, for example, is contributing to the development of the Pacific iron and steel industry by mandating improvements in mines, ports and harbors, railways, and trade channels. We now have vast numbers of trade routes, transportation channels, telecommunications

Table 1   Division of Labor among the Pacific Countries

	Market	Resources	Capital	Capital Goods	Technology	Labor
United States	4	3	4	3	4	1
Japan	3	1	4	4	4	1
Australia and New Zealand	2	3	1	1	2	1
Asian NICs	2	1	1	2	2	2
ASEAN	2	3	1	1	1	3
China	2	2	1	1	1	4

Note: Numbers indicate degree of importance, from least (1) to most (4).

networks, and air corridors crisscrossing the Pacific, and it is this infrastructure which has transformed the Pacific from a barrier to an ocean of prosperity.

Outlook for Pacific Development

So far, the Pacific region has adopted a flying-geese pattern of diversified international division of labor led by the United States and Japan. What of the future? Just as this flying-geese pattern means that the region as a whole can develop by following the lead countries, it also holds out the possibility of expanded intra-regional trade and development for all as the countries of the region expand their domestic markets and open themselves to more imports.

In trying to discern the future, let us look first at the United States. According to the 1985 *Annual Report of the Council of Economic Advisers to the President of the United States,* there has been strong plant and equipment investment in the United States as the birth of one new technology after another since the mid-1970s has led to a rebound in earnings expectations. Productivity has come out of its 1970s slump and is looking up again in the 1980s. With this upturn in plant and equipment investment, the maturation of the labor force, the moderation of wage increases, and corporate efforts for rationalization, it seems reasonable to expect that United States productivity will rise at about 2 percent per annum and that the economy overall will grow at 3–4 percent per annum in the second half of the decade. The big ifs here are how the United States handles its twin deficits—the fiscal deficit and the trade deficit—and how America's high interest rates and overvalued dollar react as a result. If we accept that plant and equipment investment is still strong, the consensus seems to be that, with federal borrowing needs sopping up most of the U.S. household savings, the country will continue to be dependent upon the capital influx from abroad to meet its capital needs, interest rates will stay high, and the dollar is unlikely to come down anytime soon. With sustained U.S. economic growth, America is likely to remain deep in the red in its international balance of payments so long as the dollar continues to be overly strong.

As noted earlier, the United States has been a major market for Asia and the rest of the world. Yet, at the same time, increasingly protectionist pressures have built up as U.S. industry has lost its ability to compete internationally in many fields. It is to be hoped that the U.S. imbalance of payments will be rectified not through protectionist measures but by correcting the dollar's exchange disequilibrium and greater export efforts on the part of American companies.

Looking next at the Japanese economy, although the Japanese international balance of payments did take a turn for the worse with the two oil crises in the 1970s, this has since been reversed and the Japanese balance-of-payments surplus is on the increase. There are a number of reasons for this. First is the fact that the economy has evolved from a resource-intensive heavy-industry economy consuming vast amounts of energy and other raw materials to a technology-intensive economy fueled by technological innovation. Second, Japanese automobiles, electronics, and other products are highly competitive in world markets in terms of both price and quality. And third, even though the growth rate has fallen from 10 percent per annum before the oil crises to 4–5 percent per annum now, Japan's savings rate remains close to 20 percent of household income, and this savings availability has enabled Japan to become a capital exporter and to achieve structural surplus in its current account. However, there is a very real likelihood that the rapid graying of the population, the expanded disbursements for social-security entitlements, and increased personal consumption may erode the savings rate, as well as that Japan may soon be exporting less and importing more as the rest of Asia industrializes and as higher Japanese wages make Japanese products less competitive in world markets. Nevertheless, it is expected that trade will continue to show a surplus and that Japan will continue to have a net outflow in its capital account for the next transitional decade or so. With the United States now a net importer of capital, the fact that the Japanese economy generates surplus domestic savings which can then be supplied to meet other countries' capital needs is a plus for world economic development.

On April 9, the Advisory Committee for External Economic Issues, of which I am chairman, produced a medium-term set of guidelines for policy measures to improve market access for foreign products, to promote growth based on increased domestic demand, to expand direct foreign investment in Japan, and to increase Japanese assistance to the developing countries. (The text of the committee's report has been circulated to you at this conference.)

The government of Japan has promised to implement the recommendations of the Advisory Committee and has announced a number of immediate measures to be taken to improve market access. The government has also committed itself to preparing an action program for market access based on the committee's recommendations by the end of July this year. Significantly, the basic philosophy underlying this effort is that of "freedom in principle, restrictions only as exceptions."

Prime Minister Nakasone appeared on television the same day, April 9, with a strong speech appealing to the people to promote imports as Japan's number-one priority.

The Asian NICs, by which I mean Korea, Taiwan, Hong Kong, and Singapore, share a very strong export orientation and aggressive corporate management as seen in their ambitious investment plans. Looking ahead, there is a need for Korea, Taiwan, and the rest to stabilize their economies by expanding their domestic markets and reining in their export dependence, as well as to contribute to the growth of intra-regional trade by opening their markets to greater imports. As already noted, it is most encouraging that these countries have begun to contribute to intra-regional economic growth and trade by offering coopera- tion, technology transfer, and other forms of assistance to the later-developing countries.

While development in the Asian NICs has already taken off, the ASEAN countries are currently on the runway, revving for takeoff. Although this development will have to be based upon industrialization, taking advantage of their abundant labor and plentiful resources, the industrialized countries can do much to speed this process with their capital and technology. And as wage levels rise in the Asian NICs, the ASEAN countries' labor- intensive products will become increasingly competitive. It is significant that these countries are shifting from import-substitu- tion industrialization to export-promotion industrialization. As industrialization and urbanization progress, it will be increasingly important to improve the social infrastructure, including trans- portation, communication, utilities, and the rest. At the same time, the process of industrialization must be accompanied by enhanced productivity and broader diversity in agriculture.

Canada, Australia, and New Zealand will continue to be im- portant suppliers of foodstuffs, energy, and other resources for the region, and even greater market expansion is anticipated as industrialization raises standards of living in the nations of East Asia and ASEAN. These three countries also have an im- portant role to play as industrialized countries providing assist- ance and technology transfer.

The independent South Pacific island states are also gaining in importance, particularly with the adoption of the Law of the Sea and its institutionalization of 200-mile exclusive economic zones.

Pacific cooperation should include measures to improve the economies of these island states by encouraging fisheries, agricul- tural production, and industrial development. Infrastructure development including inter-island transportation and the use of satellite communication should also be promoted to enhance living standards. Cooperation from the advanced countries in the region will be essential in this effort.

Although it is very difficult to predict China's future, China has been promoting more open economic policies in light of the need to modernize its economy and technology. However, the country is bound to place the primary emphasis on domestic self-sufficiency in order to provide for its one billion people. Nevertheless, as seen in the successful industrialization in Taiwan, Hong Kong, and Singapore—all of which have large Chinese populations—it is virtually inevitable that manufactured exports from China will, to some extent, come into competition with the exports from the Asian NICs and the ASEAN countries. Given their different stages of development and China's resource reserves, the economic relations between China and the Pacific industrialized countries are generally complementary. The smooth development of the Chinese economy will contribute significantly to the expansion of trade and the promotion of economic growth in the Pacific region.

Given these trends in the United States, Japan, the Asian NICs, the ASEAN countries, Canada, Australia, New Zealand, and China, what kind of a scenario can be written for the Pacific region?

For starters, the U.S. economy will retain its dynamism and the Japanese market will become increasingly accessible. Exports will continue to increase from the Asian NICs and the ASEAN countries, and China will continue on the path of opening up its economy. Although there will be persistent trade friction, growth rates in the Pacific region will continue to be higher than elsewhere. According to calculations done by Professor Akira Onishi of Soka University, the Pacific region (including North America, Oceania, and East and Southeast Asia) will see its total GDP grow from 45 percent of the world total in 1980 to 50 percent by the year 2000.

Conversely, however, it is also possible to write a protectionist scenario in which Japan does not open its markets, protectionism becomes even more virulent in the United States, exports are stymied in the Asian NICs and ASEAN countries, the Chinese economy contracts back in on itself, and economic disputes run rife. Given the fact that many countries of the Pacific region are emphasizing export-oriented policies, such a protectionist scenario could have a very adverse impact on the region's growth.

Table 2   The International Division of Labor in the Pacific

	United States	Japan	Asian NICs	ASEAN	Australia, Canada, & New Zealand	China	EEC
Agriculture	4	1	1	2	4	2	2
Resources	4	1	1	3	4	3	1
Textiles	1	1	3	4	1	4	1
Intermediates							
Glass and Aluminum	4	1	2	2	3	1	2
Steel	1	4	2	1	1	1	2
Machinery	3	4	2	1	1	2	3
Electronics	4	4	2	1	1	1	2
Services	4	3	2	1	1	1	3

Note: Numbers indicate priority orders, from least (1) to most (4).

Trends in Pacific Cooperation

As is often pointed out, the Pacific region is rich in diversity. It is a collection of countries with wide differences in ethnic background, linguistic heritages, religious beliefs, histories, stages of development, natural-resource endowments, and many other aspects. The first question in Pacific cooperation is therefore that of how we can take best advantage of this diversity in promoting our cooperation.

The second issue revolves around transport and telecommunications means—the same transport and telecommunications means that have largely eliminated considerations of distance and transformed this vast Pacific from a barrier to a facilitator of intra-regional cooperation. Supercarriers have opened the way to the long-distance, low-cost transport of resources and manufactured goods, air travel has brought the entire Pacific closer in terms of travel time, and telecommunications have made instantaneous exchanges of information possible. Clearly, the physical and technological means are close at hand to promote Pacific cooperation.

Third is the fact that, as exchanges within the region expand, the trend will be increasingly away from bilateral contacts and toward multilateral contacts. For example, it used to be that Australian iron ore was supplied mainly to Japanese steelworks. Now, however, it also supplies to works in Korea and Taiwan, and will also supply to China once the works being built in Shanghai are completed. Likewise, the trade and economic agreements between the United States and Japan have a major impact on the region's other trading countries. For example, the increase in U.S. beef exports to Japan has had an undeniable impact on Australian beef exports. Japan's efforts to lower tariff levels on plywood and boneless chicken will benefit not only the United States but also the countries of Southeast Asia. At the same time, the liberalization of Japanese capital markets and the greater internationalization of the yen as agreed between Japan and the United States will also have a major impact upon financial markets in the other Pacific countries. It is clear that these issues need to be discussed not simply as bilateral concerns but as issues of interest to all the countries of the region.

Fourth, the Pacific region includes both industrialized countries and developing countries, and the region offers an excellent opportunity to discuss North-South issues on a regional basis. Although North-South issues are often discussed at the United Nations and other forums from a global perspective, the diversity of economies in the South and the conflicting interests in the North have tended to impede the search for a global solution. Hopefully, promoting North-South dialogue on a Pacific regional basis may open up new windows of opportunity for the global dialogue. In this context, I believe it is significant that human-resources development was discussed within the general topic of Pacific cooperation last July in Jakarta at the ASEAN Ministerial Meeting with the Dialogue Countries (the famous "six-plus-five" format bringing Australia, Canada, Japan, New Zealand, and the United States together with the ASEAN six). I can only hope that some way will be found to enable Korea to participate in these discussions before long.

Fifth, given the diversity of countries within the Pacific region, it seems most unlikely that an EEC type of community structure can be achieved anytime soon. Rather, it is more realistic to work

Table 3 Production Growth

(in constant 1970 prices, annual averages in %)

	GDP		Agriculture		Industry		Manufacturing		Services	
	1960–70	1970–82	1960–70	1970–82	1960–70	1970–82	1960–70	1970–82	1960–70	1970–82
Indonesia	3.9	7.7	2.7	3.8	5.2	10.7	3.3	13.4	4.8	9.3
Thailand	8.4	7.1	5.6	4.4	11.9	9.3	11.4	9.9	9.1	7.4
Philippines	5.1	6.0	4.3	4.8	6.0	8.0	6.7	6.6	5.2	5.2
Malaysia	6.5	7.7	–	5.1	–	9.2	–	10.6	–	8.4
Korea	8.6	8.6	4.4	2.9	17.2	13.6	17.6	14.5	8.9	7.8
Taiwan	9.2	8.0*	3.4	1.6*	16.4	12.6*	17.3	13.2*	7.8	4.1*
Hong Kong	10.0	9.9	–	–4.6	–	4.3*	–	6.1	–	10.1*
Singapore	8.8	8.5	5.0	1.6	12.5	8.9	13.0	9.3	7.7	8.6
OECD	5.1	3.8	1.4	1.8	5.9	2.3	5.9	2.4	4.5	3.2
Japan	10.4	4.6	2.1	–0.2	13.0	5.6	13.6	6.6	10.2	4.1
U.S.A.	4.3	2.7	0.5	1.7	4.6	1.9	5.3	2.4	4.4	3.2

Notes: (1) OECD here does not include Greece, Portugal, or Turkey.
(2) Figures with asterisks are for 1970–78.

Source: *World Development Report*, World Bank, 1984.

for a looser and freer framework of cooperation for the region—and even one allowing stronger sub-regional ties as seen in ASEAN. The PECC (Pacific Economic Cooperation Conference) is a tripartite structured organization (with representatives from the governmental, business, and academic sectors) with the secretariat work handled between general meetings by the country tapped to host the next general meeting. While this organizational structure serves well enough under the present circumstances, it seems only reasonable that, in the longer term, we will have to consider the establishment of a small-scale secretariat somewhat after the model of the OECD Secretariat. This would probably be something along the lines of the OPTAD (Organization for Pacific Trade and Development) as discussed within the PAFTAD (Pacific Trade and Development Conference) several years ago. At the same time, PECC should also strengthen its liaison and ties with the PBEC (Pacific Basin Economic Council) private-sector business organization for regional cooperation, with the academically-oriented PAFTAD, and with such special-interest organizations as the PTC (Pacific Telecommunication Conference).

Table 4   Sector Percentages of GDP

	Agriculture		Industry		Manufacturing		Services	
	1960–70	1970–82	1960–70	1970–82	1960–70	1970–82	1960–70	1970–82
Indonesia	54	26	14	39	8	13	32	35
Thialand	40	22	19	28	13	19	41	50
Philippines	26	22	28	36	20	24	46	42
Malaysia	36	23	18	30	9	18	46	47
Korea	37	16	20	39	14	28	43	45
Taiwan	28	10*	29	48*	22	38*	43	42*
Hong Kong	4	1	39	31*	26	27	57	67*
Singapore	4	1	18	37	12	26	78	62
OECD	6	3	40	36	30	24	54	61
Japan	13	4	45	42	34	30	42	54
U.S.A.	4	3	38	33	29	22	58	64

Notes: (1) OECD here does not include Greece, Portugal, or Turkey.
          (2) Figures with asterisks are for 1970–78.
Source: *World Development Report*, World Bank, 1984.

Sixth, as noted by Indonesian Coordinating Minister Ali Wardhana at the 1983 Bali Conference, PECC's close ties to the governments of the region make it an excellent forum for policy planning in the medium and long term. It is expected that economic activity through the market mechanisms will naturally serve to strengthen the contacts and exchange within the region. Still, it would be useful to enhance the cultural, scientific, educational, and other exchanges among the countries of the region, and this will demand conscious, planned efforts by the governments, universities, and other parties involved.

Seventh, the Pacific countries should strive for cooperation in such non-military, non-political fields as economy, culture, and science and technology, thus leaving the way open for participation by countries with different political structures.

Eighth, Pacific cooperation should, in principle, be looking beyond the region itself. It is hoped that countries outside of the region—the European countries, for example—will be able to participate positively in the Pacific region's development. This must be an outward-looking regionalism, and not an inward-

Table 5   GDP Structure

	Public Consumption 1960–70	Public Consumption 1970–82	Private Consumption 1960–70	Private Consumption 1970–82	Gross Domestic Investment 1960–70	Gross Domestic Investment 1970–82	Exports of Goods and Non-factor Services 1960–70	Exports of Goods and Non-factor Services 1970–82
Indonesia	12	10	80	71	8	13	13	22
Thailand	10	13	76	66	16	21	17	25
Philippines	8	9	76	70	16	29	11	16
Malaysia	11	21	62	54	14	34	54	51
Korea	15	13	84	63	11	26	3	39
Taiwan	19	17*	68	50*	20	26*	11	59*
Hong Kong	7	8	87	67	18	29	82	100
Singapore	8	11	95	48	11	46	163	196
OECD	15	18	63	62	21	20	12	19
Japan	8	10	59	59	33	31	11	15
U.S.A.	17	19	64	66	19	16	5	9

Notes: (1) OECD here does not include Greece, Portugal, or Turkey.

(2) Figures with asterisks are for 1970–78.

Source: World Development Report, World Bank, 1984.

looking regionalism. For example, while it would be well to state a common position for the Pacific region in the new round of GATT talks, every effort should be made to avoid institutionalizing discriminatory regional preferences. At the same time, of course, it is only right that we should promote regional cooperation in such areas as financing, development assistance, personnel exchanges, and a regional scheme for compensatory financing to stabilize commodity earnings.

Conclusion

While technological advances and expanded economic interchange give Pacific cooperation the legitimacy of history, we cannot leave the birth of regional cooperation entirely to the midwife of market mechanisms. Rather, we need a steady and pragmatic approach with all of the countries of the region working step-by-step to promote mutual understanding, to conduct studies on the Pacific economy, to draw up specific action programs, and otherwise to encourage cooperation in full awareness of the mandate of history. In short, we should seek to maximize this Pacific dynamism so that it may become the driving force for dynamism throughout the world economy.

The Outlook for Pacific Cooperation and the Role of Japan

At the end of World War II, the American journalist Walter Lippmann declared that the Atlantic Ocean had become an inland sea, thus inaugurating the "Age of the Atlantic." Since then, great strides in transportation and telecommunications have expanded cultural, economic, and scientific and technological exchange among the nations of the Pacific. This progress has begun to turn the vast Pacific Ocean into another inland sea, setting the stage for the "Age of the Pacific."

The Advent of the Age of the Pacific

The major factors facilitating the advent of the Age of the Pacific are the rapid growth of the Asia-Pacific region's market economies, the deepening of their economic interdependence, and their growing share of world trade. This region, which thirty years ago was one of the poorest in the world, is now undergoing a dramatic transformation.

There have been two great waves of economic development in the Asia-Pacific region since 1960, and a third wave is now about to break. The first wave was Japan's rapid growth in the 1960s, when it achieved annual economic growth rates of more than 10 percent; today Japan, together with the United States, is a major pillar of the world economy. The second wave, in

This article is reprinted, with permission, from the Spring/Summer 1987 issue of the *Japan Review of International Affairs*. It was adapted from the text of a lecture delivered at the First Japan–ASEAN Conference, held in Tokyo, January 29–31, 1987.

the 1970s, was the fast growth of the region's newly industrializing countries: Hong Kong, Singapore, South Korea, and Taiwan. Despite the global recession caused by the two oil crises of that decade, the Asian NICs have succeeded in maintaining a tempo of economic growth greater than that of most advanced countries.

The third wave of growth will occur in China and the countries of the Association of Southeast Asian Nations (Brunei, Indonesia, Malaysia, the Philippines, and Thailand; as noted above, Singapore, the sixth ASEAN member, has already joined the ranks of the NICs). Although global recession and protectionism in the advanced countries has slowed growth in Asia and the Pacific for the past several years, the countries of the region stretching from Northeast Asia through China to Southeast Asia will maintain their growth potential and dynamism into the twenty-first century.

From the end of World War II to the 1960s, the advanced industrial nations of Europe and North America were the engines of world economic growth. The United States' economic growth and the European Community's rapid increase in both intra- and extraregional trade reflected the fact that the Atlantic region was the center of global economic and trade expansion. Subsequently, however, growth fell off rapidly, and the region was beset by a malaise that lowered productivity growth and weakened economic vitality. The center of growth shifted to the oil-producing countries and to the Latin American and Asian NICs.

The countries of the Asia-Pacific region overcame the second "oil shock" of 1979 by skillfully implementing economic adjustment policies; thus, with the recovery of the global economy in the early 1980s, the dynamism needed for regional development reappeared and they were able to continue their remarkable growth. In contrast to the Latin American countries, whose development is impeded by their heavy burden of external debt, the countries of Asia and the Pacific are today facing new growth opportunities.

One of the key factors promoting growth in these countries has been effective economic management. Their governments have promoted lively private-sector domestic investment and adopted a development strategy of actively fostering export-oriented industries. The saving rate has risen with the standard of living, enabling these countries to raise the funds needed for development domestically. In addition, the private sector has skillfully utilized the market mechanism to promote vigorous business activities. Finally, improved agricultural production has provided a solid foundation for continued growth.

Though government and private-sector efforts have made development possible, we must also note the existence of certain conditions facilitating such efforts. The region's pattern of development has been likened to the V-shaped pattern of a formation of flying geese, a pattern reflecting the unique character of Pacific development. The United States, the first Pacific nation to achieve rapid growth, became the lead country. Next, Japan achieved dramatic development in consumer goods, followed by consumer durables and capital goods. The Asian NICs and ASEAN are now following in Japan's wake.

In addition to their varied stages of development, the countries of the Asia-Pacific region differ in natural-resource endowments, religion, culture, and history. This very diversity has facilitated the flying-geese pattern of development. Each country has achieved growth by building on its unique strengths in the context of its own stage of development. This pattern of development, free of the rigid traditional North-South relationship of exploiter and exploited, offers proof that it is possible for North and South to grow and develop simultaneously, thus opening a new chapter in the history of North-South relations.

A Dynamic Division of Labor

Next I would like to describe briefly the circumstances of the countries participating in the region's development.

Access to its enormous market is one of the United States' major contributions to the establishment of a harmonious division of labor within the region. The U.S. market, the largest in the world, is among the world's most open. The United States absorbs about 60 percent of the manufactured exports of the region's developing countries. American capital, technology, and management know-how have also made a great contribution to Pacific development. In addition, U.S. military might has played a stabilizing role, thus indirectly aiding the region's economic growth.

Japan has contributed high-quality, low-priced capital goods. Japanese machinery has enabled the NICs and the ASEAN countries to improve the international competitiveness of their industries. In recent years Japan has also begun to provide more industrial cooperation, capital exports, and development assistance. Above and beyond this, Japan's success is proof that Asian countries can develop along the lines of Western models.

Industrializing through aggressive export promotion, the Asian NICs have also contributed to the region's economic development. Although Japanese and American capital is still moving chiefly into the NICs' labor-intensive industries, the NICs themselves have begun to increase production of consumer durables and capital goods.

The ASEAN countries, rich in labor and natural resources, have been utilizing these resources to increase the international competitiveness of their labor-intensive industries. The center of production in such industries is now shifting from the NICs to ASEAN. Southeast Asia, along with the Middle East, used to be called the world's tinderbox. But the formation of ASEAN, an active organization for regional cooperation, has demonstrated that the countries of the Asia-Pacific region can enjoy stability and economic development.

Australia, Canada, and New Zealand have also aided the region's development, both as major exporters of foodstuffs, coal, and ores and as advanced industrial countries that have built up complementary trade relations with such countries as Japan, South Korea, and Taiwan.

The Region's Prospects

We have seen that economic development in Asia and the Pacific has followed a flying-geese pattern, with the United States and Japan leading the way. What course will the region follow in the future?

The most important factor to take into account when considering the prospects of the Pacific economy is the direction of the U.S. economy. After World War II the United States contributed to the revitalization of the world economy by providing massive aid to Europe through the Marshall Plan, and at the same time bore most of the cost of the free trade system, exemplified by such institutions as the International Monetary Fund and the General Agreement on Tariffs and Trade. Though America's strength is not what it used to be, neither Japan nor West Germany has the wherewithal to take America's place. The United States still has tremendous potential, and will remain the major determinant of the direction of international politics and the world economy for the foreseeable future.

U.S. productivity declined in the 1970s but began to recover in the 1980s. Plant and equipment investment has risen, and the quality of the labor force is starting to improve. Wage restraint, efforts to streamline management, and other factors have had a beneficial impact.

Nevertheless, the U.S. economy cannot stand up indefinitely under the heavy burden of its huge current-account deficit; reducing this deficit has become an urgent priority. In this regard, the September 1985 agreement of the central bankers and financial authorities of Britain, France, Japan, the United States, and West Germany to lower the value of the dollar vis-à-vis that of other key currencies represented a hopeful development for the U.S. economy and for the world economy as a whole.

As stated above, the United States is the largest market in the world. Nevertheless, in many areas U.S. business is losing international competitiveness, and protectionist pressure is mounting. For the sake of the world's economic vitality, it is hoped that the United States will not try to reduce its current-account deficit through protectionism but instead will increase efforts to improve its balance of payments through policies designed to facilitate industrial restructuring and enhance competitiveness.

The Asian NICs have achieved rapid growth through a combination of export-oriented economic policies and vigorous private-sector investment. South Korea and Taiwan have recently recovered from recessions and show signs of renewed growth, though Singapore's economic problems continue. In addition to further expanding their exports, the NICs as a whole need to create greater economic stability by expanding their domestic markets on the one hand and promoting regional trade by opening up their markets on the other.

The ASEAN countries are now at the takeoff point in their economic development, but their growth rates have been slowing as a result of global recession and growing protectionism in the advanced countries, not to mention the stagnant oil and primary-product markets. The fall in the price of oil in particular has created a "reverse oil shock" for oil-producing countries like Indonesia and Malaysia, burdening them with serious budget deficits and a worsening balance of international payments. Meanwhile, the Philippines' huge external debt and political instability, as well as the stagnation of such key export markets as copper and lumber, necessitate difficult decisions in economic management. Vigorous efforts to maintain political stability have been continuing since February 1986, when Corazon Aquino took office as president, and economic reconstruction would have a beneficial effect on this process.

Despite these setbacks, the ASEAN countries retain the development potential afforded by their abundant labor and natural resources. These countries face brighter prospects than many other developing countries and should not scale down their development strategies on the basis of unduly pessimistic projections. Their international competitiveness in labor-intensive industries will continue to grow, and with this will come the need for a shift from import-replacement-directed to export-led industrialization. The promotion of economic development will also require technology and capital from the advanced industrial countries.

When assessing the future of the Asia-Pacific region, we must also carefully evaluate China's open-door economic policy, since this is one of the major variables affecting the region. If China followed the example of Hong Kong, Singapore, and Taiwan, its modernization policies would lead to both the growth of labor-intensive industries and the possibility of direct competition with ASEAN. However, in view of China's stage of development and its store of natural resources, not to mention the potential size of its domestic market, trade relations between China and the rest of the region are more likely to be complementary. The steady development of China's economy should make a large contribution to trade expansion and economic growth in the entire region. It may take some time for economic relations with China to become closer, in view of the wary attitude toward China of the other countries in the region. Nonetheless, the dominant trend is toward greater economic interdependence.

Within China itself, the problem of reconciling the open-door policy needed for modernization with the requirements of domestic political discipline has yet to be resolved. Nevertheless, as long as China's national goal of the "four modernizations" remains paramount, an open-door policy is inevitable. Though there may be occasional swings, it is hard to imagine a return to the earlier inward-looking stance.

Since China's participation in the Asia-Pacific economy would not only add a new dimension to the region's trade and economy but also exert a major influence on its future, it would behoove us to create an environment that allows China to play an active role in the region's interdependent system.

One other factor that should be examined when considering the region's future is the direction of Soviet policy. Since Mikhail Gorbachev came to power in March 1985 the Soviet Union, recognizing the urgent need for domestic economic reform, has become increasingly interested in the growth potential of Asia and the Pacific. In a speech in Vladivostok in July 1986, Gorbachev defined the Soviet Union as a "Pacific power" and made clear its intention of participating actively in the future development of the Pacific. The Soviet Union's request to take part in the Pacific Economic Cooperation Conference indicates its growing interest in the region.

At present some within the Soviet leadership are questioning the traditional emphasis on political and security concerns in Soviet policy toward Asia and the Pacific and are advocating a shift to a policy emphasizing economic priorities. We must closely watch the Soviets in order to discern their intentions. Meanwhile, it would be unwise to slow the present momentum for change by rebuffing Soviet interest in Pacific cooperation on political and strategic grounds. Peace and stability in Asia and the Pacific cannot arise from exclusionary principles but must spring from a form of cooperation that includes all concerned countries.

A Japanese Marshall Plan

How should Japan respond to the above-mentioned developments?

The two oil crises of the 1970s adversely affected Japan's trade balance, but it quickly recovered and is now recording a massive surplus. The major reason for this phenomenon is that Japan's industrial structure has shifted from one centered on resource-intensive heavy industries to one reliant on industries that feature high technology and low natural-resource consumption. Another reason is that in such areas as automobiles and consumer electronics Japan is internationally competitive in both quality and price. Finally, we can cite Japan's high saving rate.

Several factors could reduce the trade surplus. It is projected that the saving rate will fall as the proportion of elderly people in the population grows and social security payments rise. In addition, imports of manufactured goods will increase owing to rising wages and the resultant loss of international competitiveness in manufactured products. Nevertheless, for some time Japan probably will continue to run a trade surplus and will remain a net capital exporter. Of course, at a time when the United States has become a net capital importer, Japan's continued ability to use its excess domestic savings to satisfy the capital needs of the United States and other countries is desirable from the viewpoint of global economic growth. The problem is how best to use Japan's enormous saving surplus to contribute to this end.

In April 1986 I delivered a report titled "The Potential of the Japanese Surplus for World Economic Development" as a representative of the United Nations University's World Institute for Development Economics Research in Helsinki. I proposed devoting a portion of Japan's saving and current-account surpluses to the growth of the developing countries.

In September that year, Minister of Finance Kiichi Miyazawa announced that Japan was prepared to make a special contribution of SDR 3 billion (approximately $3.6 billion) to the IMF to allow a more flexible response to the developing countries' needs. In December the Japanese government announced a special contribution of $2 billion to the World Bank.

Whatever the method chosen, it is becoming increasingly important to utilize Japan's huge saving and current-account surpluses to promote the growth of the world economy. In the Asia-Pacific region alone, the developing countries urgently need to improve their infrastructure—roads, ports, electric power supply, telecommunications, and so forth. The provision of capital through such institutions as the World Bank, the Asian Development Bank, and the Overseas Economic Cooperation Fund of Japan, as well as private financial institutions, could contribute to dynamic growth in the region.

More concretely speaking, China's seventh five-year plan (1986–90) requires $40 billion in foreign capital to meet the annual growth target of 7.5 percent. Indonesia needs $2.5 billion a year in foreign capital to fulfill its development goals. Altogether, the countries of Asia, including South Asia, require no more than $20 billion annually in foreign exchange for their economic development plans. In view of the fact that Japan's net long-term capital outflows in 1985 totaled $65 billion, Japan could provide the major part of this sum on its own.

What I am proposing is a Japanese version of the Marshall Plan. I strongly hope that the Japanese government and people will realize that it lies within their power—and is their responsibility—to take the initiative in aiding the growth of the developing countries. At present almost all the capital leaving Japan is being invested in U.S. bonds, securities, and real estate. Diverting some of this money to the developing world would contribute significantly not only to Asian development but also to the global economy. Economic growth in the developing countries would raise their purchasing power, creating a larger market for the exports of the advanced countries, including Japan. Thus the economies of the advanced countries would also grow, establishing a "virtuous circle" of growth.

At the same time, Japan must continue its efforts to import more primary products and, more important, more internationally competitive manufactured products from other Asian countries. I myself believe that Japan should aim at doubling imports from the rest of Asia over the next five or six years. If Japan opened its market further and developed a horizontal division of labor with other Asian countries, economic relations between Japan and the rest of Asia would expand dramatically.

Pacific Cooperation: Problems and Prospects

Regional interdependence and the need for cooperation. The economic development of Asia and the Pacific over the past twenty years has increased the economic interdependence of the countries in the region. Our task now is to manage and develop this interdependence in such a way as to foster a better balance among countries and ensure the region's stability and prosperity. The most import aspects of this task are maintenance of an open international economic system and industrial restructuring.

Strong economic growth is causing dynamic changes in the international division of labor among the countries of the region, and comparative advantage is shifting; the development of the NICs is part of this process, but so is trade friction, and protectionism often strengthens in countries that wish to maintain the status quo.

Industrial restructuring is unavoidable if we are to protect the free-trade system that has fostered the region's export-oriented economies and promote the development of economic and trade relations based on the free-trade principle. We must also expand trade within the region. In 1985 trade within the Western Pacific region, including Northeast Asia, Southeast Asia, and Oceania, accounted for only 15 percent of the region's total trade, while trade with the United States was close to 40 percent. In contrast, trade within the EC accounted for about half of all EC trade, while trade with the United States amounted to only 10 percent.

Increasing interdependence is leading to a growing recognition that some form of regional cooperation is the most effective way of dealing with issues of common concern. Close consultation on shared problems and on the implementation of cooperative measures to identify and resolve economic disputes before they develop into political crises will promote the region's resilience and stability.

Steady progress in Pacific cooperation. The concept of economic cooperation among the countries of the Pacific has been debated among scholars, business people, and government officials for the past twenty years. The first person to articulate the issue was Professor Kiyoshi Kojima of Japan's Hitotsubashi University. As early as 1965, he sought to define Pacific cooperation, calling for a Pacific free-trade zone along the lines of the EC. A group of Japanese scholars interested in this issue have explored regional economic cooperation since 1968 in the Pacific Trade and Development Conference. Meanwhile, the Pacific Basin Economic Council, initiated by a group of business people in 1968, has helped deepen understanding of the region's interdependence.

The Pacific Economic Cooperation Conference was established in September 1980, on the occasion of the Canberra Seminar convened at the behest of Prime Minister Masayoshi Ohira of Japan and Prime Minister Malcolm Fraser of Australia. The founders of the PECC understood the need to focus on existing problems in a pragmatic and flexible way. The PECC searches for areas in which there is a recognized potential for cooperation and seeks formulas for successful cooperation. The PECC's tripartite composition—government officials, academics, and business leaders—is an appropriate one for promoting Pacific cooperation at the present stage of development.

As it broadens its scope of activities, the PECC is becoming one of the most authoritative bodies promoting Pacific cooperation, and its work will become increasingly important as time passes. The PECC considers and recommends policy measures to enhance cooperation, policy planning, and the prevention of friction through free and frank exchanges of views, at the same time maintaining close links with the governments of the participating nations. Task forces comprising specialists from each participating country explore concrete methods of cooperation in such areas as trade, investment, finance, technology transfer, energy, fishing, livestock, and animal feed.

One indication of the progress made in Pacific cooperation over the past several years was the decision made at the July 1984 meeting in Jakarta of the ASEAN foreign ministers and their dialogue partners from other Pacific region countries and the EC to establish a "six plus five" formula for intergovernmental talks on economic development in the Pacific region. In accordance with the proposal of Indonesia Foreign Minister Mochtar Kusuma-Atmadja, the six-plus-five formula included, in addition to the six ASEAN foreign ministers, the foreign ministers of Australia, Canada, Japan, New Zealand, and the United States. It was agreed that six-plus-five consultations would be held once a year and would cover topics in two general areas: economic developments affecting the Pacific region and proposals for specific cooperation projects. The first such project designated had to do with the development of human resources. Working-group meetings in Jakarta in the fall of 1984 were followed by a conference of representatives of the eleven participating governments and the ASEAN secretariat in 1985.

Major issues facing the PECC. It is still too soon to predict the final outcome of the Pacific cooperation initiative. At present, consensus among the participating countries forms the basis for activities, and it would be counterproductive to force the pace of progress. At this point we must concentrate on strong and persistent efforts to increase real cooperation, with faith in our ultimate success. It is most important to expand activities gradually, on the basis of shared interests, procedural flexibility, and decision by consensus. The importance of ASEAN initiatives cannot be overemphasized. Pacific cooperation must also promote the private-sector activities that have played a central role in producing the dynamism of Pacific economic development, at the same time remaining open to the rest of the world.

Three points regarding our future efforts deserve emphasis. First, we must deal with the problem of turning ideas into actual policies. We can see from the activities of the PECC task forces that concrete plans for Pacific cooperation are materializing. Government-level consultations among the participating countries are desirable to determine how each country is to formulate specific policies and how the costs associated with policy implementation are to be distributed. In raising this point, I would like to call attention to the proposal to establish a Pacific Cooperation Research Fund, made by the delegation of the Japan National Committee for Pacific Economic Cooperation at the fifth general meeting of the PECC, held in Vancouver in November 1986. This proposal will be discussed at the sixth general meeting, to be held in Osaka in May 1988.

Second, although Pacific cooperation has focused mainly on trade and economic issues, we must also promote cultural and educational cooperation. An understanding of one another's history, culture, and present circumstances is a prerequisite for smoother relations among the nations of the Pacific. While recognizing that money and goods are the main forms of exchange among the Pacific nations at present, we must also reaffirm the importance of comprehensive cooperation, which includes the exchange of people, information, and culture. I wish to stress the need for governments to make conscious efforts to promote cultural, educational, and personal exchange rather than limit themselves to the economic area, where to some extent the market mechanism works automatically.

The third point has to do with the issue of "open regionalism" and the extent of national participation. Our ideal is a form of Pacific cooperation that is open to all countries. But the political realities of the region complicate the automatic application of this principle. Under the circumstances, the only way to realize open regionalism is to strive to include all countries that share the objective of regional interdependence and cooperation and wish to contribute actively and constructively to this end.

Toward Dynamic Pacific Cooperation

In conclusion, I would like to emphasize three points that have an effect on the achievement of true Pacific cooperation.

The first is that the export-oriented economies of Asia and the Pacific, which are responsible for the region's economic dynamism over the past twenty years, are now facing difficulties because the free-trade system on which they depend is under assault by new waves of protectionism from the advanced industrial countries. Protectionist measures of any kind impede the functioning not only of bilateral trade but also of the entire global trading system.

In today's economic environment of growing interdependence, a cooperative approach to trade and economic problems aimed at upholding and further developing free trade is the only way to ensure mutual long-term benefit. Trade and economic problems should be resolved according to rules established by multilateral consensus rather than by bilateral negotiations. The Pacific cooperation framework facilitates the creation of such rules. If the nations of the Pacific cooperate to uphold an open and free trading system, they will be in a position to offer international leadership.

The second point is that because the countries of the region are at different stages of development, Pacific cooperation provides a golden opportunity to address the North-South problem at the regional level. This problem has been debated at the global level in such forums as the United Nations, but the diversity of the economies of the South and the conflicting interests of the countries of the North have made a global approach difficult. North-South dialogue at the Pacific-region level could afford a new springboard for fruitful international dialogue.

The Asian NICs have already achieved economic takeoff, and the ASEAN countries have begun the takeoff process. Since the international competitiveness of ASEAN's labor-intensive industries will strengthen as wages continue to rise in the NICs, the ASEAN countries can expect to develop export-led economic growth. Japan, the United States, and the other advanced nations of the region can facilitate ASEAN's takeoff by providing capital and technology.

In addition, the advanced countries should help the South Pacific nations develop their economies, providing aid in such areas as fishing, agriculture, and tourism. There is also a great need for aid to improve transportation and communication between island nations. Such cooperation could help make the Pacific region a model for solving North-South problems.

The third point is that though the region has untold potential for development, various political problems still stand in the way. The problem of Kampuchea is one such hindrance to stable development. U.S.–Soviet tensions also affect the region deeply. The region's potential wealth could make it a bone of contention between the superpowers.

It is unrealistic to expect that conflicts rooted in ideology or political systems can be resolved by economic means alone. Nonetheless, economic strength can contribute indirectly to the gradual relaxation of tensions. Though the region's development so far has been limited to trade and economic transactions, this has formed a firm foundation for fruitful exchange in other areas as well. For the first time in history the nations of Asia and the Pacific have a common basis upon which to build comprehensive exchange. This common ground provides an excellent opportunity for pursuing the long-term objective of widening and deepening interdependence among countries of differing cultures, systems, and beliefs.

Environmental Protection
and Economic Development:
Guidelines for Sustainable Growth

Because the costs of preventing environmental pollution accompanying economic development do not necessarily contribute directly to expanded production, it used to be thought that environmental protection and economic development were contradictory concerns. This feeling was especially strong among the developing countries at the time of the 1972 United Nations Conference on the Human Environment, these countries contending that poverty was the ultimate environmental problem and that they therefore had no choice but to give economic development the priority over environmental protection. However, it has become increasingly obvious that environmental degradation in the developing countries imposes its own constraints, not only on these countries' own economic development but upon growth worldwide. For example, the destruction of tropical forests for agricultural, fuel, and timber uses not only deprives future generations of the use of these tropical forests but also means that we forever lose those genetic resources residing in the tropical forests. The loss of genetic diversity in turn means forfeiting the possibility of developing new strains and other products for agricultural, pharmaceutical, and other uses. People are thus becoming increasingly aware of the grave consequences of environmental degradation.

Poverty has been a primary cause of environmental destruction in the developing countries in that development has been seen as essential to the effort to eradicate poverty. Accordingly, it is increasingly coming to be viewed as imperative that the

This paper was presented to the Secretary General of the United Nations Environment Program (UNEP) in 1987.

developing countries see environmental protection and economic development as the two sides of the same coin and seek to attain both ends.

The industrialized countries have experienced many different varieties of environmental pollution in the course of their economic development. In Japan, for example, we have seen industrial effluent result in such terrible afflictions as the mercury poisoning in Minamata and industrial air pollution in such debilitating conditions as the racking asthma of Yokkaichi. These are just two of the better-known and most-feared examples of the kind of pollution-induced illnesses that have accompanied industrial development. Learning from these bitter lessons, the leading industrialized countries have moved in the past fifteen years to enact and enforce strict environmental regulations and to improve the quality of their environments. This improvement is symptomatic of some degree of success in reconciling the need for industrial development with the equally important need for environmental protection. Nevertheless, with the expansion in the scale of economic development, there is an increasing possibility that the failure to spend on environmental protection may inflict costs on society well in excess of any savings gained by the negligent company.

The environment is basic to continued human survival, and long-term prosperity for mankind is inconceivable unless we ensure that future generations are also able to receive full benefit of the blessings of nature. Yet, at the same time, development is also necessary in order to solve the problem of poverty in the developing countries and to enable all peoples everywhere to live civilized lives in a better environment. Environmental protection and economic development must thus be seen as mutually complementary concerns. Working from this perspective, the World Commission on Environment and Development established in 1984 has emphasized the need for all peoples to join hands in an effort for sustainable development worldwide. In so doing, it has defined sustainable development as progress in the human society to meet the needs of the present generation while not foreclosing the ability of future generations to meet their own needs.

Calling upon all institutions in all countries to work both on their own and in cooperation with each other for sustainable development, the World Commission on Environment and Development set forth the following eight basic principles in its February 27, 1987, Tokyo Declaration:

Reviving growth.

Changing the quality of growth.

Conserving and enhancing the resource base.

Ensuring a sustainable level of population.

Reorienting technology and managing risks.

Integrating environment and economics in decision-making.

Reforming international economic relations.

Strengthening international cooperation.

Because it is important to observe these principles in order to integrate environment and economics and to ensure sustainable development, it might be well here to dwell a little on their meaning and significance.

Reviving Growth

Countless numbers of people in the developing countries are in a state of absolute poverty, unable to meet even their basic human needs. This situation imposes an excessive burden on the environment, and is why poverty is a major source of environmental degradation. At the same time, this environmental degradation not only affects the many people living in the developing countries but also threatens the very survival of the entire community of nations, both developing and industrial.

It is thus imperative to promote economic growth, especially in the developing countries. Eradicating poverty in the developing countries will require at least 3 percent per-capita annual GNP growth in the developing countries as a whole, including the redistribution of wealth. Taking population growth into consideration, this means per-annum GNP growth of at least 5 percent in Asia, 5.5 percent in Latin America and Africa, and 6 percent in West Asia.

Because the developing countries' economies are closely interdependent with those of the industrial countries, it is also important that there be economic growth in the industrial countries to stimulate and revive growth worldwide. The medium-term outlook is for 3–4 percent per-annum growth in the industrial countries. This is both the minimum level of growth needed for these industrial countries to fulfill their international economic responsibilities and an economically sustainable rate of growth assuming that it is resource- and energy-conservative.

The developing countries need massive capital financing to pay for the imports needed to support rapid growth, and their growth is also crippled by these countries' debt accumulation. There must be international cooperation to sharply increase the flow of capital to the developing countries as well as to stabilize commodity prices so as to stabilize income levels in the low-income countries dependent upon commodity exports. At the same time, emergency international action is needed to resolve the debt crisis.

Changing the Quality of Growth

Even if growth is restored, this must be a different kind of growth from before. Just as it must be more energy- and resource-conservative, it must renew natural assets, improve income distributions, and reduce the susceptibility to economic crisis.

Economic growth must be sound growth compatible with the stock of natural resources. As such, economic development must pay full heed to the increase or decrease in the natural assets. Income distribution is another important component of the quality of growth, and there are times when it may be more desirable to have gradual growth with income redistribution advantageous to the impoverished classes than rapid growth that exacerbates income disparities. It is often better to promote small owner-tilled farms than to embark upon agribusinesses run by giant corporations. Likewise, the need to lessen the susceptibility to natural disaster, price collapses, and other crises may well imply an imperative to adopt low-risk technologies and to enter into contracts that are relatively immune to market fluctuation.

If growth is to be sustainable, it is not enough simply to increase the number of economic coefficients that are taken into consideration. Rather, there must also be a strong priority on education, health, clean air and water, natural beauty, and other non-economic values intimately connected with human needs and welfare. Protecting the interests of disadvantaged minorities is also an important consideration.

Economic and social development can and must be mutually complementary. Improving education and health also contributes to enhancing human productivity. Social development to promote the spread of education and other opportunities among people who are at a disadvantage also contributes to further promoting economic development.

Conserving and Enhancing the Resource Base

Sustainability requires the conservation and enhancement of such environmental resources as clean air and water, forests, soil, and genetic diversity. Major policy changes are needed if this is to be done while still maintaining the high levels of consumption in the industrial countries, ensuring that the developing countries are able to attain at least the minimum necessary levels of consumption, and responding to the pressures of population increases. This is also part of our moral responsibility to future generations and to all manner of non-human life.

One of the most urgent issues is that of conserving and enhancing the resource base for the primary industries cultivating and harvesting agricultural, forestry, and maritime resources. Unless this is done, it will prove impossible to meet the needs of an expanding population. The expansion of farmlands has reached its limits in many parts of the world, and forestry and maritime resources have been exploited to the brink of depletion. While it is possible to raise farmland productivity with the development and use of new agricultural technologies, any technology that carries the danger of reduced genetic diversity, contaminated water tables, or residual toxicity on crops is liable to create serious long-run ecological problems even if it does lead to a short-term increase in productivity. It is imperative that ecologically sound means be employed. Likewise, care must be taken in using forestry and maritime resources that harvests do not exceed replenishment. Ambitious efforts must be made in reforestation and fishery cultivation.

We are likely to run up against the limits to our energy resources sooner than the limits to our other finite resources. The first issue with energy resources will be the limits to supply, and the second issue is the environmental problems arising from their use. In order to resolve these issues, it is important both to develop cleaner energy resources and to promote energy conservation in all aspects of modern life, including industrial technologies, agriculture, and transport.

In considering the issue of conserving resources, it is important to prevent the fouling of air, water, and other resources. It is thus imperative that all countries rigorously enforce environmental regulations, promote low-waste technologies, and anticipate the environmental impact of new products, technologies, and wastes so as to prevent environmental pollution.

Ensuring a Sustainable Level of Population

While the requirement of sustainable growth makes it imperative that populations be held to ecologically sustainable levels, the developing countries are experiencing rapid population growth, and lowering their population growth rates has become an important issue.

In the industrial countries, income growth and an increased social role for women have resulting in lower birth rates. It is important to take a similar approach in the developing countries. In effect, population policy should be integrated with such other economic and social development policy concerns as women's education, health and medical care, and efforts to enhance the livelihood base of the poor. Because there is so little time for solving this problem, it is also imperative that the developing countries promote the spread of family planning policies as a more direct means of holding population growth to sustainable levels. In fact, such policies are one aspect of social development in that they recognize the right to self-determination of couples and women especially.

Population growth in the developing countries has been particularly rapid in the urban areas, far outstripping the urban areas' ability to accommodate these people. As a result, much of the population increase finds itself living in slums and subjected to polluted air, contaminated water, dangerous exhaust furmes, and other environmental hazards. While it is obviously important to provide adequate amenities for urban populations, it is also necessary to prevent these urban concentrations by seeking to expand employment and other opportunities in outlying areas.

Reorienting Technology and Managing Risks

The developing countries' capacity for technological innovation must be vastly strengthened in order to execute sustainable development more effectively. In so doing, because the industrial countries' technologies are not necessarily those appropriate to the developing countries, there is a need to develop appropriate technologies suited to the developing countries' own requirements. And in all countries, technology must be reoriented so that it is fully compatible with environmental concerns. This means the public sector must provide incentives to ensure that private-sector technological development takes environmental concerns into consideration and that the public sector must itself take the initiative in developing environmentally sound technologies.

Just as technology creates risks, so does it offer the means for their management. Atomic power, electrical and telecommunications networks, high-speed mass-transit systems, and other technologies exhibit considerable fragility above a certain point. It is thus imperative that legal, institutional, and organizational arrangements be made and systemic provisions be put into place for design safety, accident prevention, crisis management, damage containment, and other means of minimizing the risk that the use of such technologies entails.

As new technologies come into wider use, there is the danger that they may pose hazards to the environment in unexpected areas and unforeseen ways. It is therefore necessary that national and international mechanisms be instituted to assess the potential impact of new technologies in all phases of their production, use, and disposal before they become widespread. Similar mechanisms are needed for checking river diversion, forest clearance, and other major interventions in the natural ecosystem. Likewise, it is imperative that the kind of no-fault liability introduced in Japan to provide indemnification for the victims of air and water pollution be introduced on a global scale. It is also necessary to promote greater public participation and appropriate access to the relevant information in making public policy on environmental and development issues.

Integrating Environment and Economics in Decision-making

Environmental and economic goals can and must be mutually reinforcing. Yet, environmental and economic goals are generally seen as conflicting when individuals and group pursue their own short-term interests heedless of the impact on others. Most of the environmental and developmental problems that we face today have their origins in personal decision-making that refuses to accept any responsibility for the decision's impact on others.

Sustainability requires the enforcement of wider responsibility for the impact of policy decisions. It is especially important that policy decision-makers be responsible for the impact of their decisions upon their national environmental resources. If this is to be done, it is imperative that legal, institutional, and organizational arrangements be reformed to pursue the common good. In effect, the pursuit of the common good demands not only legal reforms but also that the general public have the information and ability to participate in decisions affecting the environment. It is especially indispensable that large numbers of informed and experienced people make their views felt on large-scale project decisions.

In taking environmental concerns into consideration in the decision-making process, the focus should be not on the symptoms but on the sources of environmental degradation. Accordingly, it is imperative that environmental policy outgrow its traditional emphasis on emission regulation, effluent treatment, or industrial siting and that environmental concerns be an integral part of tax policy, investment and technology decisions, trade incentives, and the entire range of development policies. The need to prevent pollution demands that the decision's potential ecological impact be taken into consideration alongside the economic, trade, energy, agricultural, and other facets of policymaking. Moreover, this multifaceted consideration including ecological concerns must prevail not only at the local and national level but at the international level as well.

Reforming International Economic Relations

Long-term sustainable growth can only be attained in the developing countries with a combination of these countries' own bootstrap efforts and complementary support from the industrial countries. Sadly, however, many of the developing countries are resorting to ecologically destructive development and foreclosing the possibility of long-term sustainable growth in a desperate bid to pay off their external debts despite the deterioration in their terms of trade engendered by the collapsing prices for those primary commodities on which they are economically dependent. Likewise, many of the developing countries beset with burdensome external debts are finding it difficult to attract new capital and are forced to adopt austerity budgets in an effort to wring the money for debt repayment from their already weak economies, a need that in turn results in increasing the pressure on natural resources, reducing the funding and personnel available for environmental protection, and slighting environmental considerations in the formulation and implementation of development policy. Broad-ranging reforms are thus needed in capital, trade, and technology flows to enable these countries to achieve growth consistent with environmental protection.

The flow of capital to the developing countries has to be enhanced, both quantitatively and qualitatively. Quantitatively, there has been a decline in the level of official development assistance and a sharp falloff in commercial lending and export credit financing. As a result, there is a need to expand the amount of financing available to the developing countries through the World Bank, the International Development Agency, and other multilateral institutions as well as through bilateral agencies. At the same time, realizing that past development assistance has not always been sufficiently mindful of ecological concerns and has sometimes run contrary to the interests of sustainable development, it is imperative that there be a qualitative enhancement of development assistance for sustainable growth.

Responding to the deterioration of the developing countries' terms of trade that has resulted from the structural slump in commodity prices will mandate revising commodity agreements to provide the financial and funding resources for price supports and efforts to escape economic dependence on single commodities. Likewise, the governments of the developing countries must strive to curtail resource exploitation and to encourage resource renewal so that the pace of development can be held within sustainable levels.

Sustainable development also demands the development and widespread use of new technologies for agricultural production, renewable energy resource systems, pollution prevention, and other ecologically compatible development means. When patent issues and other concerns pose impediments to promoting international technology exchange, international coordination is needed to resolve these constraints. Likewise, it is essential that the developing countries pursue ambitious research and development, on their own and in cooperation with other countries, so as to acquire an indigenous technological capability.

Strengthening International Cooperation

With the poverty-induced environmental degradation in the developing countries and the affluence-induced conspicuous consumption in the industrial countries, environmental pollution and ecological devastation have become global concerns transcending national borders. Rising levels of carbon dioxide in the atmosphere, the depletion of the ozone layer, the clearing of tropical forests, the encroachments of desertification, the damage of acid rain, the endangerment and extinction of wild species, and the pollution of the world's oceans are just a few of the many examples of this global threat. Environmental problems on a global scale are thus forcing everyone to take an active part in seeing that the constant efforts for economic coordination in an increasingly interdependent world are supplemented and integrated with equally determined efforts to preserve the environment for the greater good of the entire global community. The addition of this new dimension of environmental considerations to the agenda of international issues means that these problems are even more important and even more urgent, and it should be clearly understood that the effort to resolve these environmental problems is in everyone's mutual interests.

If we are to resolve these environmental problems and achieve sustainable development, there must be a higher priority on environmental monitoring, assessment, research and development, and resource management in all fields of development that have an international impact potential. This in turn requires a high level of commitment by all countries to the satisfactory working of multilateral institutions and to the making and observing of international rules in such fields as investment, trade, and technology. At the same time, explicitly realizing that national interests may not always coincide but that cooperation for the effective preservation and utilization of shared environmental resources is imperative for sustainable growth in everyone's best interests, there must be constructive dialogue in these areas of short-term conflict. New dimensions of international cooperation for sustainable growth are essential to human progress.

The Emerging Prospects for Development and the World Economy

It is a great honor for me to be able to present my views on development and the world economy from this platform. I still remember vividly the long and trying months from March to June 1964 when the first session of UNCTAD was held here in Geneva. I was a member of the Japanese delegation to the conference. The first conference had some elements of creative confusion, trying to elaborate a mechanism where Western countries, socialist states, and developing countries could jointly endeavor to consider ways to promote trade and development. Since then, I have participated in the activities of UNCTAD in various capacities. In the course of these years of my involvement in UNCTAD as well as in various activities in other places, I had the privilege and the pleasure to work with Dr. Prebisch. The many and varying virtues he had are well known. Among these, the quality of his which impressed me most was his ability to combine deep ethical commitments and the rigorous scientific analysis of economic issues in considering complicated questions of development. Based on these two major concerns, Dr. Prebisch's approaches to development and the world economy appear to have evolved pragmatically, addressing key issues of the day. I would like to present my views in the same spirit. I will first, identify briefly key issues which face us now; second, present a historical retrospect from the viewpoint of dynamism of the North-South dialogue, and, last, offer my thoughts on areas where actions are possible and useful.

This chapter is the text of the Third Raoul Prebisch Lecture, delivered July 9, 1987, in Geneva to an UNCTAD plenary session.

Issues in North-South Relations

The global economy is now faced with dangerous possibilities of a recession, after several years of a growth path, however feeble it has occasionally been. The imminence of it originates in adjustment requirements of an enormous proportion. The United States government is trying to reduce its huge budget deficit and has to find ways to reduce the trade deficit. Indebted developing countries have to reduce their domestic demands and to export as much as possible. While some countries, such as Japan, have decided to expand government spending, the gap in the global context between demand-generating efforts and demand-reduction requirements points to a recession.

I would now like to quote some parts of the Economic Declaration of the recently held Summit at Venice. "We can look back on a number of positive developments since we met a year ago. Growth is continuing into its fifth consecutive year, albeit at lower rates. Average inflation rates have come down. Interest rates have generally declined. Changes have occurred in relationships among leading currencies which over time will contribute to a more sustainable pattern of current-account positions and have brought exchange rates within ranges broadly consistent with economic fundamentals. In volume terms the adjustment of trade flows is under way, although in nominal terms imbalances so far remain too large."

How would Dr. Prebisch see the global situation we are in? He might see some similarities of the problems we are facing with those he encountered in the 1930s as a young economist and a high government official in his country, Argentina. But, I suppose, he might also look at the issues before us in the light of his own experiences of the whole of the past half-century. I also would like to present my views on those issues briefly, based on the experiences I have gone through in the past several decades.

Diversification of the interests of countries

The first issue which comes to my mind is the diversification of the interests and developmental stages of countries. Of course, the differences of the interests and perceptions among developing countries were already significant in 1964 when the first session took place. However, the degree of these divergences has increased in the past fifteen years to such a level that it has become impossible to consider just a set of policies which are equally effective in all developing countries. Beyond some simple typologies of development policies, we now need to consider various elements in elaborationg policies in individual developing countries. Upon my insistence, the Report of the Committee for Development Planning elaborated this point somewhat in 1979. I suggested four categories of developing countries then: OPEC and other oil-exporting countries, newly industrialized countries, poorer developing countries, and others. While it is essential for developing countries to maintain political solidarity, it is increasingly important for the world community to recognize different categories of countries which can benefit from and contribute to the world economy in different ways. It seems that there is now clearer recognition of this point. In the course of the intervening eight years, the global economic situation has again changed dramatically. The major impacts of this alteration on the divergences of developing countries are two-fold. Firstly, the salience of oil-producing countries in the world economy has diminished considerably. While there may be some possibilities that these countries might again become an important group in the world in the 1990s, they cannot be conceived of as a category of countries in the present world economy. Secondly, some countries in addition to the newly industrialized countries have emerged in the course of the past ten to fifteen years as major forces in the world economy. This emergence is due, to a large extent, to the successful management of their economic policies in their struggles with the turbulence of the world economy. In the present situation, it appears, therefore, that there are three categories of countries which need to pursue different policy objectives in the world economy.

The first category of countries can be called *major emerging economies*, which comprise newly industrialized countries and several other countries whose economic performances in the past fifteen years of turbulence have been significantly better than others (such as China, India, and Thailand). These countries can benefit more by integrating themselves progressively into the international economic system which is now dominantly market-oriented.

The second category of countries consists of *poorer developing countries*, which include not only the least developed countries as recognized by the United Nations but also twenty or thirty other developing countries whose economic performances have been stagnant. The viability of the national entities of these countries is increasingly becoming a global issue. While national efforts to combine attempts at revitalizing national economies and a fresh look at nation-building requirements are essential, it is also important for industrialized countries to respond more positively to these double efforts of poorer developing countries, as promised at, for example, the Special Session of the United Nations on Africa last year.

All other countries will need to learn from the experiences of themselves and of others, in particular those in the emerging-country category during the past two to three decades. Rich experiences of the developing countries themselves will be the biggest source of inspiration for these countries. Some devices to make this mutual learning possible may have to be considered. Industrialized countries will have to listen to the presentation of these countries more attentively once these countries have learned from each other's experiences.

Relative roles of the government
and the market in the development process

The second issue is related to the roles to be played by the government and the market in the development process. This question was a highly ideological issue twenty years ago. The discussion of this subject was largely rhetorical. However, it appears that this issue has now acquired a measure of pragmatism and seems amenable to useful discussion. The following three considerations are of particular importance.

1. In broad terms, it is important to liberalize microeconomic areas, whereas it should be essential to articulate broad guidelines within which macroeconomic policies are to be established.

2. Another factor is related mainly to developing countries. It appears that stronger government intervention is more effective

for those countries which attempt to catch up with more developed countries than for those countries which are already at the forefront of the world economy.

3. The third dimension is the requirement for planners to read the market signals carefully and to incorporate them in their planning work. This means planning with market forces rather than planning against market forces.

Low prices of commodities

The third issue is the question of low prices of commodities. Some observers even suggest de-linkage between economic performances and commodity prices. While prices of commodities are indeed low on practically all fronts, it is particularly important to differentiate between commodities in analyzing even the current situation. For example, in examining agricultural commodities in Africa, it is essential to differentiate between cash crops and food crops. Considering that there is a relatively easy changeability between the two, this rather banal distinction can have important policy implications. For the purpose of enhancing the capacity of individual countries to maximize this flexibility, it is important to examine positive contributions that various technologies can make through such a mechanism as the Consultative Group on International Agricultural Research. In other commodity areas as well, differentiation between commodities should be able to elaborate approaches to break out of the present situation. Thus, while there is certainly a structural element in the present situation of low prices of commodities, there are ways to improve the supply and demand equilibrium.

Indebtedness of developing countries

The next issue which characterizes the current situation of development and the world economy is the gravity of the indebtedness question of developing countries. The interdependent nature of this issue is now well known. The one-trillion-dollar debt of developing countries has a significantly depressive impact on the world economy. In the face of the slow growth of the world economy, in spite of the efforts at the Western Economic Summit and other places, the export prospects of indebted countries are not bright. With regard to the problems which Latin American indebted countries are facing, we are now forced to learn three lessons.

The first lesson is that recycling of surplus savings practically only through commercial banks is a vulnerable endeavor. In the course of the latter half of the 1970s, there were many proposals for recycling OPEC money, including some which could have combined private channels and the official interventions. I myself proposed an idea jointly with Bob Roosa, Armin Gutowski, and others in *Foreign Affairs* in the January 1975 issue. However, what in fact happened was the recycling of most of those OPEC surplus savings through commercial banks, an action which at that time was praised as being very efficient. This efficiency, however, was achieved, in some cases, by sacrificing rigorous observance of bankability tests.

The second lesson is that it requires tremendous efforts on the part of the Latin American leaders to persuade their people to reduce their high propensity to consume. This is one of the major points which Dr. Prebisch stressed just before passing away. Unless external financing is invested in activities which are likely to develop into areas of comparative advantage, the debt burden originating in that external financing will inevitably become impossible to bear.

The third lesson is the increased need for improved capacity of the world community in economic forecasting or prediction of likely development. This exercise comprises not only pure economic analysis but also examination of political economy. The second oil shock of 1979, combined with staunch non-accommodating policies of the OECD countries, led the world economy into the recession of the early 1980s which triggered Latin American debt problems. In the late 1970s, real interest rates reached zero, or even negative, and the dollar exchange rates were very low. Awash with liquidity, international banks resorted to considerable levels of salesmanship, in particular in Latin American countries. This situation changed dramatically in a few years' time as we all know very well. Living in a world where uncertainty is prevailing, improved capacity for forecasting political economy, though not easy, will contribute significantly to avoiding the repetition of the Latin American type of indebtedness problems.

With regard to the indebtedness problems of sub-Saharan countries, we have learned three lessons in hard ways.

The first lesson is that the official development aid increased significantly in the wake of the famine in these countries in the early 1970s without carefully measuring the impact of the aid. Action was seen to be more important than its effect. The external aid, in the form of lending, led to unbearable debts in recipient countries.

The second lesson is that without appropriate policy mixes in the medium- to long-term context in individual recipient countries, no amount of aid will be able to surmount the problems of hunger, but will lead only to burdens of indebtedness.

The third lesson is that it is essential for donors to respond more positively to the adjustment policy efforts of individual African countries as agreed at last year's Special Session of the United Nations General Assembly on the critical economic situation of Africa.

The focal point for considering the debt of these countries is the Paris Club. There have been improvements in the functions of this forum. The recent meeting of the Western Summit agreed on this point as follows:

> For those of the poorest countries that are undertaking adjustment effort, consideration should be given to the possibility of applying lower interest rates to the existing debt and agreement should be reached, especially in the Paris Club, on longer repayment and grace periods to ease the debt-service burden.

To the extent that these various elements which led developing countries into the indebtedness trap exist, some Asian countries are also suffering, though to a lesser extent, from the same problems.

Given these lessons which we have been compelled to learn, it is important to recognize that all the relevant parties, such as the governments of creditor countries and of debtor countries, the IMF, the World Bank and the commercial banks, will have to be involved in attempting to solve the problems of indebtedness.

Relations between domestic policies and the international environment

The next issue is related to the linkages between domestic policies and the international environment. One important aspect of this recurrent issue is the question of broad policy choices between export-oriented growth and import substitution. While there are different mixes of the two ingredients which should be appropriate for individual countries, it is, in principle, desirable to increase export orientation as much as possible. There has been a broad understanding of the effect in recent years. However, import substitution policies are gaining ground again in some policy circles. This new trend is apparently related to protectionist tendencies in the industrialized countries. When it is difficult to increase exports due to the unfavorable international environment, it is natural for some people to begin to think about going back to import substitution policies. This resembles ominously the climate of the 1930s when, according to Dr. Prebisch, Latin American countries had nowhere else to go but to domestic markets, owing to increasing protectionism in the developed countries. This is a typical case of a vicious cycle. He observed as follows:

> When did import substitution begin in Latin America?
> During the great world depression, when the monetary
> policy of the United States and the enormous rise in customs
> duties shattered the whole system of bilateral trade and
> payments that had been working very well. The slump in
> our countries' exports was formidable. And import substitution was the only way out. I had an active part to play at
> that time, and I do not remember that in the existing situation there was anyone crazy enough to say "The thing is
> not to substitute domestic production for imports but to
> export manufactures." Export manufactures where? To a
> world that was out of joint and where protectionism was
> a normal way of safeguarding economies? Import substitu-

tion was the only solution possible. It was not a doctrinaire imposition. It was imposed by force of circumstances.

In the face of the slow growth of the world economy, it is, in general, necessary to attempt to generate domestic demands in developing countries. As one might say, "growth begins at home." This may, in some circumstances, include import substitution to some extent. This approach can be valid in the current circumstances for medium to large developing economies. With regard to smaller countries, expansion of intra-regional trade and investment should be able to optimize growth gains in the generally unfavorable international climate. More broadly, South-South trade is becoming increasingly important due to slow growth in industrialized countries. With increasing differentiation among developing countries, South-South trade, in fact, should become more productive if trade liberalization among developing countries is achieved. These efforts should be pursued as an integral part of the global endeavor to liberalize the trading environment as much as possible.

The roles of industrial countries and developing countries are becoming only relative in producing a trading climate. In the current situation where there are certain signs of increasing protectionism in some industrial countries, it is for developing countries—in particular those which are more industrialized than others—to attempt to improve the international climate by maximizing openness in the international environment.

Weakening multilateralism

The last current issue, as I look at development and the world economy, is the question of weakening multilateralism. Despite the difficulties multilateralism is facing now, the broad trend toward increasing multilateralism is a natural historical tendency. Given increasing economic interdependence as well as technological developments in, in particular, transport and communications, which make it easier to get together, multilateralism will become an increasingly important element in international life. In considering this issue, it is essential to differentiate between forum organizations and operational bodies at all levels of multilateral endeavors (sub-regional, regional, inter-regional, and global). The major objective of forum organizations such as this body, UNCTAD, is to build up elements of legitimacy in the international community. Understandings arrived at in multilateralism are seen to constitute "common goods." To put it differently, the weakening multilateralism in forum organizations means decreasing elements of legitimacy in the world community. Unfortunately, we are witnessing this tendency.

The major objective of operational bodies such as the World Bank is to de-politicize the actions. For instance, aid policies, which tend to become highly political instruments in the bilateral context, can be de-politicized by such bodies as UNDP and the World Bank. Weakening multilateralism in operational bodies tends to generate an increase in politicization of the relevant actions.

Among various issues which the world community faces in the field of development and the world economy, these six are the ones that I see as the present major questions.

The Dialogue in Retrospect

Let us now review the broad context of the North-South dialogue in which these issues have been dealt with—the major objectives of the North-South dialogue being to enhance development of developing countries, and to gradually integrate developing countries into the international economic system. It is important to examine the dynamism of the dialogue in order to look into prospects for development and the world economy.

Among various facets the North-South dialogue has, it is particularly important to consider it as a political movement of the developing countries. Like any other political movements, such as labor movements and student movements, the North-South dialogue has three phases: mobilization, peak, and decline. The major factors which cause this dynamism are leadership, organization, and ideology, while the economic environment in which the dialogue is carried out is not negligible. Reflecting the wax and wane of these factors, two cycles of the North-South dialogue appear to have been completed. The first cycle harvested such fruits as global systems of preferences for trade and the 0.7 percent of GNP target for ODA. This cycle began with the preparatory meetings in 1963 for the first session of the conference and ended in the early 1970s. The leadership of this period was marked by the activities of Dr. Prebisch. Organizationally, this body, UNCTAD, was created, and the Group of 77 was formed.

The second cycle began immediately after the end of the first cycle in the early 1970s. Its ideological focal point was the New International Economic Order. The real forces behind the NIEO movement was the oil power of OPEC. In contrast to the emphasis on trade (GSP) and aid (0.7 percent target) in the first cycle, it was the area of commodities which became the major focal point among various activities which were dealt with in several North-South forums. However, given the broad nature of the NIEO, the focus tended to be lost, and with it, the power of the developing countries. Therefore, while the major fruit of the second cycle was the Common Fund, the forces behind it were not strong enough to implement it. At the same time, the recession of the early 1980s set in. The declining phase of the second cycle has been continuing in the course of the 1980s.

The industrialized countries maintained reactive attitudes throughout these two cycles of the North-South dialogue. They have been institutionalizing themselves, partly owing to the pressures of the developing countries throughout these years. These have taken various forms, including the Western Summit and various new committees at the OECD. The major drawback of institutionalization of the Western countries has been to encourage these countries to consider ways to re-establish some equilibria, mainly among themselves. In a way, pressures of the developing countries in the North-South dialogue have encouraged this tendency. This is not a particularly healthy trend. For example, the balance of trade disequilibria between, on the one hand, the United States and, on the other hand, Japan and the Federal Republic of Germany could be approached from the viewpoint of global balances including the developing countries. However, this question tends now to be treated as an issue between the United States and the surplus countries in such forums as the Western Summit and the OECD. Instead, recycling of part of the surplus into developing countries would enable them to increase their imports from the United States, thus reducing the trade gap of the United States.

Development and the Role of UNCTAD

Enormous amounts of effort, both political and intellectual, have been devoted to maximizing prospects for development and the world economy in recent years. The World Commission on Environment and Development, of which I was a member, chaired by Mrs. Gro Harlem Brundtland of Norway, has also attempted to examine these aspects considerably in the past three years. In its report, entitled *Our Common Future*, we have pointed out as follows:

> Humanity has the ability to make development sustainable— to ensure that it meets the need of the present without compromising the ability of future generations to meet their own needs. The concept of sustainable development does imply limits—not absolute limits but limitations imposed by the present state of technology and social organization on environmental resources and by the ability of the biosphere to absorb the efforts of human activities. But technology and social organization can be both managed and improved to make way for a new era of economic growth. The Commission believes that widespread poverty is no longer inevitable. Poverty is not only an evil in itself, but sustainable development requires meeting the basic needs of all and extending to all the opportunity to fulfill their aspirations for a better life. A world in which poverty is endemic will always be prone to ecological and other catastrophes.

Thus, the issue of sustainable development has to be considered from a global perspective. The major task of enhancing prospects for development and the growth of the world economy, then, is to break out of the North-South bind. Major disequilibria in trade and finance need to be addressed, not only between key industrialized countries, but in a broader context where developing countries should be involved. It is important at this juncture to aim for building up policy approaches to address the complicated tasks by producing creative patchworks, rather than to aim for an ambitious comprehensive package. The major elements of these patchworks should be as follows. . . .

Surplus savings to be transferred to developing countries

As we observed in a recent report of the WIDER (a recently established institution in Helsinki under the United Nations University), where I serve as chairman of the governing board, "the complementarity between the urgent resource requirements of developing countries for increased investment and growth, and the availability of capacity in developed countries which may otherwise become idle on an unprecedented scale, has never been as striking as it is today." However, as I pointed out earlier, we have learned from the experiences of the recycling of the oil dollars that channeling surplus savings to developing countries only through private routes tends to invite indebtedness problems. Government actions on the part of surplus countries are required. The Japanese government has recently announced specific actions for recycling $20 billion or more toward developing countries.

Surplus savings do exist almost always in some economies in the world community. In the 1940s and the 1950s, the surplus savings of the United States were a main feature in the world economy, in the 1970s those in OPEC countries, and in recent years those in Japan and the Federal Republic of Germany. While each surplus economy has its own con constraints, it should be useful to consider the policy options available for it to rechannel its surplus savings to developing countries. It would be important to examine this from a global perspective as well and it would be for UNCTAD to play a constructive role in this context.

Global indicative guidelines

A related activity that would be useful is to attempt to arrive at some broad indications of development and the world economy for the coming years. Some good works exist already. They have been done by a few international organizations, including UNCTAD, and by some private forecasting groups. Based on these, it would be possible to elaborate broad indicative guidelines for development and the world economy. Strengthening the exercise of the annual *Trade and Development Report*, UNCTAD could attempt to perform this function. For individual countries, particularly for developing countries, these indicative guidelines will be useful in considering their own policy options.

To advance this logic a step further, it is essential for individual developing countries to have stronger capacities in making policies and in implementation of the policies. Based on some major studies, there are indications that the strongest correlation exists between development and the quality of government. It appears that various relevant factors such as capital and raw materials are not by themselves the determining forces for development, but that the capacity of government to organize available resources for productive purposes is the most crucial factor which makes a difference in development.

There are two ways to strengthen the government's capacity in this respect. The first approach is a rather traditional one— namely, technical assistance. This is, in fact, pursued by various international bodies, bilateral donors, and some professional associations. It should be useful to do research on what is being done in this area and to map it out. Perhaps UNCTAD might consider doing it. Then it should be possible to identify gaps. Consideration should be given to filling these gaps by multilateral and bilateral agencies.

The second approach is to devise a mechanism through which individual developing countries can learn from the experiences of each other. Perhaps the richest potential resources developing countries have are their own experiences of both successes and failures in the past two to three decades. It is important for the world community to make arrangements for turning these potentials into real resources. One way to do so might be to establish a forum where interested developing countries could learn from the experiences of each other. UNCTAD may be able to undertake such a function.

Strengthening commodity markets

There is no magic in attempting to deal with the current situation of commodity markets. As I suggested in a session of the Committee for Development Planning in the late 1970s, it is essential to distinguish four categories of countries in considering commodity issues. They consist of the following: resource-rich rich countries, resource-rich poor countries, resource-poor rich countries, and resource-poor poor countries. The impact of the price behavior of commodities is different, depending on these categories of countries. The first task of the international community must be to enhance the analytical capacity of the prospects of the commodity markets. Considerable efforts have already been made to comprehend these markets by various bodies, notably by UNCTAD. It should be possible to enhance this capacity of UNCTAD significantly. UNCTAD should continue to play a major role in the commodities field, particularly in analysis of their prospects. A good and reliable analysis in this area is bound to affect both multilateral and bilateral donors and other investors, including developing country governments and private entrepreneurs.

The major new demand generators of commodities should be the emerging countries which I referred to earlier. These are the countries which are rapidly increasing manufacturing capacities, in particular in highly commodity-consuming product lines. Enhanced analytical capacity should make it possible for the international community to have a better grasp of this new trend.

At the same time, high technologies—in particular, new materials and biotechnology—might make it possible for commodity-producing countries to control production better than before. This might become a new weapon against the formidable factors of the structural elements.

The debt problem

The problem of indebtedness of developing countries is deteriorating slowly but, unfortunately, steadily. In order to tackle this problem, an approach based on inter-linkages among debt, trade, finance, and growth has been discussed in various forums in recent years. Indications of recent months point to a need to emphasize growth in this list. Reflecting the concerns over indebtedness questions in the context of inter-linkages among these policy elements, a number of broad agreements have emerged recently. The policy packages addressed to the so-called Baker countries and some sets of understandings with regard to poorer countries, least-developed countries, and African countries which have been formulated by UNCTAD and the United Nations General Assembly have been pursued. These would have been correct approaches. But in reality the partial implementation of them on the part of all relevant parties is bringing about the current difficult situation. What we are seeing is a series of sporadic and unilateral decisions on the part of some indebted countries as well as on the part of some banks.

The policy approaches to be taken are, therefore, either to confirm the existing Baker packages and UNCTAD/United Nations "understandings" more strongly and to try to implement them, or, in addition, to attempt something more. My assessment of the situation is tilting toward the latter—namely, to try to do something more.

Broad approaches toward policies on indebtedness in addition to these past commitments are twofold. With regard to bank loans, broadly speaking, additional actions should be based on the indications coming from the secondary markets of these loans. Individual banks are already taking some measures, and they need to be encouraged to further elaborate their schemes, which should be aimed at ensuring steady flows of capital into developing countries. As mentioned earlier, a large-scale recycling of savings from surplus countries to developing countries will be required for the fundamental solution of debt problems. Because surplus savings are mostly accumulated in the private sector, government or multilateral financial institutions should provide measures for reducing investment risks by strengthening guarantees, insurance, tax incentives, or subsidies.

With regard to indebtedness originating in official development assistance, consideration should be given to strengthening the commitments made in this organization in 1978 and thereafter. Further actions on the part of donors with regard to the coverage of countries as well as to the terms and amount of the commitments could be sought. They, however, should be accompanied by an improvement of the policies of indebted governments.

These additions will contribute significantly to the improvement of the climate of the international community. Given the uncertainty prevailing over the financial markets, this psychological dimension is of particular importance.

The patchwork of these policy actions will need to be elaborated in various forums, some of which will be existing multilateral institutions, while others will be more flexible arrangements but of a multialteral character. This policy-making process in the area of development and the world economy will gradually build up a sense of legitimacy in the international community, a factor which is sorely needed now. Thus, as I see it we stand now at the starting point of the third phase of the North-South dialogue. This phase, however, is significantly different from the previous two phases. This time, it is not the Southern countries only which set the tone of the dialogue: It has to be the joint task of both the North and the South. Individual countries will, at the same time, need to break out of the bounds of the North and of the South. They will need to form various patterns of partnership depending on the issues involved while political solidarity of developing countries may need to be maintained. It is going to be a complicated endeavor, requiring enormous capacity for intellectual insight and imagination on the part of the global community. Overseeing the progress on various fronts of discussion and negotiation will be of particular importance. I believe it is the biggest challenge for UNCTAD to perform this task in the third cycle of the North-South dialogue.

Index